Achieve Anything In Just One Year

Be Inspired Daily to Live Your Dreams and Accomplish Your Goals

JASON HARVEY

Amazing
LIFE PRESS

First Published 2010
Reprinted 2014

Published in Canada by Amazing Life Press

www.amazinglifepress.com

Library and Archives Canada Cataloguing in Publication Data:

Harvey, Jason
Achieve anything in just one year: be inspired daily to live your
dreams and accomplish your goals / Jason Harvey.

ISBN: 978-0-9813639-0-5
eISBN: 978-0-981-3639-1-2

1. Self-actualization (Psychology).

2. Goal (Psychology). 3. Success. I. Title.

BF637.S8H295 2009   158.1   C2009-906450-2

Introduction

Josh gets up every morning to prepare himself for the day ahead without enthusiasm. He dislikes his job and dreads the traffic he will likely face. Each morning, he tries to think up a new excuse for getting out of his evening plans so he can just come home and hit the couch — and try to forget the whole day.

He groans at the mere sight of his roommate, Ben, and his constant sunny attitude — particularly his morning energy. But then, what does Ben have to be gloomy about? He loves his job, takes great vacations, and always lucks into opportunities.

It isn't luck. Ben decided a long time ago that he didn't want to make a living. He wanted to make a life. He commits every day to finding ways to achieve his goals — from simple ones like finding a new place for lunch to more complex objectives, like mapping out his career and planning his next travel adventure.

Ben is passionate about helping young people and works with at-risk youth twice a week. He joined a business-networking group and "lucked" into meeting a well-known entrepreneur who came to speak to the group. At the end of the presentation, Ben introduced himself to the woman who turned a simple idea into a multi-million-dollar business. He invited her to visit the youth group. Ben knew she shared his passion for giving kids a better chance to thrive. Two weeks later, she funded a scholarship and some much-needed equipment to the center — and offered Ben a job.

Josh, on the other hand, just lets life happen. He is content to grumble about the wrongs in his world, accepting a dreary fate. He watches people like Ben who seem to just win at everything all the while believing that good fortune just isn't in the cards for him.

Do either of these people reflect your own attitude toward success? Are you just "showing up" in your life or are you taking an active role in guiding it to reach your full potential and achieve your dreams?

Doreen is a stay-at-home mom. Before the birth of her first child, sixteen years ago, she was a computer technician. She has thought of going back to work for the past few years, but feels she is out of touch with today's technology. She knows about employment training for people returning to the workplace, but continues to put off finding a course in current trends and technology.

Rather than make a decision—and a commitment—Doreen dreams about feeling more valued. Meanwhile, she spends her days running errands for her husband, kids, neighbors, and friends who are working moms. They love that she is always available.

Carla chose to stay home to raise her children. She also opted to go to school with them, to volunteer. After volunteering—as classroom "mom", field trip chaperone, and PTA president, the school offered Carla a part-time job as a classroom aide. She loved getting paid to spend time with kids, helping them to learn and grow.

Working as a classroom aide, Carla discovered she not only had a talent for inspiring kids, but she found immense joy from it. Less than two years later, she went back to college at night to earn her teaching degree. She is now teaching full-time with plans to get her master's degree within two years.

Tanya and Devon live and work in the city, but love to spend weekends visiting the country. They have a favorite inn—in fact, they were married there—and enjoy the outdoor recreation. Tanya does not like her job. She mentioned to Devon that she would love to relocate to their rural getaway to run a small business. He told her that they should aim for working hard, saving money, and retiring early.

However, Devon is not the best money manager. They never seem to be able to put away much money because the cost of city living and weekend escapes just about equals their salaries.

Tanya sees her dream drifting away. As for Devon, well, he just drifts.

Karen and Andrew met while working in a large advertising agency. She was an account executive; he managed the graphic design group. For three years, they put in long hours — including many weekends — developing strategies and campaigns for clients. Karen brought in several key accounts, working closely with the clients, who trusted her insight and decision-making. Andrew had talent as a creative director, but had some difficulty managing his temperamental team.

Their relationship grew, both personally and professionally. They were discussing marriage when the agency, hit by the recession, decided to downsize. Andrew survived the first lay-offs, but was let go in the second round.

Andrew told Karen that the job loss was not a bad thing. He considered it an opportunity to do what he had always wanted — start his own small design firm. Karen used her strategic talents to help him with his business plan. Six months later, she left the agency to join Andrew, giving up a guaranteed salary to take charge of her future, which she knew would be with Andrew.

Have you spent your life so far thinking and wishing about having something more? What is holding you back from achieving your dreams? Have you created your own obstacles? Dreaming is free. And it is fun to think about what you might do if you won the lottery or if you could afford the luxuries that you see others have or if you simply had the freedom to do whatever you want.

Most people who haven't reached their potential have a long list of excuses for why they haven't.

The time is not right.

I need to save more money first.

I just can't up and change my life that easily.

It's just a dream.

While you are busy making excuses, other people are busy seeking opportunities, people like Ben, Carla, Karen, and Andrew. They chose not to wait for things to come to them, but instead navigated the path to their desired futures.

Your life is rich with possibility, and you are the only one who can discover the opportunities that will allow you to live your dreams. You must open your eyes to what can be, envision the life you want, and take the steps to get yourself to that place.

I challenge you to stop postponing the joy you deserve. Take control of your happiness. Learn how to make the decisions that will continue to elevate your mind and your spirit. Turn your wishes into goals and then attack them with the vigor you never knew you had. You have made a great start by picking up this book. This is the perfect opportunity for you to change your life — literally staring you in the face.

Jackson, an honor student in high school, was accepted into a prestigious university with a scholarship. Soon he found that coming from a small school to a large college where the best of the best studied was more challenging than he expected. He was not accustomed to studying hard. The answers always came easily, and he managed to get A's on papers he churned out without much effort.

He enjoyed the freedom of being away from home and spent more time partying with his new friends than studying. Jackson got the first "C" grade of his life in his first semester of college. He received three of them. Not only was Jackson devastated, his parents were shocked. He felt like he was in way over his head.

If he did not dramatically improve his grades next semester, he would lose his scholarship. He considered transferring to a less challenging school, but hated to admit he had made a mistake in choosing this one. His parents encouraged him to take a semester off and consider his choices, but he felt doing that would be automatically admitting failure.

Like Jackson, Alison was an honor student. Unlike him, she worked hard at earning her grades. Even while she battled non-Hodgkin's Lymphoma during high school, she did not allow herself to accept anything less than her best. Alison graduated with her classmates — in spite of the many days she was too ill to study. She finished high school cancer-free and with a 4.0 grade point average.

Alison went on to a highly ranked college, which she funded with grants and scholarships that she had aggressively pursued. She didn't want her parents to have student loans alongside the medical bills that had amassed during her cancer treatments. While in college, Alison used her experience as a cancer survivor to speak to groups of young patients, motivating them to keep pushing and not cave in to the disease. She also made the time to participate in races and rock climbing events to raise money for cancer research.

Alison graduated college with honors in three and a half years, earning a degree in Communications. She received an offer for a public relations position with a national non-profit organization. She accepted, on the condition that she could delay her employment so she could go to Haiti to help the earthquake victims.

Alison never let anything stand in her way. As a child, her parents thought she was stubborn, but as an adult, she used that trait to continually push forward, to achieve results, and to never stray from her dreams.

In *Achieve Anything In Just One Year*, I present a year's worth of mindful exercises that will give you a daily personal challenge. None of these exercises will require more than a few minutes of your time each day, so they do not require a massive commitment in that regard. Every assignment will build on the previous one, so you accumulate a wealth of knowledge, ideas, and guidance to rebuild, reshape, and redefine your new, improved life.

Step by step, you will discover insights into yourself and others. You will learn why you make the choices you do. Whom do you spend your time with and why? What do your relationships add to your life? What makes you happy and what needs to change in order for you to have a more joy-filled life?

With every turn of the page, you will gradually craft a new perspective. You will begin to see opportunities that you might have otherwise overlooked.

Achieve Anything In Just One Year is a roadmap to achievement. This volume of self-development is based on experience gained during my fifteen years as a Certified Life Coach. Through the evolution of my coaching clients and my own personal journey, I accumulated tremendous insight into how to break through the barriers we create to derail our success. My methods breakdown every obstacle that blocks your path and show you ways to navigate them. If lacking confidence, self-awareness, patience, focus, passion, or other traits prevents you from fulfillment, you will learn how to build those skills, one action at a time.

If you were told that you cannot succeed, that you lack experience, or that you are simply not good enough, you will learn how to prove every naysayer wrong! But first, you have to prove it to yourself.

I have coached hundreds of people who believed that something was missing from their lives, something that would link them to success. What they all had in common was that their "missing link" was buried under a heap of self-doubt, fear of change, complacency, or some other form of negative thinking. Don't allow your life to be less than exceptional. Give yourself 365 days to become the person you have always wanted to be, to live the life that you know you deserve. All it takes is the commitment to grow and the courage to explore what is out there.

Your new life starts right now. Turn the page.

"Faith is taking the first step even when you don't see the whole staircase."

Martin Luther King, Jr.

What will your future hold? Have you even thought about it? Are you afraid to think about it? Are you looking forward to the future, or are you dreading it? Why?

Are you willing to have a little faith? What is faith? Sometimes it is described as a strong belief in something for which there is no proof. If that's the case, then faith is exactly what you need right now.

You can't predict the future. What you can do is let go of the baggage of your past and move forward without expectations. There is no evidence to prove this book will change your life. Take that first step in faith. Walk boldly into this endeavor, and have faith that if you are simply willing to make one small change at a time, you will begin to see huge results. You don't need to see the whole staircase. You don't need to put any limitations on your future. Just take that first step toward change.

Your lesson today is easy and fun. You get to dream about your staircase. Your assignment is to get a notebook. You can go to a bookstore and pick out a fancy journal or find a quirky spiral notebook at your local drug store. It can be silly or pretty or bold or non-descript. The only requirement is that you take it with you wherever you go. Keep that notebook with you for at least a week and write down your dreams whenever they pop into your head. It doesn't matter if they are impossible. Don't judge them. Just write them down. Have faith. Take that first step.

Day 2

"It is our choices that show what we truly are, far more than our abilities."

J. K. Rowling

You shape your future every day through the choices you make. That's sort of a hard one to swallow, isn't it? It would be much easier to say you are a victim of circumstances. Then you don't have to act. Your choices create your reality. They are far more important than aptitude or circumstance.

Say you have a boss who is constantly criticizing your work. They pick on you so much that you are starting to mistrust your ability to perform your job. You can choose to believe your boss, or you can trust yourself and leave the doubter in the dust. Think about how you respond to people who make you feel small. Why are you giving them power?

Does your level of education define you? Does it limit you? That, too, is a choice. You may not think you're smart enough to earn a degree or apply for a better job. Is that really true, or did you choose not to do the work? There are a million ways to add to your abilities, and they don't all come with huge price tags or scary entrance exams. Have you thought about seeking a mentor or applying for an apprenticeship? Have you even explored your talents to find out where your aptitudes lie?

Today, your assignment is to observe your choices. Look at every decision you make, from the food you eat to the time you spend on various tasks, to the people you choose to hang out with. Are you making choices that limit you or choices that nurture you?

"Whatever you can do, or dream you can begin it. Boldness
has boldness genius, power and magic in it."

Goethe

A couple of days ago, you started a notebook of dreams. How is that
going? Have you written anything down yet? If you haven't, what are
you waiting for? Get busy! You are not going to change by just reading
this book. If you have been working on your dream notebook, pat
yourself on the back. Good job! You are taking that first step in faith.

Today's lesson is about boldness. It's a wonderful word that means *to
have courage, to plunge forward even when there is risk involved.* To be bold
also means *to be clear or distinct.* Bold type is stronger. It stands out.

Be bold about your dreams. Take risks. There is genius in being bold,
because it is the opposite of being shy and uneasy. It shows direction
and commitment. You can either apologize for your life, or you can
step up to the plate and go for it. What do you have to lose? A boring
and unfulfilling life?

You don't have to even believe in yourself to be bold. It's like
standing on the high dive for the first time. You don't have to know
what it's going to feel like to plunge into that cold water. You just
have to dive off.

Your assignment today is to look at some of your dreams. Pick one.
What can you do to boldly go in the direction of that dream? Is there a
clear and distinct move you can make today that will start to hurl you
toward that goal? Would it really be so scary? What first step can you
take in faith? The results may be magical.

Day 4

"Remember there's no such thing as a small act of kindness.
Every act creates a ripple with no logical end."

Scott Adams

You are a powerful being. Do you realize the immense authority you
have at this very moment to influence the world?

If you are skeptical of this fact, now is the time to test it. Your
assignment today (and every day forward if you choose) is to do at
least one nice thing for someone else. It can be nothing bigger than
offering a smile and a hand to an elderly woman in the grocery store
or not honking at the guy who cuts you off in traffic. You have no
idea of the ripple effect you set in motion when you scatter small
acts of kindness around. They change the people you touch, and
they change you.

There are two rules to keep in mind when carrying out this assignment.
One, you have to be sincere. Don't compliment someone on their bad
haircut and then make fun of them behind their back. You must be
honest and sincere when carrying out each act of kindness.

The second rule is you must not expect a single thing in return. Try
not to take credit for the act. Anonymous acts of kindness are the
best. Don't worry about getting praise for your actions. You will
be rewarded by a jolt of excitement and happiness when you carry
out your good deed unnoticed. Don't believe it? Try it, and see how
you feel.

Here is a little secret: acts of kindness are not completely selfless.
The ripple reverses itself, and you will begin to feel good from the
inside out.

"Destiny is not a matter of chance, it is a matter of choice; it is not a thing to be waited for, it is a thing to be achieved."
Winston Churchill

Destiny carries with it an unfortunate connotation. It sounds pre-determined, unchangeable, and inactive. Some people tend to think of destiny in the same way the main character sees her fate in the opera *Carmen*. She reads in the tarot cards that she's going to die, and what happens? She dies. Not a darn thing she can do about it. It's her destiny.

That's not reality. What you choose to do every single minute of every single day shapes your destiny. Don't sit around like Carmen in front of the bull ring waiting for destiny to come upon you. Choose your destiny before it chooses you.

Winston Churchill said destiny is a thing to be achieved because it takes real effort to fulfill your destiny. You can't sit around waiting for destiny to show up. You must act. It's time to own up to what is going on in your life today. What are you doing to steer the boat? Did you throw your life into cruise control a long time ago, or are you actively pointing yourself in the direction you want to travel?

Your assignment today is to take one step toward achieving your destiny. Chart your course. Look at your list of dreams and pick one thing you want to achieve by the end of this year. Congratulations! You have a destination and a timeframe. Now, what can you do to launch your journey? Is it compiling a list of recruiters to call? Is it getting on the Internet to search for a long-lost friend? You don't have to reach your destination today. Just start the journey. Soon your destiny will be clear.

Day 6

"To accomplish great things, we must not only act, but also dream, not only plan, but also believe."

Anatole France

You are destined to do great things in your life. It is okay to believe that. It's true. In order to accomplish great things you must start small and think big. Allow yourself to imagine the impossible. You may start with a phrase like, "I would like a job I enjoy going to every day." That's a great dream. Now go bigger. Try something like, "I would like to be an influential person."

Feel free to get specific and maybe even be a little selfish. No one will see this homework assignment but you. "I would like to travel the world" or "I would like to be a millionaire" is perfectly acceptable, if it is your dream. Nothing is too big, too silly, or too ridiculous. What can you imagine if you have no rules or boundaries? Add to your dream list whenever you can, and read through your dreams every day. Don't forget them.

Dreams mean nothing if they are not followed by action. Here is your new assignment: start another list of Action Items in your notebook. This is a list of tasks you never seem to get around to doing. It may include items such as: clean out the garage; wash the windows; send a letter to your great aunt who is bed-ridden; learn a craft; take a load of old clothes to a charity. There should be nothing earth-shattering on this list. "Take over the world," for example, would not be a good choice. This is just a list of simple things. You don't have to do any of them today. Just create the list. What does this have to do with dreams? You'll see.

"There are two cardinal sins from which all others spring:
Impatience and Laziness."

Franz Kafka

I want it now! (But I don't want to have to do anything to get it.)
Sound at all familiar? One of the biggest obstacles to achieving
your dreams is laziness. It's hard to reverse sloth. You think about
cleaning out your closets, but you are glued to *Seinfeld* reruns you've
watched a million times. How can you catapult yourself off the
couch and into action?

You must move, no matter what. You don't have to find the cure to
cancer today. Just find something simple that needs to be done and
do it. The best antidote for laziness is putting one foot in front of the
other. Don't listen to the little voices in your head that whisper, I'll
start tomorrow. Ignore the equally damaging voices that whisper, "I
should have done this three months ago." Just go. Don't think. Do.

Impatience is another looming roadblock. Maybe you've done the first
few exercises in this book, but you're not seeing results. Therefore,
you're thinking about re-gifting this book to your brother-in-law for
Christmas. He's a big, fat loser. He probably needs it worse than you,
right? Wrong. Don't let impatience halt your progress. Hang on. Don't
leave before the miracle occurs.

Your assignment today is to turn off the TV. Pick one action item and
do it. Do not even consider the results or the rewards. Just launch
yourself into action. When you're done, congratulate yourself. You've
conquered laziness and impatience today.

Day 8

"Alone we can do so little; together we can do so much."

Helen Keller

You do not get any extra points for accomplishing things alone. In fact, one of the great keys to success is teamwork. Everyone has different talents and abilities, and when you pool your resources, you tend to witness amazing results. It just might be the big cosmic joke of humanity. Alone it is impossible, but together all things are possible.

A very important lesson in success is to acknowledge that some people are just better at certain tasks than you are. So if you can't beat 'em, join 'em! Band together with people you admire and see how powerful you are when united.

Helen Keller was deaf and blind and therefore had very little opportunity to connect with the outside world. Her potential for greatness was almost wasted. Then Annie Sullivan broke through her isolation. Together, they formed a bond and a way to communicate. Annie Sullivan took Helen Keller by the hand and brought her out of her isolation and into the world. She helped her achieve her dreams. Alone, Helen Keller would have accomplished very little. Together they did so much.

Through hard work and cooperation with her teacher and others, Helen Keller broke through her barriers and became a model of achievement. She was a prolific American author and lecturer, and she was an activist in many causes, including women's suffrage and worker's rights.

Today, your assignment is to think about your partnerships. Do you have any? Did you recently lend a hand to someone? Have you accepted help? Why or why not?

"What lies behind us, and what lies before us are small matters compared to what lies within us."

Ralph Waldo Emerson

A very important point to consider while you are working through this year is that your past and your future are totally irrelevant to achieving your dreams. They are insignificant details. What you want to concentrate on this year is what you've got going on inside.

You want to touch that flame in your soul that will allow you to do great things. It doesn't matter if you're not proud of your past accomplishments. It doesn't matter if the uncertainty of the future terrifies you. What matters is doing that internal inventory to find out who you are and what you want out of life.

There is a powerhouse of potential locked inside you. How are you going to choose to use it? Would you rather keep it hidden and controlled, so that you don't stick out in a crowd? Or would you secretly like to see what would happen if you unleashed your true potential on the world? Are you willing to take responsibility for yourself and your actions?

Your assignment today is to write a definition of yourself. Define yourself in three sentences or less. Then write down five things you really like about yourself and five things you wish you could change. Finally, if you could look deep inside, what color do you imagine your soul to be and why? Do this exercise quickly, and don't spend too much time pondering your answers. Write down the first things that come to mind, and then leave it. Keep this definition in your notebook, and you will refer to it again a few months from now.

Day 10

"It's kind of fun to do the impossible."

Walt Disney

Do you get overwhelmed easily? Is it hard for you to finish things you've started? If something seems impossible, would you rather forget it and move on to something easier? Most people don't like to attempt the impossible, but Walt Disney has a wonderful twist of logic when it comes to this word.

It really is fun to do the impossible. It's like throwing a surprise party. You catch people off guard. You show them that their limitations don't apply to you. It's also a little like playing make-believe. What if you pretend a task isn't impossible? You might just find a way to accomplish it if you don't know the goal is supposed to be unattainable.

Why not? No one actually expects you to succeed, so go for it! There is a freedom in attempting the impossible. Failure is expected, so you have nowhere to go but up. And who defined it as impossible, anyway? How do you really know it can't be done until you try?

Cultivate your devilish side today. You don't have to accomplish the impossible, but it might be fun to practice the improbable. Think about something positive you could do that would completely shock people who know you. Let's say you absolutely hate getting up in the morning. What would happen if you got up very early one morning, participated in some sort of physical exercise, and then brought breakfast to your family or co-workers? That might just send some of them into cardiac arrest. "You did what? But you hate the morning! It could be fun."

"You are the average of the five people you spend the most time with."

Jim Rohn

Yikes! It might be time to find some new friends.

Seriously, you are influenced by the people with whom you spend the bulk of your time. Who are those people? Think through a typical week in your life. Who do you hang out with most? Is it your family, people at work, or members of a church group, a book club, a hiking group? Who are your closest friends? Who do you go to for advice?

Some people respond to this statement with a feeling of helplessness. They didn't choose their five people. They're stuck with the group they have due to circumstances beyond their control. That is completely untrue. You cannot cry victim here. You have every right to choose the people around you. The controls are in your hands and no one else's.

Seek out people you admire, and spend time with them. Do you have an elderly relative who holds a wealth of information about your heritage? Why not sit at her feet and let her tell you about your family? Is there someone at work you really admire? Sit down with them in the lunchroom and start a conversation.

Your assignment today is to take a critical look at the five people you spend the most time with. Are they individuals who inspire you? Do they make you laugh, or do they bring you down? Do they belittle you, or do they encourage you? Do they nurture you and allow you to grow, or do they squash your dreams every chance they get? You are influenced both positively and negatively by people around you. It is time to choose your friends wisely.

Day 12

"Inspiration is wonderful when it happens, but the writer must develop an approach for the rest of the time . . . The wait is simply too long."

Leonard Bernstein

Inspiration is not just for writers. It is a wonderful asset for achieving your dreams in any walk of life. Finding inspiration, though, is an interesting and sometimes frustrating journey. Most of us wait for it to hit, like nomads in the desert searching the sky for the possibility of rain.

Leonard Bernstein suggested that you can do more than wait. Develop a plan for the off time. Set an approach to life when you are not bubbling over with inspiration. You can accomplish just as much on an average, uninspired day, if you are in the practice of cultivating inspiration. The work is just a bit more tedious.

One terrific way to cultivate inspiration is to start a journal. Get in the practice of writing in your journal every day. If you don't know what to say, write "I don't know what to say." Pretty soon you'll get bored with that statement and write down what's really on your mind. The key to journaling is honesty. This is not an assignment you will ever turn in to a teacher, so say what you really feel.

When you journal, you are turning over the earth of your mind and soul and getting it ready for planting ideas. Journaling is a non-judgmental task. Just write down what comes to mind. Let your pen on the paper be an extension of your thoughts. Do not try to think about what you are going to say first and then write it down. This is not meant to be a perfect composition. The action is much more important than the result.

"Never worry about numbers. Help one person at a time, and always start with the person nearest you."

Mother Teresa

It is easy to worry about the numbers. "I'm not spending enough time with my children." "I don't make enough money in my job." "I only made it to the gym once this week." "I gave a donation to a charity, but they need so much more." That kind of worry leads to a feeling of being overwhelmed, and that's a dangerous place. When you feel overwhelmed, you are precariously close to giving up.

Don't let yourself go down that dark alley. Concentrate on the present. What can you do right now that would cause a positive ripple effect? Is one of your children struggling with math homework? Go help them right now. Is there a part-time job you can pick up a couple of nights a week to boost your income? Apply for it. Have you pursued new job opportunities recently that would include an increase in salary? It can't hurt to look. Do you feel fat and flabby today? Go for a walk or get yourself to the gym no matter what. Concentrate on what you can do today, and force yourself to drop your worries about tomorrow every time they surface.

One of the best ways to get out of the funk of worry is to be helpful to someone else. It immediately takes your mind off of your own problems, and it feels good. Are you a member of a volunteer organization? You don't have to necessarily join the Peace Corps to help. What can you do in your community today to help someone other than yourself? You will be surprised to see how reaching out to others will eventually help you.

Day 14

"You have achieved success if you have lived well, laughed often and loved much."

Author Unknown

If you died today, would you be able to look back on your life with satisfaction, or would you feel like you missed out? Life is not merely meant to be endured. It is really meant to be celebrated every step of the way. Are you having fun yet?

Don't wait for the big pay-off before you start enjoying your life. There is no proof to support the idea that successful people must pay their dues by toiling endlessly and forfeiting happiness for a number of years until they reach their goal. You can actually be happy and enjoy life all along the road to success. It's true! Take off your blinders and look at the scenery. There is so much out there for you to experience. Life is a journey, not a destination. You have a 100 percent chance of dying, but it's what you do between now and then that counts.

One of the greatest measures of success is friendship. Have you lived well with your friends and family? Do you isolate yourself from them, or do you get together and share laughter and love?

How do you define success? Is it purely monetary? What makes your life good? Do you agree with this quote? The definition of a successful life is different for everyone. It is up to you to define when and how you achieve success.

Your assignment today is to write down five things in your life for which you are grateful and five ways in which you are successful today.

"If we all did the things we are capable of doing, we would literally astound ourselves."

Thomas Edison

What are you capable of doing? Do you have any idea? Have you ever tested your limits? Thomas Edison suggests that very few of us have a clue about our real capabilities. What might we accomplish if we work together using our resources to their fullest? It is an awesome thing to consider. How wonderful it would be to be part of a world where we all explored our capabilities. Is that a ridiculous dream? Not necessarily.

The first step in discovering your capabilities is to try new things. You have no idea what you are capable of until you try. Janet always thought it would be incredible to climb a mountain, but she wasn't in very good shape. She set a date in early September and gave herself a year to work up the nerve. She walked with her best friend, Judy, four or five times a week. They started out walking around the block, but every week they increased their distance just a little. By August, the ladies were hiking nearly twenty miles a week.

Janet chose a relatively "easy" first mountain to climb. It was over 14,000 feet at the summit, but she could walk it without climbing gear. On the scheduled day, the sun shone brightly, and Janet huffed and puffed and stopped every few feet as she reached the summit, but she did it! The view was astounding. Janet hadn't known what she was capable of until she tried.

Your assignment today is to try something new. If you don't like it, you never have to do it again. Remove the chains that limit you and jump in to the unknown.

Day 16

"In real life, I assure you, there is no such thing as algebra."
Fran Lebowitz

This may come as a great relief to those of you for whom math is not your strongest subject. The point of this quote is not to offend the mathematicians of the world. It simply points out that you don't have to be brilliant in everything in order to be successful in life.

Lucky for us, real life offers numerous options for success. Your job is to find out which one fits you the best. Have you truly explored your talents? A good place to start is with things that actually interest you. You may be drawn to them because you have a certain aptitude in that area.

Andrew always loved the theatre. Ever since his parents took him to see *Peter Pan* in the second grade, he has been enthralled with the spectacle of a live stage production. As soon as he was old enough, he auditioned for plays, but he soon discovered performing in front of a crowd was not one of his true talents. He was crushed, but he remained on the periphery of the stage like a moth to a flame. Finally, someone put him to work hanging lights. Andrew is now an award-winning lighting designer. He makes magic on the stage through his artistic use of color and light. It took him a little while to figure it out, but he found his calling and achieved a level of success he never could have dreamed of when he was seven years old.

Your assignment today is to become a detective. Search for clues that might lead to your hidden talents. What do you really enjoy in life? What gets you excited? Think about all aspects of those items. Do you have an undiscovered talent hiding within them?

"The greater danger for most of us is not that our aim is too high and we miss it, but that it is too low and we reach it."

Michelangelo

Are you bored with your present life circumstances? It might be because you set your goals too low. No one likes to fail, but people often over-compensate by setting goals that are too easy to obtain. They reach them, and then they coast as long as they can, resisting a challenge or a new opportunity. They feel safe and secure in their accomplishments, even if they lead a slightly unfulfilling life.

This approach to life is a little like the duck-pond game at a carnival. Every duck has a number on its belly, so everyone is a winner. It's the safest game at the carnival, but the prizes are usually pretty crappy. Do you want to have the guarantee of obtaining a prize, any prize, even if it's a crappy one? Or would you rather go for the giant stuffed animal in the difficult game where very few winners emerge?

That's a tough choice. You want to win. If you lose, you have nothing to show for your trouble. But what are you going to do with the mediocre toy once you win it? It will probably be discarded in a week or so when you move on to more exciting diversions.

Your assignment today is to take a look at where you are aiming. Examine the targets you have set in your professional life and your personal life. Are you aiming too low? If you haven't even set your goals, your assignment is to find a few targets and take aim. It is very difficult to achieve success without seeing a goal before you. Find your targets and aim high.

Day 18

"A sense of humor is part of the art of leadership, of getting along with people, of getting things done."

Dwight D. Eisenhower

Cultivating a sense of humor is one of the best weapons in your arsenal of success. Humor is healing and unifying, and it can also lead to great accomplishments. Why is humor such an effective weapon? It might be because laughter is something to which everyone relates. It allows people to see their commonalities rather than their differences.

If you want to be a leader, you must not take yourself so seriously. Life is too important to be taken seriously! Poke a little fun at yourself. Admit it when you fail, laugh, and move on. You will gain more admiration by taking responsibility for your foibles than by trying to cover them up.

If you find yourself acting as a mediator between disparate parties, humor is also a handy tool. Use it to release tension and help each side get a glimpse of how the other side sees things. If you can get people who disagree with each other to laugh at their situation for a moment, they will relax and be more receptive to a mutually agreeable solution. Humor releases tension and loosens people up so that they are willing to work together toward a common goal. It takes the heat off for a moment so that parties can cool down and get back to being productive.

Your assignment today is to look for examples of how humor can help in various situations in your life. Where can you apply humor to mend a relationship, ease someone's burden, or bring people together?

"Music washes away from the soul the dust of everyday life."
                                        Berthold Auerbach

Music is extraordinary. It is an amazing tool for inspiration. Whether you are a fan of chamber music or Led Zeppelin, you probably know how effective music is in altering your mood. If you are feeling frazzled, soothing tones can bring your pulse down to a manageable level. If you are lethargic, a driving melody will pick you up faster than a cup of coffee.

Music does have the power to wash off the dust of everyday life, to transport you, and to adjust your mood, so take advantage of its influence. Consider your array of choices. Through today's technology, you have melodies throughout the centuries and across the globe at your fingertips. You may find you really have a connection to Gregorian chant, a form of music that was first notated back in the 10th century. The contemporary music of Tina Turner might make you feel powerful and energized. South African music provides a mind-boggling choice of styles from folk tunes to jive. Beethoven's Pastoral Symphony has the magical ability to transport you to a country scene and trap you in a driving rain storm.

Does music play a part in your daily life? Do you ever take time out to stop what you are doing and actively listen to your favorite tunes? Explore how music affects you. Find out more about its positive and powerful influence. It is one of many art forms that have a direct line into your soul.

Your assignment today is to get down and boogie! Spend at least ten minutes listening to music and observe how it affects your mood.

Day 20

"You must take personal responsibility. You cannot change the circumstances, the seasons, or the wind, but you can change yourself."

Jim Rohn

Personal responsibility: two words that will give you the key to success. You are responsible for everything you do in life. If you truly want to change, you must start by looking in the mirror. It takes courage to take personal responsibility. It would be much easier to blame someone or something else for your problems or shortcomings.

Susan grew up in a small town. Her parents were abusive, and she had very few successful role models around her. She got pregnant when she was sixteen years old and dropped out of high school to raise her child as a single mother.

There were of host of people, places, and things Susan could blame for her situation, but she decided to take a different route. Susan couldn't change the tiny town where she was born; she couldn't change her parents; and she couldn't pretend the little girl she held in her arms didn't exist. She only had the power to change one thing—herself. That's exactly what she did. Susan went to night school and got her GED. She read about a company she really admired in the newspaper and applied for an entry-level job. Once she had a foot in the door, she went back to night school and earned a bachelor's degree, which led to her first of many promotions. Susan changed herself, and that changed her circumstances.

Your assignment is to think of at least one situation where you avoid personal responsibility. Make a plan to change yourself and take responsibility for your actions.

"Imagination is everything. It is the preview of life's coming attractions."

Albert Einstein

Imagination is not a tool reserved for children. It is a very useful instrument for success. When was the last time you took imagination out of your toolbox? Is it old, rusty, neglected, and hidden under all of the other tools? It's time to clean it off and play a little.

There is a very practical use for imagination. If you can't imagine your life changing, then it's simply not going to happen. Albert Einstein nailed it when he said imagination is a preview of coming attractions. You have to think something up before you can bring it into reality. If we didn't use our imagination, we would never have invented airplanes, or the Internet . . . or indoor plumbing. Think of all the new ideas that pop up in our world every year. Are you astounded by the ability some people have to create new things? You possess that same capability within you. You can put it to good use simply by playing.

Today's exercise is fun, and you may think it's a little silly. Your task is to practice using your imagination. Give yourself permission to let your mind wander all day. Imagine your perfect life. Where do you live? What is your job like? Who do you hang out with? There are no rules here. You can live in a castle and be president of the world if you want.

Now, become even more childlike. Imagine you are a superhero, and you can use your powers to help three people. Who will you help and how?

This exercise may feel a little ridiculous to you, but it has a purpose. You are stretching your mind to visualize the impossible. That is a key ingredient to success. Have fun!

Day 22

"Only those who will risk going too far can possibly find out how far one can go."

T.S. Elliot

Are you willing to take risks in order to achieve success? That's not such an easy question. This book is about achieving success one day at a time. The idea is that you can take small steps and reap great rewards. It sounds safe, not risky. But you also have to be willing to go out on a limb at some point. You have to step a little too far into the wilderness in order to find out what you might be missing. Are you willing to do that?

What would happen if you took a risk and failed? Would it be so terrible? Many of us are terrified of failure, but maybe it's not so bad. Think about failure for a moment. If you try something new and fail, what will you do? You will pick yourself up and try something else. That's not really the doomsday we make it out to be.

You cannot find success without also experiencing failure. They are twins attached at the hip. Almost every great person in history experienced an equal measure of failure before finding success. You have to be willing to get a little egg on your face if you want the big prize.

If you are afraid of risk, imagine that superhero you were yesterday. That person wouldn't be afraid. Pretend you are fearless today. Walk up to the person you have admired from afar and ask him or her on a date. Talk to your boss about the raise you deserve. Reach out to the person you fought with months ago and swore you would never speak to again. Conquer your fear by experiencing it and moving through it. You don't know what incredible things you will find in that wilderness.

"Most folks are about as happy as they make up their minds
to be."

Abraham Lincoln

Bill shuffled through life like Eeyore in Winnie the Pooh. He was
always sad. He just couldn't catch a break. It seemed as though a dark
cloud followed Bill around, and he never got to feel the sunshine.
Friends and family tried to snap him out of his funk, but he was a
hopeless case. They suggested he see a doctor about his depression,
but he ignored their recommendations. Bill watched other people
who seemed to be happy, and he assumed they were faking it. Life
was hard. Every time he thought things were going to get better, he
was knocked right back down in the gutter. Why even bother?

Your first reaction to this story may be to empathize with Bill or at
least feel sorry for him. But Bill chooses his sadness every day. He
picks that gray, dingy sweater out of his closet and decides to put it
on. He chooses to concentrate on his sadness and not turn it around
by accepting the help and suggestions of people who care about him.

You cannot choose your circumstances. Life throws curveballs at
everyone on this planet. You *can* choose your reaction to life. You have
the power to select your mood just like you pick out your clothes.
If you wake up feeling melancholy, you can take action to replace
those thoughts with happier ones. Maybe you like the feel of that old,
gray sweater. Maybe it's more comfortable. Are you choosing sadness
today? It's completely up to you.

Your assignment is to experiment with the power you possess to be
happy (if you want to be). List ten things that make you happy and do
at least three of them. Then, do at least two random acts of kindness
for someone else. How do you feel?

Day 24

"If you want to be happy, set a goal that commands your thoughts, liberates your energy, and inspires your hopes."
Andrew Carnegie

One way to find happiness is to create goals. Unhappy people tend to be aimless. They are stuck in a cycle of despair that leads nowhere. If you set just one goal, it may become your lifeline out of despair and toward hope. Goal-oriented people have drive and purpose in life. They want to get up in the morning, because they have a plan to make their life better. They are looking forward to what the day will bring, not dreading it.

Your assignment today is to set a really exciting goal. It should be something that will take up your thoughts for awhile and require some imagination and creativity. It can be a totally frivolous goal, but choose something that will make you proud when you've achieved it.

Maybe you are short on cash, and your brother's birthday is coming up in a few weeks. Set a goal to create a unique gift using your own skills and imagination. This few weeks of creativity will liberate your thoughts and will probably lead to ideas in other areas of your life. You might end up so proud of the result that you can't wait for your brother to open his present.

Happiness does not happen randomly. It is the result of a series of actions. You have the power to make conditions right for happiness. You can choose happiness today by setting a goal that will command your thoughts, liberate your energy, and inspire your hopes.

"Success is not the key to happiness. Happiness is the key to success. If you love what you are doing, you will be successful."

Albert Schweitzer

So many of us have this idea reversed. Success is not the key to happiness. Happiness actually has to come first. If you are engaged in what you are doing and you enjoy it, you will be successful.

Kate loved her job, but she always adopted a stern expression at work. She felt as though people took her more seriously if she was somber.

Finally, a wise co-worker asked, "Kate, do you like your job?"

"Why, yes," she replied, a bit startled.

"Then, if you're happy, let your face know it."

Happiness is the key to success, and it is also contagious. If you love what you're doing and you let yourself experience the joy of taking part in that action, you will be glowing with inspiration. Other people pick up on that. They will be drawn to you, because they want what you have.

Your assignment is to find something you love to do. Don't just pick something you sort of enjoy. Find something you love to do. It doesn't have to be the same thing you do for a living. The thing you love to do might be a volunteer activity or a hobby. Try out some new ideas if you don't have a clue about what that thing is. Join a club or audit a class at your local community college. Experiment to find out what brings you joy and then take part in it. Success will be soon to follow.

Day 26

"Face the worst. Believe the best. Do the most. Leave the rest."
Bishop Mel Wheatley

Whenever you feel stuck in life, it can be very difficult to find a way out of the darkness. This quote gives you a flashlight to navigate through the shadows. If you stick with these simple directions, you will emerge into the light before you know it.

Face the worst. What is going on in your life that you are avoiding? You will have to face it sooner or later, so you might as well get it over with and stop worrying about the ramifications. Face your problems head on and deal with them.

Believe the best. It is a waste of time to worry about bad things that might happen. If you're going to let your mind wander, why not imagine a positive outcome? Believe the best will come to you. You deserve the best. Believe it will happen. If it doesn't, you're no worse off. You can deal with a less-than-ideal situation if and when it occurs.

Do the most. Do whatever you can to ensure you will end up with the best possible results. Have you done everything you can in a given situation, or are you hiding and hoping for the best? You need to do the footwork if you want to reap the benefits.

Leave the rest. There are aspects of life that are completely out of your control. Leave them alone. You are powerless over them. You can leave them to your god, to the universe, to chance, whatever works for you. Just let them be. Conserve your efforts for things you can change.

Your assignment today is to use this roadmap the next time you hit a roadblock. Take stock of your situation by examining each of these four principles.

"A wise man will make more opportunities than he finds."

Francis Bacon

Joe was a lucky guy. It seemed like opportunity followed him everywhere. His projects at work always came out on top, he was in great shape, he had tons of connections, and he smiled all the time. It was nauseating! Some people just have all the luck.

In truth, Joe's circumstances had very little to do with luck. He created opportunities rather than waiting for them to show up. Joe looked at everything he experienced as a way to grow and improve and learn something new. He observed others, and he tried new things. Soon, he saw opportunity budding all around him.

Joe had a friend who went to the gym regularly during lunch, so he decided to give it a try. He found the midday exercise to be exhilarating. It gave him a jolt of energy for the rest of the day and cleared his mind of the issues he had faced that morning. As a result of trying something new, Joe found a way to increase his concentration at work and also get in shape. He observed a colleague, tried something that person found to be helpful, and created an opportunity to get in shape and become more productive at work.

Joe didn't wait for his doctor to tell him it was time to get rid of a few pounds. He didn't wait for his friend to invite him to the gym. He noticed what was going on around him, and he created his own opportunity.

Your assignment today is to write down three ways in which you can create opportunity in your life. You have one week to follow through and make at least one of those opportunities a reality.

Day 28

"Gather ye rosebuds while ye may,
Old Time is still a-flying;
And this same flower that smiles to-day
Tomorrow will be dying . . . "

Robert Herrick

You have very few second chances in this life. Are you willing pass by a good opportunity? The flowers of chance are opening all around you. Do you see them?

Pick those lovely flowers of opportunity while they are blooming, because you may never get another chance. Gather precious moments with your children. Take a walk under the stars tonight, because they are too stunning to ignore. Give a project at work everything you've got, because you may not have a chance to go back and fix it later. Play in the snow, because it's in your front yard right now. Listen to the music of the waves when you sit on the beach, because you may never hear such a beautiful melody again. Stand up and volunteer for that committee that is a little outside of your comfort zone, because now may be your only opportunity to do it.

Experience as much as you can in this wonderful world, because your stay here is finite and often far too short. You don't know if you will get a second chance, so snatch up opportunities when you see them.

Grab on to life with both hands. Experience it. Don't just go through the motions; don't just get by. Be an active participant. You will find success in your experience. Your assignment today is to actively participate in your day as if it was your last day on earth. Make the most of everything you do. Enjoy every little moment.

"While we stop to think, we often miss our opportunity."
Publilius Syrus

We've been talking for the last several days about opportunity, and the one thing that keeps popping to the surface is living in the here and now and taking advantage of what is before you. Opportunity is strongly linked to living in the present rather than regretting the past or worrying about the future. You must act when opportunity shows up, and you can't take action if you are not paying attention.

The quote above from the 1st century B.C. shows just how long humans have been looking for opportunity and finding the best ways to capture it. Grabbing opportunity has more to do with instinct and less to do with thinking. It's a gut reaction to something new and exciting and potentially noteworthy.

Many of us tend to think of opportunity in business terms: a new job opportunity, an opportunity to make more money, an opportunity to show your boss what you're worth. Opportunity also takes other forms. A random call from your mother may be an opportunity for you to tell her you love her. A solicitation from your favorite charity in the mail may be an opportunity for you to give back to your community.

Your assignment today is to look back through the previous week and list times when you have missed an opportunity. Journal for about fifteen minutes or so about why you didn't grab on to those opportunities and what you could do in the future to make a different choice.

Day 30

"A missed opportunity is worse than a defeat."

Anonymous

This is the last day in our miniseries on opportunity, and it's a sobering quote. Can missed opportunity really be worse than a defeat? Yes, it can! When you miss an opportunity, you didn't even bother to show up for the game. It's not as if you made an attempt and lost. You didn't play.

It is worse than defeat, because you have no idea if you might have won. Every opportunity is a chance for success, and you can't win if you don't play. Are you in the game? Or are you standing on the sidelines watching the players go back and forth, never taking part in the action yourself?

It is risky to act when you see an opportunity, but you will never move forward if you don't get in the game. You cannot obtain success if you do not grab onto opportunity. If you latch on to an opportunity and fail, you actually have achieved a certain amount of success. You know for certain what doesn't work, and you can explore other options. If you miss the opportunity, you are left with nothing.

You may think it's safer to stay away from opportunity, but when you do not participate in life, that, too, is a choice. You are making a decision not to grow and learn and stretch yourself. You are actively choosing not to achieve success when you let opportunity slip by. That's not safe at all.

Your assignment today is to get in the game! Don't miss an opportunity when you see one.

"If you're walking down the right path and you're willing
to keep walking, eventually you'll make progress."

Barack Obama

Are you on the right path? Is your life filled with activities that help
you and others to flourish, or do you tend to partake in behaviors
that send you on a detour away from success? If you are completely
honest with yourself, you will know the answer.

You know intuitively if you are on the right or wrong path. You are
aware at some level of whether or not you engage in behavior that is
healthy mentally and physically, or unhealthy. When you are headed
down the wrong path, and you know it, you might want to think
about why you chose that road. Do you gain some amount of comfort
from not living up to your potential? Why did you choose to be where
you are? You do not have the luxury of saying it's not your fault. You
are not a victim. You choose every step of your journey.

Sometimes the more difficult task is to stay on the right path once
you've found it. You may have an inkling you're headed in the
right direction, but you're not getting the results you would like
quickly enough.

That's where patience comes in. You must be willing to keep walking,
even if you don't reap rewards immediately. You are in control of the
path you choose, but you can't mandate the amount of time it will
take you to reach success. However, if you are on the right path, you
will eventually make progress. You will find success.

Your assignment today is to take a look at your path. Are you on the
right path or the wrong path? Are you getting impatient?

Day 32

"My little [note]books were beginnings—they were the ground into which I dropped the seed . . . I would work in this way when I was out in the crowds, then put the stuff together at home."

Walt Whitman

Your very first assignment was to get a notebook. You may have discovered by now that having a notebook with you at all times can be extremely handy. Numerous successful individuals keep a notebook with them to jot down their ideas whenever they think of them. Do you keep your notebook handy? That is your assignment today.

Why? There is one very good reason: you never know when inspiration will hit. Walt Whitman was a wonderful observer, and he found many seeds of creative inspiration when he was out and about. He didn't want to forget his best ideas by the time he returned home. Inspiration is a fleeting thing. It is front and center in your mind at one moment, and then the next minute it vanishes.

You may take a walk on a beautifully crisp blue morning and witness a hawk flying against the bright sky. The scene inspires you to write down a few lines. Those lines may become a poem, a song, or a new advertising campaign. They may even motivate you to use similar colors when you remodel your living room. Who knows?

The words Walt Whitman jotted down were beginnings. He recorded scraps of ideas and then put them together and worked on them more carefully at home. The notebook was a net to catch all of the ideas that floated to the surface. Walt Whitman did not judge the ideas he wrote down in his notebook. He knew they weren't the final product. They were the ground into which he dropped the seed.

"My first notebook was a Big Five tablet, given to me [at age five] by my mother with the sensible suggestions that I stop whining and learn to amuse myself by writing down my thoughts."

Joan Didion

Joan Didion's mother was no dummy. Her "no whining" attitude laid the groundwork for a great American writer. Joan Didion is yet another example of using a notebook as a tool for success.

A notebook is outwardly such a simple and unassuming item — boring even. But put it in the hands of a human being, and it has unlimited possibilities. It may become the next great novel or the plans for an invention or a sketch that will later become a sculpture.

Your assignment today is to stop whining and grab your notebook. Take it outside or to a quiet corner in your home or to a coffee shop, wherever you feel comfortable. Now, spend about thirty minutes amusing yourself. Write down whatever comes to mind; draw pictures; doodle in the margins; turn it upside down if you want or write in circles instead of along the lines. Break whatever rules you think exist for writing in notebooks. You don't have to start on the first page. You can start at the end if you want. Today is a play day.

Did you bring a pen or pencil? Maybe you should try crayons instead . . . or markers or watercolors and a paintbrush. What other object could you use as a writing utensil? This assignment is not a college thesis. Your degree does not depend on it. Who cares what kind of silliness you create? The point is to amuse yourself and no one else. Have a little fun today!

Day 34

"[John F. Kennedy] relishes notable writing, and has ever since he started collecting examples of good prose and putting them in a bound book, which he was still doing when he started running for president."

Benjamin C. Bradlee

You are not the only one with good ideas. Another way you can fill up your notebook is by writing down quotes from others that inspire you. One of the best ways to achieve success is to learn from others. John F. Kennedy collected quotes to inspire him, to remind him of significant ideas, and to help him along the road to success.

You have endless resources at your fingertips with the Internet. You can look up quotes on just about any subject. You may also pull good prose from a book you are reading or a newspaper article. Is there a colleague you admire at work? Write down some of the things they say as a way to learn from their behavior.

Sometimes the best quotes come from children. Are there any wise little ones in your life? Did they say something recently that was unusually wise or funny? Write it down. Don't let their words be lost in the chatter that surrounds everyday life.

Your assignment today is to write down three quotes in your notebook that came from someone besides you. How do those quotes make you feel? Are they inspiring? Depressing? Funny?

On Day 27 you were given a week to turn an opportunity into a reality. Have you had a chance to do that yet? If not, what are you waiting for? Get to work! You will come across hundreds of opportunities every day. Grab on to one of them. If you did it, way to go!

"You can observe a lot just by watching."

Yogi Berra

Leave it to Yogi Berra to state the obvious. He has been both cheered and jeered for his malapropisms, but sometimes the obvious is exactly what you need. Keep it simple. Yogiisms are part of Yogi Berra's charm and part of his success.

How can you simplify your life today? One great way to do that is to become a good observer. Drop your agenda and expectations and turn your vision to others. It is amazing what you will pick up if you get out of yourself and watch the world from another's perspective. It will give you the opportunity to become a better friend, a better spouse, a better coworker, and a more-well-rounded individual. Observation is quite a useful tool for success.

Your assignment today is to pretend the world is new. You just landed here on Earth, and there is nothing you can assume about human nature. Your task is to simply observe without judgment. Discard everything you know and start over objectively. Watch and take note. Jot down the things you find interesting in your notebook.

What are some important things you notice? How do people come together in a crisis? Who is the first to reach out and help? How do others react to that person? Can you identify people who are only concerned about their own well-being? How are they treated by others? Make a list of observations you would like to emulate and those you would not want to repeat. Through all of this, keep it simple. Watch and listen and learn.

"A few observations and much reasoning lead to error; many observations and a little reasoning lead to truth."

Alexis Carrel

Julie managed fifteen employees in a house cleaning service. She was walking by the window of her office and stopped to observe some of her employees loading a van to start the day. Angela was talking on her cell phone and pacing back and forth while the other employees loaded vacuums and mops and other equipment into the back of the van.

Julie shook her head and flicked her pen against her crossed arms. Obviously, Angela was not pulling her weight. Just yesterday she left a job early. Julie made a mental note to pull Angela aside at the end of the day and give her a final warning or she would have to find another job.

Did Julie make the right decision? How many observations did she use to come to her conclusion? The answer is two. Is that enough? Why didn't Julie go outside and ask Angela about her phone call? Is there a reason she didn't go directly to the source? Did she ask Angela or any of the other employees why she left early the day before? Should she have done so?

How many observations do you collect before you make a decision? The more observations you can assemble, the more accurate your picture. Your task today is to count the number of observations you gather before making a conclusion. Count them; write them down in your notebook; and work to increase the number throughout the day. More observing and less contemplating will get you closer to the truth.

"Thinking is more interesting than knowing, but less interesting than looking."

Johann Wolfgang von Goethe

Goethe created a continuum with this quote. Knowing is the point when you arrive at the finish line. It's the end of the game. Thinking is more interesting than knowing, because you are engaged. It's enjoyable to allow your mind to turn over ideas and create new solutions. The best of them all is looking. Looking contains a surprise factor. You can never be quite sure what you'll find when you look. It's exciting. It also takes the pressure off you. You are not creating what you see. You are simply taking note of it.

Observation is not a difficult task. It is a discovery. Enjoy your chances to observe what's going on around you. They will be exhilarating, and they can lead you back down Goethe's continuum. Looking is thought provoking, and thinking will help you to become more knowledgeable. It is a continuous cycle of learning.

You give yourself more ammunition for success if you increase your observational skills. Observations are fuel for thought and knowledge. Your assignment today is to continue to collect observations in all aspects of your life. Observe how your son brushes his teeth; observe how the woman at the bus stop holds her packages and sighs while she waits for her ride; observe how the tips of your boss's ears turn red right before he starts yelling at his employees.

Again, this task is not drudgery. Make it fun — but avoid making others uncomfortable. Your goal here is not to become a stalker. Just pay attention to what goes on around you.

Day 38

"Speak little, do much."

Benjamin Franklin

Do you talk about the great things you want to do in life but never get around to actually accomplishing them? If you want to achieve success, now is the time to put your words into action. This is the point where many individuals get discouraged. It's fun to dream up lofty accomplishments, but when it comes to the part where you have to put in some real work, the exercise loses some of its appeal to the average person.

But you are not average. This is where you have the opportunity to separate yourself from the pack. You will find that taking action is not as tiresome as you imagine. You don't have to do anything that requires too much sacrifice. You just have to act.

You will now break away from the crowd simply by doing. You've already worked on becoming a good observer. That is one type of action that will lead to success. What are other things you can do today to send you on the road to achievement?

Don't put undue pressure on yourself. You don't have to come up with something brilliant. Just button your lip and get off the couch. That's a great first step. Do you have unfinished projects around the house? Pick one and do it. You will feel great when you're finished. Don't get overwhelmed by all of the things you've left undone. Just pick one job and complete it. You can worry about other stuff another day.

Your assignment today is to pick one thing around the house that you have been meaning to complete and finish it. When you're done, congratulate yourself with something fun and a little frivolous.

"When your work speaks for itself, don't interrupt."
Henry J. Kaiser

You are now becoming a person of action. How does it feel? It can be quite a powerful experience. Even a little bit of work gives you a large return in the form of pride and accomplishment.

Jonathon became a man of action. He started with little tasks and stayed in motion, and soon he found he was accomplishing things he never thought possible. He even built a workroom onto his house where he could follow his dream of woodworking.

When Jonathon's wife entered his newly finished workshop, she gasped as she gazed around. She had always known he was quite an artist when it came to woodworking, but she had no idea he had the gumption to follow through with something like this. Jonathon started many projects in the past, but he finished very few. Just months prior, she had been badgering him to get his unfinished woodblocks off of her craft table in the basement.

"This is beautiful!" She smiled.

Jonathon hiked up his pants and looked around, busting with pride. "Yep, I thought I would start off by building you a birdhouse; then I'm going to re-do all of the cabinets in the kitchen; next, I think I'll design and build an entertainment center for the living room . . ."

Your assignment today is to continue to be a person of action. Don't interrupt your efforts with talk. Get back to work.

Day 40

> "A superior man is modest in his speech, but exceeds in his actions."

Confucius

Jonathon's wife in yesterday's story was at first impressed by his new workshop, but then she became immediately skeptical of his actions when he started to talk big about his future plans. At that point, she had only seen him carry out one project to completion. She didn't have much evidence to suggest he would finish all of the other schemes he boasted about.

You must remember to be modest in speech even when you start to become a person of action. You will want to talk about what you've done, because you're happy about your accomplishments. You are proud that you made a very important change in your life. That is a great triumph! But avoid the temptation to talk about what you've done. Pile up more actions instead to build your success.

Push forward in the action category, and you will be happily surprised with the results. You don't have to tell anyone what you are doing. They will look at the evidence and realize you are someone who gets a job done. No further explanation is necessary at this point.

Your job today is to exceed in actions. Today you will avoid lethargy and stay in motion. Find out just how much you can accomplish in twenty-four hours. At the end of the day, make a list of everything you did in your notebook. How does it look? Could you have done more? This list is for your eyes only. Don't show it to anyone else. The next day you will get back into action and keep the secret of your success to yourself.

"When I stand before God at the end of my life, I would hope that I would not have a single bit of talent left, and could say, I used everything you gave me."

Erma Bombeck

What a wonderful demonstration of success it would be if you could say at the end of your life that you used up every single bit of talent you possess! It would be incredibly satisfying to know that you put all of the materials you were given to good use and built a happy and fulfilling existence. Now is your chance to make that happen.

There is really no need to conserve your talents. There is absolutely no reason to wait to use the skills you have been given. Don't save your smarts for a rainy day. In fact, you are doing yourself a disservice by not using up your talents right now and sharing them with the rest of the world. You may find that you have a treasure within you that increases the more it is given away.

When you share your gifts in a way that betters the world around you, you will be blessed with riches beyond measure. You can consider yourself an immediate success, because you have been a positive force on earth.

What do you want to be able to say at the end of your life? Do you want to say I used everything you gave me, or do you want to say, I have a little bit left over? The talents you don't use today are wasted. Do you want to live a wasteful life or a fulfilling life? The choice is yours.

Your assignment today is to use your talents. Don't hide them or save them for just the right moment. You have a vast supply. Share your gifts with the rest of the world.

Day 42

"You may never know what results come of your action, but if you do nothing there will be no result."

Mahatma Gandhi

This is the final day in a short series on action, and the message is simple: if you do nothing, that's exactly what you'll get—nothing.

You can't predict the future, so it is impossible to know what results will come from your actions. They may be good or bad. It is understandable that you would have some trepidation about taking action when you are unsure of what might happen. You could fail. You also might be successful. There is no guarantee one way or the other.

Gandhi makes one very important point, though, and that is if you do nothing, there will be no result. You have no chance of winning. When that truth is brought to light, it makes the decision to take action quite a bit easier.

You picked up this book because you have a desire to be successful. You have a yearning to live up to what you know deep down you are capable of being. The only way you can do that is to take action.

Today, your task is to dig deep and consider actions that you can take right now that will lead to your success. Life is unpredictable, so you do not have the luxury of waiting any longer. Act now! If you do nothing today, you will receive nothing in return. How much better will you feel about yourself if you take action this very moment? There is a brand new world outside waiting for a contribution only you are uniquely qualified to give. Take action today.

"Far away there in the sunshine are my highest aspirations.
I may not reach them, but I can look up and see their beauty,
believe in them, and try to follow where they lead."

Louisa May Alcott

This quote from Louisa May Alcott gives a striking depiction of the beauty of aspirations. Aspirations are goals floating high in the sky and shining in the sunlight. When you feel discouraged, you can look to them, believe in them, and follow them.

Every successful person fills their own imaginary sky with aspirations. It helps them to reach further and try harder and achieve more than they would have if they kept their face to ground and never looked up to the heavens.

One very important secret that successful people have discovered is that they do not have to achieve those highest aspirations. They simply have to strive for them, to follow where they lead. The final result is much less important than the journey toward that shining goal.

What do your aspirations look like? Are they sparkling in the sunlight like those of Louisa May Alcott? Are your dreams displayed openly in your mind's eye? Or are they hidden in the darkness under piles of blankets or deep in a cave? Do you hide your highest aspirations even from yourself?

Your assignment today is to draw a picture of your aspirations. What do they look like? Are they diamonds sparkling in a midnight sky? Are they a strong flowing river that runs through a verdant forest? Draw a picture of your dreams.

Day 44

"I have been impressed with the urgency of doing. Knowing is not enough; we must apply. Being willing is not enough; we must do."

Leonardo da Vinci

Just when you thought you were done with all of that talk about action, here it is again. You can't escape it! It is the main ingredient for success, so you will continue to be nudged toward doing. The wonderful thing about action is it's not hard. It requires a tiny bit of bravery to put one foot forward and get moving, but that's it. You don't have to study to get into action. You just have to do it.

Marion's doctor told her that her diabetes was becoming worrisome, and she really needed to lose weight and change her eating habits if she wanted to live a happier and healthier life. Marion listened intently to the doctor and was willing to make a change.

She bought a library full of self-help books to help her lose weight. She read them all and studied the pros and cons of each in preparation to make a change in her life. She did so much to prepare for change that she was practically an expert on nutrition and exercise, but Marion was still fifty pounds overweight, and her blood sugar levels were out of control.

Knowledge and willingness do not mean much if they are not followed by action. Do you find yourself in an endless cycle of preparation today? It's time to break out of it and start doing. You will learn so much more by taking action.

Your assignment is to write down three ways you can take action today, and then actually do those three things. Don't prepare; don't wait until you're willing; just do them.

"I've learned that people will forget what you said, people will forget what you did, but people will never forget how you made them feel."

Maya Angelou

How do you make people feel? Have you considered that? It is so important to be a positive influence on others. You can create an entire string of success by lifting others up and applauding their accomplishments and acknowledging their talents and good deeds.

Think of how many times you have noticed something good about someone else and neglected to acknowledge it. You know how wonderful it feels when someone pays you a compliment or congratulates you on a job well done. Do the same for others and see what happens.

Find ways to bring out the best in people around you. Concentrate on someone other than yourself for awhile. This is not a contest. Thinking of someone else will not put you behind on the road to success. It does not diminish your own talents. Spend some time concentrating on how the people around you feel. How can you help them feel better? What can you do to bring them success?

Your actions create a ripple effect that influences how others feel. Consider how people feel as a result of the things you do. Do you make people feel happy and safe and loved? Do you make others feel comfortable? Or do you worry people and leave them feeling like they are on pins and needles around you? Do you have a calming influence on others, or are you more like a tornado that tears through their lives?

Your assignment today is to observe how you make others feel.

Day 46

"A person's faults are largely what make him or her likable."

Anne Lamott

It's hard to be perfect. Thank goodness it's not a requirement for success. In fact, one of the unifying factors of humanity is our faults. We all have flaws, and the person who is aware of that and can laugh about it is much more likable than one who tries to appear perfect.

What are your faults? Do you know? Your assignment today is to make a list of your character defects. Be as honest as possible. You can start with the seven deadly sins as a guideline. They are lust, gluttony, greed, sloth, wrath, envy, and pride. Every single one of us probably touches on each of these sins at some level.

You do not need to be exhaustive in your list of faults. The object of this lesson is not to throw you into a deep depression. It is simply an exercise in awareness. It is important to be aware of your blunders so that you can work on them, but it is also important to note that we all have faults. We are all fallible. We are the same in that respect. No one is free of flaws. Everyone has some difficulty to overcome.

You can achieve success by dealing with your shortcomings and having a sense of humor about life when you fail. How boring it would be to be perfect. There would be nothing to work on! Find the humor in your faults, but never stop working to overcome them. We all gain a bit of comfort in knowing that nobody is perfect. You can help others feel better by admitting your faults and dealing with them rather than attempting to give the impression of perfection.

"In a Nutshell: Six Ways to Make People Like You —
Principle 1: Become genuinely interested in other people.
Principle 2: Smile.
Principle 3: Remember that a person's name is to that person the sweetest and most important sound in any language.
Principle 4: Be a good listener. Encourage others to talk about themselves.
Principle 5: Talk in terms of the other person's interests.
Principle 6: Make the other person feel important — and do it sincerely."

> Dale Carnegie

A couple of days ago, your assignment was to observe how you make others feel. What did you discover? Maybe you found out some pretty embarrassing facts about how you treat people. You might even have realized that people in general annoy you. You are not a people person, and you have no intention of becoming one.

If that is even remotely the case, it is time to readjust your thinking. You need people, and people need you. So get over yourself and start reaching out. Today you have a chance to put some principles into practice that will help you concentrate on others and help them feel great.

It is important for you to be genuinely interested in helping others and listening to their points of view if you want to have any chance of achieving success for yourself. You cannot know how rewarding it is to care about others until you make it a consistent part of your daily life. Your assignment today is to put Dale Carnegie's principles to work. Forget about yourself for awhile and take a real interest in the people around you. Start with people you see every day. Do you even know the names of your neighbors? You can't fake this task through half-hearted efforts at sincerity. You must be authentic.

"I can honestly say that I was never affected by the question of the success of an undertaking. If I felt it was the right thing to do, I was for it regardless of the possible outcome."

Golda Meir

It is impossible to predict whether or not a particular undertaking will be successful. So how do you choose which goals to strive for? Golda Meir has a terrific rule to go by: Ask yourself which one is the right thing to do.

There are many ways in which you can measure achievement. Happiness, influence, money, charity, and love are just a few ways in which you can evaluate your success. But the evaluation usually comes after the endeavor. You want to develop a clear sense of direction long before you look back on your choices. How do you know that you are on the road to success?

Think about what goes into your choices. Why did you choose your current job? How did you end up with the friends who surround you? Why do you choose to get up at a certain time in the morning or sleep in? Why did you decide to spend a holiday away from your family?

The most important test is to ask yourself if you did the right thing. The outcome really doesn't matter if you know that you did what was right. If a project fails miserably, but you know you did the right thing, then you are still successful. If you are not selfish, and you reach out and help a person in need, you are successful.

Your assignment today is to ask yourself with each decision you make if you are doing the right thing. Change course if the answer is no.

"Those whom you can make like themselves will, I promise
you, like you very well."

Lord Chesterfield

The last few days you have been concentrating on others. You may
be starting to feel like you are trying to win some sort of popularity
contest. What is the big deal about getting people to like you?

It is a big deal to want people to like you, because if they do, it means
you make them feel good about themselves. Who wants to hang
around someone who makes them feel small or ugly or incompetent?
If you are well-liked, then you are successful at helping others feel
good about who they are when they are with you.

It is important to stress again that this should never be a disingenuous
undertaking. You have to honestly cultivate a desire to bring out the
good in someone else. Highlight their strengths and compliment their
achievements. Lift them up. Don't make up things that aren't true and
fill people with hollow compliments just to complete this task and
move on to your own success.

When you really search for the good in others, you end up finding out
what is good about you. If you are able to have empathy with another
human being, you have the right stuff to be a strong leader, a good
friend, and a valuable person to be around.

Your assignment today is to continue to develop your skills in
making people like themselves. Practice the delicate balance between
compliment, encouragement, and belief in someone or something
other than yourself.

Day 50

"Life is about becoming more than we are."

Oprah Winfrey

Fifty days ago, you picked up this book and made a commitment to yourself to become more than who you thought you were. You knew that deep down you had more to contribute to the world, so you chose to explore new avenues of success through these pages. It is time to review your progress thus far.

First, you wrote down your dreams. Then, you took note of the choices you have made so far in life. You practiced a few random acts of kindness, and you took initial steps toward achieving your destiny. You followed those first steps with actions that would lead you toward new and exciting goals.

Next, you reviewed your partnerships and the people you spend time with on a regular basis. You started to define yourself and had fun imagining the impossible. You jotted down your thoughts and ideas in your journal and noted all of the things for which you are grateful. Gratitude was paid forward when you helped someone else.

You conducted experiments by trying something new and searching for your hidden talents, and then you re-examined your goals in life. You cultivated your sense of humor and played with the power of music. You took risks, practiced fearlessness, and seized opportunities. Finally, you paid attention to others and how you could be of service to them.

Congratulations! You have accomplished quite a lot in a few short weeks. Are you still reaching for more? Can you imagine what the rest of the year will hold?

"It's loving and giving that make life worth living."

Anonymous

In the movie *Home Alone*, a child's dream comes true when he thinks his annoying family has vanished into thin air. He is suddenly free to do whatever he wants. He stays up late, eats ice cream for dinner, watches movies that he's not supposed to watch, messes up his big brother's room, and tries out his dad's deodorant and after-shave lotion. He has a wonderful time alone . . . for a few hours.

Then suddenly, the child comes to the realization that he's just not having that much fun on his own. He misses the love of his family, and he longs for a chance to share his life with them again.

Have you ever wished that everyone would just leave you alone and stop bothering you? Have you ever longed to have everything to yourself, just for one day? Be careful what you wish for.

The truly good things in life are loving and giving. They far exceed material possessions, power, or prestige. Why is that? Have you considered why a simple hug from a friend when you need it the most can completely turn your day around? Have you experienced what it feels like to give to someone who really needs your help?

Your assignment today is to get out your notebook and recall two or three experiences you have had that involve loving and giving. Then journal for a few pages about how loving and giving bring extra meaning to your life. What are ways in which you can add larger portions of those two ingredients to every day?

Day 52

"Life is a game — play to win."

Al Neuharth

Jo Ann trudged through life. Everything was a chore to her. There were very few things she enjoyed in her day, and her sour mood made that very clear. She believed that life was work — hard work — and the people surrounding her were idiots. Jo Ann felt that she would be successful if she played the martyr and grudgingly fixed everyone else's mistakes. She knew how to do things right, and that was her claim to fame.

What is life to you? Is it a chore? Is it drudgery? Do you feel grumpy most days? Does it seem to you like the object of your existence is to get through life, not to enjoy it?

Today's exercise will provide you with an alternate perception of life. Think of life as a game. Stop taking yourself so seriously and start having a little bit of fun. Think of the way you dive into strategies when you play a game. You get right into the action and react to what is going on around you with energy and vibrancy. You can be fearless and take a few risks, because it's just a game. But you are never too reckless. You play to win.

Your task today is to play the game of life. Whenever you start to take yourself too seriously, stop and think of what you would do if you were simply playing a game. What is the next move you want to make? What would be the right move? How can you play to win?

Energize your day by turning your thoughts upside down. Try out a risky move that may be just the right strategy to bring you success. If it doesn't work, no big deal. It's just a game. Laugh at your failures and learn from them. Then get back on the board and try a new strategy. Life is a game — play to win.

"Man is born to live, not to prepare for life."
                                                Boris Pasternak

You are born to live. That is a fairly obvious statement. However, many of us don't do what we were born to do. We don't live. Instead, we spend far too much time *preparing* for life. What exactly are we getting ready for? If we look around, we will find we're in the midst of it already.

Imagine you are the winner of a luxurious train trip. You can take anyone you want with you, and the journey promises to be filled with loads of exciting sites, spectacular events, and a few surprises. The train is pulling away from the station, and rather than hopping on, you choose instead to rearrange your suitcase in the terminal. That sounds ridiculous, doesn't it?

Think about your life right now. Are you rearranging your suitcase, or are you getting on that train? Are you preparing for life, or are you living it?

Your assignment today is to take a page of your notebook and draw a line vertically down the center of the page. On the left side of the line, list at least five ways in which you are preparing for life instead of living it. On the right side of the page list strategies you might use to change what you're doing. How can you stop preparing and start living? What can you do today, at this very minute, to change your inaction into action?

Life is a journey that is just too wonderful to pass up. Get on the train!

Day 54

"Remember no one can make you feel inferior without your consent."

Eleanor Roosevelt

As you navigate your road to success, you will come across roadblocks. We have mentioned them a few times already, and today we will talk about one particularly ominous one — individuals who make you feel inferior.

Do you have a boss, a coworker, a family member, or a friend who makes you feel like you are unworthy of having a successful life? Who is that person? It may be difficult to point them out, especially if they are someone you admire. Nevertheless, it is important to identify them. You must clearly label your roadblocks in order to find a way around them. Who makes you feel inferior?

Your assignment today is in two parts. First, write down who makes you feel inferior. List them by name. Then, write about what that individual does specifically to make you feel substandard. Do they make fun of you? Do they criticize your work? Do they ignore you? What actions do they take to make you feel bad?

The second part of your assignment is to take personal responsibility. You had a chance to complain about what they do to you in part one. Now, you must own up to the fact that you are allowing them to do it. You are giving them consent to make you feel bad. Open up your notebook again, and write about how you can change that. What can you do to take away their power? They cannot make you feel inferior without your consent. You know the truth, and you are in no way inferior to that person. Take responsibility for yourself and take back your power.

"The louder he talked of his honor, the faster we counted our spoons."

Ralph Waldo Emerson

On Day 38 you worked on putting your words into action. You found out that it is often better to speak little and do much. Today, we will revisit that concept in a slightly different way. Actions almost always speak louder than words, and in fact, words will have a negative effect on your character if you don't follow up with appropriate actions.

In the quote above, Ralph Waldo Emerson pokes fun at people who boast about themselves. They usually come across as untrustworthy, and we tend to question their behavior. You may know of someone who is a big talker. They sing their own praises whenever they get the chance, but they don't actually do all the things they say they do. In fact, they are often missing in action when it's time to do some real work.

Now for the tough question: are you one of those people? What do you talk about the most? Does it have anything to do with your reality? Do you talk about all of the wonderful trips you plan to take around the world, but the truth is you've really only taken one vacation, and it was two hours from home? Do you boast about what you would do if you ran the company, but you never take any concrete steps to become part of a management team? Do your actions match your words?

Your assignment today is to shut up. Refrain from talking about yourself. If you do good work, people will notice. You do not need to tell anyone how wonderful you are. If you do great deeds, those actions will speak for you. Trust that you will get the attention you deserve if you make the right choices and put your words into action.

Day 56

"I have been through some terrible things in my life, some of which actually happened."

Mark Twain

Samantha had a gift for imagining worst case scenarios. She spent a lot of mental energy thinking about what might happen to sabotage the good things in her life. When she got a promotion, Samantha worried for days about what would happen if she couldn't handle the added responsibilities of her job. Her mind wandered through horrible scenes where she failed on projects and ended up being fired by the boss who originally promoted her.

She took those images with her to work every day and wore them like a heavy coat. Pretty soon, Samantha began to believe in her terrible imaginary things, and her misgivings showed up in her actions. Every day she was more paralyzed by fear and less effective in her job. She was living out her negative fantasies.

Do you have an active imagination? Imagination is a very powerful tool that may have a positive or negative effect on your everyday life. Your assignment today is to test that power. Use your imagination to visualize great things happening in your life. Imagine a successful presentation at work or a productive meeting. Imagine a fun day with relatives, free of bickering and pettiness. Imagine people turning to greet you when you enter a room, because you glow with excitement and positive energy. Drop any negative thoughts that enter your mind today, and concentrate on happy, useful, and positive visualizations. At the end of the day, write about your experience.

"You never know how a horse will pull until you hook him to a heavy load."

Bear Bryant

Bear Bryant was a long-time coach at the University of Alabama who was known for his trademark houndstooth hat. He was also a man of few words, but his carefully chosen gems are terrific phrases to ponder.

Consider what Bear Bryant is saying in the passage above. You really don't know what you are capable of achieving until you hook yourself to a heavy load. It is natural to want things to go your way and grumble about the obstacles in your life. On the other hand, if those difficulties weren't there, you would never have a chance to discover your true power.

You are not likely to unleash all of your potential unless you are forced into situations that require every bit of energy you hold. This year your goal is to achieve success, so every time you find yourself carrying a heavy load—celebrate! You are being handed exactly what you need to achieve more than you ever dreamed possible.

If you do not experience defeat, sorrow, pain, or setbacks along your life journey, then you will also never experience the uniquely satisfying achievement of pulling through those difficult times. On Day 52, we talked about life as a game you play to win. Do you want to miss that experience? If there is no challenge, there is no game.

Your task today is to look at your burdens with new eyes. Consider them as opportunities for success and chances to unleash your true power. You have no idea of your capabilities until you are hooked up to that heavy load.

Day 58

"The true measure of a man is how he treats someone who can do him absolutely no good."

Samuel Johnson

Eleven days ago you explored Dale Carnegie's six ways to make people like you. You discovered during that lesson that your efforts to make people like you are in vain if you are not sincere. Today you will have another chance to practice compassion toward others.

There are so many ways to measure success, but one of the most enduring examples is your interaction with those around you. You must develop a real interest in others. It's a waste of time to go through the motions. You have to mean it. Look around you today and follow that old rule of treating others as you would like to be treated. Today you will come into contact with a number of people. Each one of them has their own story, their own obstacles, and their own triumphs. What can you do to treat them well? How can you make their day better?

Practice helping others without expecting anything in return. Do not underestimate the difference you make when you do something nice for someone who can do absolutely nothing for you in return. Every positive action you take on behalf of others builds your power and influence. You are creating an atmosphere of respect and love, and that is an incredibly rich environment for success.

Your assignment today is to give all your attention to others. Treat those around you as if they are unique and very special to you, because they are. Do not even entertain the thought of what you might get in return.

"I think it pisses God off if you walk by the color purple in a field somewhere and don't notice it."

Alice Walker

Are you a good observer? It is a crucial tool for success, but it comes in several parts. You must observe what is going on around you, but you also need to have an appreciation for what your five senses pick up.

When was the last time you noticed the color purple in a field? Have you recently stopped to savor the smell of a hot meal before diving in? What does your lover's hand feel like when you hold it in your own? Can you appreciate the fascinating melody of children laughing, or does the sound simply annoy you? Do you relish the hot, strong taste of your first cup of coffee in the morning?

Your assignment today has three parts:

1. Stop.

2. Notice.

3. Appreciate.

Stop for a moment. Stop running through your life as if it is a race, and the first one to the finish line wins. Next, look around and use your five senses to take in your environment. Finally, appreciate everything you notice. You are part of a very intricate and wonderful world. Find some gratitude in your heart for the gifts that surround you.

Day 60

"Think what you feel, say what you think, do what you say, feel what you do."

Eric L. Mott

Today's quote is the first in a series that will delve deeper into aspects of personal responsibility. If you look a little closer, you will find it is a circular guide to living a successful life.

Let's break it down. The first part of the quote is think what you feel. That has to do with authenticity. Think about what you truly feel about your life. Are you living the life you want to live? Are you allowing your true feelings to surface, or are you masking them in some way?

The second part of the circle is say what you think. This section deals with honesty. Do you say what you think? Or do you spend a lot of time trying to figure out and say what people want to hear? Where do you score on the honesty meter?

The third portion of the circle is do what you say. It is imperative to have integrity in your life. Can you be counted on? Do you follow up on what you say you will do, or do you usually find excuses to get out of a promise?

The final part that brings the quote full circle is feel what you do. Practice mindfulness in all areas of your life. Do you experience life, or are you numb to what goes on around you and how you influence the world?

Your assignment today is to write down this quote on a sticky note or a piece of paper and keep it with you at all times. Take it out and ponder it whenever you get a chance. It will become a cornerstone for your work the next few days.

"We need to find the courage to say NO to the things and people that are not serving us if we want to rediscover ourselves and live our lives with authenticity."

Barbara De Angelis

Living an authentic life takes courage. You are presented with opportunities to veer off your true path every single day, and one of the hardest things to do is say no to those temptations.

You are not a feather floating aimlessly in the wind. You have a purpose in this life, and you are in control of achieving your destiny. Do you know what it is? Are you living an authentic life right now, or are you allowing people or things to distract you from your true identity and purpose?

Your assignment today is twofold. First, spend some time writing in your journal this morning. Write honestly about your dreams and desires for your life. Do not be afraid to put down on paper what you really want to achieve. Try very hard not to limit yourself. Let the truth come to the surface. What do you feel destined to do? You do not need to worry at this point about how you will achieve success. Just keep writing with truth in your heart, and you will begin to rediscover your authentic self.

The next part of your assignment is to practice saying no. You have uncovered some of your dreams. Now, you need to stay on the right path to achieve those dreams. If a person asks you to get involved in something today that you do not feel good about or that you strongly believe will lead you away from your true destiny, say no. The more you unearth your authenticity, the easier it will be for you to respectfully decline the detours.

Day 62

"Serve others for they are reflections of the same Entity of which you are yourself another reflection. No one of you has any authenticity, except in reference to the Original. Feel always kinship with all creation."

Sri Sathya Sai Baba

When you zero in on authenticity, it is easy to become a bit self-absorbed. You are working very hard to discover your authentic self, which means you are concentrating on you. But truthfully, it's not all about you.

If you want to live an authentic life, you must acknowledge the fact that you are connected to everyone and everything around you. You are not an island. You are part of humanity, and everything you do affects creation.

Think about the statement in this quote that says others are a reflection of the same Entity of which you are yourself a reflection. How do you know you are smart? Because someone outside of yourself has found value in your knowledge. How do you know you are funny? Because you see a smile reflected in a friend's eyes. How do you know you have been disrespectful? Because you read the rejection on your victim's face.

When you serve others, you are also serving yourself, because you are inseparable, just like drops of water in the ocean. Look at your reflection in a still pond. It is not you, but it is a part of you. You are similarly a reflection of the elements that surround you. If you serve others, their gratitude will be reflected back to you in various ways. If you reject those around you and disregard their own authenticity, you are setting in motion a ripple that will eventually come back and disrupt your own life.

Your assignment today is to serve others and observe your kinship with creation.

"Every man has three characters – that which he exhibits, that which he has, and that which he thinks he has."

Jean Baptiste Alphonse Karr

Alphonse Karr was a French critic and novelist who lived in the 1800s. He was known for his fresh perspective and his biting sense of humor, and he brings up a very important point in this quote. Many of us have multiple personalities. We have a character that we exhibit to the world; a true character buried somewhere deep inside; and a third character that we think is the truth, but probably has no basis in reality.

Today your task is to honestly look at your three characters through journaling. How do you portray yourself to the world? Are you outwardly pleasant to others, but inside you are seething with jealousy or outrage? Do your outsides match your insides?

Next, write about the characteristics you assume are part of your general make-up. What do you think you're like? Are you serious, trustworthy, emotional, or silly? Name about ten adjectives that you believe describe your character.

Compare your list of characteristics with your earlier journal entry. Do they match up, or is Alphonse Karr correct in his assessment? Do you feel sometimes as though you have multiple personalities: the person you show the world, the person you are inside, and the person you wish you were? What can you do to unify your character?

Today's task is a difficult one, and it requires a large dose of honesty. The closer you can get to the truth, the further you will travel on your road to success.

Day 64

"The authentic self is the soul made visible."

Sarah Ban Breathnach

You've been doing a lot of digging the last few days to unearth your true self. How do you feel? It can be a painful process, but the results will be extraordinary. It is an incredible experience to discover the diamond in your soul and bring it out into the light to sparkle and shine in its unique brilliance.

Today is an assessment day. How have you been doing on your authenticity homework? Are you honest with yourself as you write in your journal? Is there more that you have not yet uncovered about your true self? Drop your fear and do it today. There is no time to waste.

Your authentic self is yearning to be made visible. Can you imagine what it would be like if you were transparent to the world? What kind of power would you feel if you allowed your true brilliance to emerge, rather than keeping it hidden under layers of fear and doubt?

If you make your authentic self visible, you will be living without regret or doubt or fear. When the truth is evident, there is nowhere to hide, no secrets to keep. You are open to receive and give fully to humanity. Doesn't that sound exciting? What are you waiting for?

Are you afraid that your true self might be rejected? You're right. There may be people who try to put you down for living an authentic life. But they hold absolutely no power over you. If you make your soul visible, you have the power of truth on your side.

"Honesty is better than any policy."

Immanuel Kant

You are now moving into the next part of the circle that was discussed on Day 60: honesty. You have already spent a lot of time with honesty as you worked to discover your authentic self, and you have an opportunity now to continue to make it an integral part of your everyday life.

Honesty is better than any policy. When you are in doubt over what to do in a given situation, the best tactic is to be honest. There is always a spot in your soul where you can draw on the truth. That place of honesty should be the core of all of your decisions.

Are you honest? Or do you spend more of your time developing policies that you think will help you get what you want? Honesty is not easy. Sometimes the honest road looks a little more harrowing than other directions. It can be a difficult path, but the route is always more direct, and the rewards are always greater. They may not be rewards that include money and prestige, but they will most likely include peace of mind, serenity, and happiness.

Your assignment today is to observe your actions. Were you honest? Did you take credit for something you didn't do at work? Did you let your husband paint the kitchen a color you really don't like, because you didn't want to start an argument? Did you keep the extra dollar bill a cashier gave you by mistake? Did you say you were "fine" when really you felt depressed? Make a mental tally of how many times you are honest today.

Day 66

"Nobody can boast of Honesty till they are try'd."

Susanna Centlivre

It's pretty easy to say, "Sure, I'll be honest. Sounds like a noble idea. Why not?" But you will never truly know if you are capable of honesty until you are tested. Honesty is not easy. It carries with it great rewards, but it is hard to put into action in certain situations.

What if your boss asked you to slightly alter some of the accounting books in order to give the business a tax break? Would you do it? If you practice honesty every day, the answer is simply no. However, when a situation like this comes up, you may start to consider the consequences of your actions. Then the decision is not so easy. If you refuse, will you be fired? How will you support your family?

Nagging questions about consequences may lead you on a detour from the truth. You start to rationalize your actions. What difference will one little change make in the big scheme of things? It will help the company, and you will keep your job. Maybe it would be safer not to make any waves. Next time you'll stand up to your boss, but right now you need to worry about supporting your family. Soon the line between true and false is smudged.

It is very important to be vigilant in your quest to live an honest life. Integrity is so important if you want to achieve lasting success and be proud of your accomplishments. When you are faced with a chance to smudge the line between truth and falsehood today, your job is to choose the honest path. Do not consider the consequences. If you are honest, the details will take care of themselves.

"Hamlet: To be honest, as this world goes, is to be one man picked out of ten thousand."

William Shakespeare

When you picked up this book, you had a desire to achieve success. You are learning every day about ways in which you can triumph in life and be that one person in ten thousand who stands out from the rest. Here's your chance.

An honest person is the exception rather than the rule, as William Shakespeare points out through the words of Hamlet. If you want to be exceptional — if you want to stand out in a crowd — it is time to practice honesty in all of your affairs. Are you up for that challenge?

Before you give this honesty thing a real shot, you might want to explore some of your deep-down feelings on the subject. Do you truly believe that honesty is the road to success? Or are you skeptical? Is there a voice in your head saying, "Wait a minute, there are hundreds of successful people in the world who do not exhibit an ounce of honesty."

You can certainly find dishonest people in positions of power across the globe, but they are not the ones to emulate. What kind of life do you want to live? If you want to stick out in a crowd as an example of living a great life, choose honesty as your path to success. You will be happier, and you won't have to waste time looking over your shoulder and wondering when you will be caught in a web of lies.

Your assignment today is to write down five successful people you admire for their honesty. List the traits they have that you would like to adopt.

"If you tell the truth you don't have to remember anything."
Mark Twain

Another great advantage of honesty is that it's uncomplicated. If you tell the truth, you don't have to remember your stories. You don't have to keep track of the lies that you told people. Telling the truth is simple.

Johnny just didn't feel like going to work. There was new-fallen snow up in the mountains, and he was yearning to take a day off and hit the ski slopes. The problem was that he didn't want to use any more vacation days that month. He had a bank of sick days but only two vacation days left. So Johnny made up a little lie. He left a message for his boss early in the morning, before he would be in the office.

He plugged his nose and made his voice sound scratchy. "I'm sorry, sir. I have a terrible cold. I won't be coming in to work today."

Johnny grinned at his ingenuity as he piled his gear into the SUV and took off for the mountains. It was a great day of skiing. The lines weren't long, because it was a weekday, and the sun shined brilliantly on the sparkling new powder.

Johnny stopped in at the ski lodge for a quick lunch, and his heart sank when saw a familiar face. It was his boss's teenage son, who was on a high school skiing trip. As the young man walked toward him, smiling, Johnny's mind raced for a plausible story to coincide with the lie he told the boy's father that morning.

Have you been in a similar situation? Your assignment today is to journal about a time when you were caught in a lie. How did you feel?

"Have the courage to say no. Have the courage to face the truth. Do the right thing because it is right. These are the magic keys to living your life with integrity."

W. Clement Stone

You are now moving into the third section of the circle mentioned on Day 60. This part concentrates on integrity. Living your life with integrity is the real essence of becoming a success. You have started to shine a light on various truths in your life, and today you are encouraged to continue to practice doing the right thing in all situations.

If you have hidden from the truth in the past, it will be difficult to change your automatic, everyday actions. Cut yourself some slack. No one is perfect. Living your life with integrity does not happen immediately, especially if you have practiced patterns of behavior that are not truthful and take you away from an honest path.

Your goal today is to change your patterns and practice integrity. Tape a slip of paper to your bathroom mirror that lists three things:

1. Have the courage to say no.

2. Have the courage to face the truth.

3. Do the right thing because it is right.

Repeat this list out loud every morning when you get ready, and use these magic keys to live your life with integrity. They are tools at your disposal, but you have to have the courage to pick them up and use them.

Day 70

"Integrity without knowledge is weak and useless, and knowledge without integrity is dangerous and dreadful."

Samuel Johnson

On the road to success, you are constantly searching for knowledge. It is one of the essential elements of your journey. Integrity is nothing without knowledge. It's like having a beautiful new car and no gas. There's nothing wrong with the automobile. It looks great, and it's in perfect working condition. But it won't take you anywhere without fuel.

On the other hand, knowledge without integrity is dangerous. History has provided numerous examples of what happens when individuals armed with knowledge but lacking in integrity come to power.

In 1958, Mao Zedong implemented a five-year plan in China called the Great Leap Forward. It was intended to be a Soviet model for expansive economic growth. Unfortunately, the model was not successful, and subsequent efforts to mask its failure resulted in the malnutrition, starvation, and death of millions of Chinese citizens. If Mao and other leaders in his party would have had the courage to deal with the truth of the situation, countless lives would have been saved. But they wanted their new brainstorm to be a success, so they dropped their integrity and lied about the results.

There is no single element that will give you success. You must combine the best-known tools, sharpen them, and practice using them every day. Your assignment is to research three historical figures that combined knowledge and integrity with winning results. What can you learn from their examples?

"Whatever happened to integrity?"

Anonymous

Let's talk to your cynical side today. You've been working hard on lofty goals like integrity, honesty, and authenticity. Be candid now; is there a part of you that thinks this stuff is a little idealistic?

Do you buy into the idea that you must have integrity in order to truly achieve success, or do you think that's a little naïve in the real world? Do you admire people who do whatever it takes to claw their way to the top? Or do you respect people who put integrity, honesty, and authenticity ahead of immediate material goals?

Get out that journal again and allow yourself to write down what you really feel. It is absolutely okay to doubt. Are you skeptical of this approach that says you must practice doing the right thing in order to achieve success? Visualize what your life will look like when you become a success. What does it include? Are you alone, or are you surrounded by friends and family? Are you happy, or are you discontent and overworked? Are you proud of your accomplishments?

Give your doubt and apprehension a voice today. Don't stuff those feelings. Let them out. Try to specify your skepticism. Do you think the honest approach will work, or are you doubtful? What do you think about the statement that integrity is gone in our society today, and now you have to look out for yourself if you want to get ahead? Do you believe that? Do you consider yourself an idealist or a skeptic?

Day 72

"One of the truest tests of integrity is its blunt refusal to be compromised."

Chinua Achebe

Yesterday, you gave your skeptical side a voice. Today, you are going to give your idealistic side an opportunity for rebuttal. Feelings of doubt and skepticism are important to recognize and face, but what do they accomplish? They usually succeed in putting limits on you and your ability to achieve success. They create barriers.

An optimistic attitude removes barriers. You may consider a cheerful outlook to be idealistic and not based in reality, but who cares? Do you want to live a life with limits or one that is completely open to the possibility of success?

Your job today is to remove all barriers. Write down your perfect life. Do not be remotely realistic. Write a fairytale with yourself as the main character. If you had an unbelievably successful life today, what would it look like? Who would share it with you? What would you be doing? Where would you live? Take away all limits, and let yourself dream.

Now, why can't you have that life? What's stopping you? You have the will to succeed, and you are building your integrity through the exercises suggested in this book. You have taken steps to live up to your true potential. Doesn't it feel good to reach for goals you never thought possible? Do not be discouraged, and whatever you do, do not allow compromise. You deserve to live the life of your dreams — right now. Remove your barriers; argue with the skeptical voice in your head; and go for it.

"The most precious gift we can offer others is our presence. When mindfulness embraces those we love, they will bloom like flowers."

Thich Nhat Hanh

Wouldn't it be great if you had a limitless supply of gifts to give others? You do have one very precious and unlimited gift to give, and it comes with a catch. If you don't give it away, its value in this moment is lost forever. That very special gift is your presence.

When you are present and mindful of what's going on around you, you give the gift of yourself, and that has a value that cannot be measured. Think about how it works when you are on the receiving end. Do you have a great friend who is always there when you need to talk and who is genuinely interested in your life and your happiness? How does it feel to stand in the sunlight of that person's attention? It's great, isn't it?

On the other hand, have you tried to have a conversation with someone who has no interest in talking with you? It makes you feel insignificant and small and maybe even invisible. Offering your presence seems like such a small thing, but mindfulness is extremely powerful. Your presence is a gift, and if you do not participate actively in the moment, you are devaluing your life as well as the lives of those around you.

Your assignment today is to practice mindfulness. It is the final portion of the circle that was introduced on Day 60. Whenever you start daydreaming about the past or the future, bring yourself back into the moment and participate in life. It is one of the greatest gifts you have to offer. This is not a dress rehearsal. You will never have these moments again.

Day 74

"People will do anything, no matter how absurd, to avoid
facing their own soul."

Carl Jung

Today's lesson is a sort of check-up. How are you doing on some of
these soul-searching exercises? They're not as easy as they seem, are
they? Have you been avoiding facing your own soul? Are you afraid
of what you might find hidden within yourself? Or are you afraid you
might have to actually do some of the work to achieve success when
you find out that you are more than capable?

Jenny started reading this book a few months ago, but she stopped
short at around Day 20. Today, she is not happy. She finds that she is
irritable and quick to point out the flaws in others. What triggered her
mood shift?

Maybe the work got just a little too uncomfortable. Jenny didn't
appreciate facing her own soul. She didn't like having to take personal
responsibility for her life. It was so much more comfortable to blame
others for her lack of success. She was in a bad marriage. Her husband
put limits on her, because he wanted her to stay home and raise their
children. She knew she was far smarter than those around her in her
part-time job, but she wasn't able to prove it, because she couldn't
work full time and also be available to pick the kids up from school.
It wasn't her fault. She had been dealt this deck of cards, and she had
to live with it.

Jenny preferred to remain stuck and grumpy rather than facing the
true desires of her soul. Are you facing your soul today, or are you
looking for a distraction to avoid this ultimate confrontation?

"As long as we have practiced neither concentration nor mindfulness, the ego takes itself for granted and remains its usual normal size, as big as the people around one will allow."

Ayya Khema

Mindfulness is not just a gift you give to others. It is a way for you to have an accurate picture of life and your place within the world. Mindfulness is an opportunity to keep your ego in check. If you numb yourself to the world around you and choose to believe only select ego-boosting people and your own fantasies, you are not living in reality, and you will not achieve success.

Concentrate on what is going on outside of you. Notice the world and other people, and acquire as much knowledge as you can from the things that surround you every day. Use all of your senses to experience life. Concentrate on learning and participating rather than maintaining your image and status. You cannot achieve if you are not teachable. Practicing mindfulness gives you a constant lab and classroom and a lot of new opportunities for success.

Your assignment today is to take mindfulness to a more intense level. Concentrate on what is going on around you. Find out what happens when you intensely focus on all of the things that take place outside of yourself. It is a fascinating exercise. Try to jot down your experiences throughout the day. Then, at the end of the day write down a top-ten list of things you learned by concentrating on humanity and elements of this world. Make sure you incorporate all of your five senses into this exercise.

Day 76

"Fundamentally mindfulness is a simple concept. Its power lies in its practice and its applications. Mindfulness means paying attention in a particular way: on purpose, in the present moment, and non-judgmentally. This kind of attention nurtures greater awareness, clarity, and acceptance of present-moment reality. It wakes us up to the fact that our lives unfold only in moments. If we are not fully present for many of those moments, we may not only miss what is most valuable in our lives but also fail to realize the richness and the depth of our possibilities for growth, and transformation."

Jon Kabat-Zinn

Mindfulness is such a valuable tool to build your awareness and stack up opportunities for growth and transformation. Today you will nurture your practice of mindfulness.

The quote above is a little longer than most of the quotes in this book, but it is a beautiful description of the benefits of mindfulness. Read the passage several times, and then make a pact with yourself. Promise to concentrate on mindfulness for at least one week by reading this passage every morning and then sitting quietly for five minutes with your eyes closed, concentrating on nothing but the rhythm of your breath. Then launch into the day with total abandon. When you find your mind wandering, gently bring your attention back to the moment and revel in your ability to participate fully in every single instant.

Practice the art of paying attention without judging. When you are actively participating and focusing on the day, you will not have an opportunity to judge. Judging takes you away from the moment. Stay in the present and reap the benefits of your increased awareness.

"When a thing is funny, search it for a hidden truth."

George Bernard Shaw

Humor is another terrific instrument that is very useful for building your success. It allows you to not take yourself too seriously, and it also softens the blow of a difficult hidden truth. It is sometimes hard to look at defects of character and work on them, but humor provides a sort of cushion that gives you room for change.

If you can laugh at yourself, then you are aware of your shortcomings. You can deal with them with a much lighter heart than you would through tools like fear, anger, or disapproval. Humor gives you the opportunity to respond with an action, rather than retreat in remorse or shame or guilt.

Woody Allen is one of the most prolific artists of our time. He is a successful writer, actor, director, playwright, musician, and comedian. One of his sharpest tools is humor. He pokes fun at his own neurosis, nervousness, and intellect, and even at his Jewish heritage and his identity as a true New Yorker. The reason Woody Allen is so funny is because his humor is based in truth. He can poke fun at himself, and that is endearing. It strikes a common chord with humanity. We're all imperfect, and that's funny when you think about it.

Your job today is to poke fun at yourself. Don't worry about looking good all the time or being perfect. You'll never attain those goals. The world loves imperfection, so show them what you've got. Bring out your truth through humor. Don't beat yourself up. Laugh at yourself and be open to change.

"He who laughs, lasts!"

Mary Pettibone Poole

Laughter is the secret weapon for happiness and success. It is the magic elixir that will change your outlook and probably lengthen your life. Why is it so healing and helpful? Who knows? If you are skeptical, give it a try and find out for yourself how it can transform your life.

You have a great assignment today. Your job is to laugh. That's right, laugh. No excuses. It doesn't matter if you just got fired, your dog died, and your wife kicked you out of the house. Find a reason to laugh. It will heal you.

It's not that easy to just spontaneously break into laughter, so what can you do to get the ball rolling? Here are a few suggestions:

Rent a funny movie.

Call an old friend and talk about the stupid things you did when you were kids.

Spend about an hour with someone under the age of five.

Go to a comedy show.

Get underwear with smiley faces on it, and wear it to an important meeting. Your colleagues won't know what you're hiding.

Practice a random act of kindness on your grumpy neighbor.

Whatever you do, don't take yourself seriously, and let that laughter bubble up and start to heal you from the inside out.

"A good laugh is sunshine in a house."

William Makepeace Thackeray

Mary sat at the reception encased in a wall of grief. She buried her husband that morning, her best friend for over fifty years. She wasn't sure if she could ever be happy again. The bitter cold outside mimicked the brittle, icy hardness she felt in her heart. She had the uneasy feeling that at any moment she might shatter into a million pieces on the floor, and there would be nothing left of her. But that didn't happen. She held her cup of tea stoically on her lap and halfheartedly listened to the continuous stream of condolences that floated past her.

One of Mary's grandchildren was summoned to play a tune on the violin to cheer Grandma up. Mary grimaced as the six-year-old tucked her little violin under her chin and started to play one of three tunes in her repertoire. Unfortunately, the child had no idea that there were words to the song she played. It was an old traditional tune, and the culminating line was, "The old gray goose is dead."

Mourners started to shift in an uncomfortable silence at the end of the performance, and then suddenly Mary started to giggle. Her giggles soon erupted into a huge belly laugh, and her granddaughter joined in, not really knowing why. Soon, the entire room was rolling with laughter. It was as if a burst of sunshine filled the room, and the healing began.

Your assignment today is to never underestimate the power of a good laugh. Take every opportunity to laugh today and every day. This is far too important a journey to be taken seriously.

"Never laugh at live dragons."

J.R.R. Tolkien

All right, so there's a time to laugh and a time to run! But seriously, all of this information the last few days about laughter and happiness may be a little nauseating if your life is in crisis. You can't slap on a happy face and pretend everything is okay if it's not. The laughter therapy suggested two days ago in no way promotes insincerity or pretends certain realities in your life do not exist. Your laughter must be genuine. It has to burst forward from the depths of your soul. Sometimes real life prevents that from happening.

That is when you need to look at what is blocking you from happiness. What stops your laughter? Seek out those live dragons and face them. Are you grieving over the loss of a loved one? Are you in fear of financial ruin? Do you face the demons of addiction every day and lose?

Face your dragons and fight them head on. If you want to bring laughter back into your life, you need to clear out the scary stuff to make room for the sunlight. Give names to the dragons you face. Write them down in your journal today. Be honest and jot down specifically what blocks you from happiness. Then pick at least one of your dragons and devise a plan to battle it and win.

Live dragons aren't funny at all, but dead ones are hilarious, because they can't hurt you. Pick your battles today, and defeat the dragons that block your happiness. Be brave, and your reward will be a soul that is overflowing with joy.

"Let every man shovel out his own snow and the whole city will be passable."

Ralph Waldo Emerson

Wouldn't it be great if everyone just did what they were supposed to do? The world would be a much better place. But who is in charge of the plan? Do you want to be? That might be your problem. There are nearly seven billion people in the world, and every single one of us has a different agenda.

Now, here's a news flash. You are not in charge. You don't get to control whether or not your neighbor shovels his own snow, so stop wasting your time worrying about it. You are powerless over the actions of others. If you want to be successful, concentrate on your own actions. What can you do to make this world a better place? How can you contribute?

It is so easy to get stuck complaining about the actions of a boss, a spouse, a friend, a relative, or a co-worker and blame them for sabotaging your road to success.

"If she would have just done her job, I wouldn't be in this mess!"

Does that line sound familiar? Has it come out of your mouth recently?

If you want to lower your stress level and move forward in life, you must stop worrying about the actions of others. Take personal responsibility and take action. What can you do to create change? What actions can you take to reach success?

Your assignment today is to leave other people alone. You cannot control them, and they probably don't care about your opinion. Concentrate on what you can do to change your life, and focus on how you can be helpful to others rather than how you can boss them around.

Day 82

"As you make your bed, so you must lie on it."

English Saying

Jimmy was not happy with his situation. He was deep in debt, and he resented the daily calls he received from creditors. He never picked up the phone, because he was afraid of who might be hounding him for a payment. On top of that, he hated his job. It didn't allow him to make enough money to pay all his bills. His response was to put forth a halfhearted effort and call in sick often. Jimmy was under so much stress, he had no idea how to change his life. Success didn't even cross his mind. He was worried about survival.

How did Jimmy end up in this situation? Was it just bad luck? The truth is, Jimmy overspent, and then he hid from his responsibilities rather than facing them. If he wants to change, he has to take personal responsibility for his situation. He has to admit fault and make a change. Jimmy made his bed, and he is going to have to lie on it. His situation is the direct result of his own actions.

This is not a tragic story. Jimmy has the power to change. He can face his creditors and work out a payment solution. He can show up at work and put in an honest effort that might lead to a promotion, or he can apply for a better job with a higher salary. But if Jimmy chooses to hide and not take responsibility, his crummy situation will just get worse.

Your assignment today is to look at the bed you made. What is your present situation? What actions did you take to get where you are today? What can you change in order to improve your life?

"Refuse to be average. Let your heart soar as high as it will."

A.W. Tozer

You are not average. There is no one on this earth exactly like you. You are unique, and you have special gifts to share. Are you letting your gifts out of the bag, or do you hide them from everyone — including yourself?

It is comfortable to fit in, to not stand out in a crowd, but that is not what you were made for. You were made to soar as high as you dare. You are uniquely qualified to bring your special talents out and follow your heart, but it feels risky to step away from the group. It's frightening to fly without a safety net. You must have the courage to refuse to be average. You are throwing away your innate gifts if you fit in with everyone else.

Let your heart soar. Open up and follow your instincts for success. It is a thrilling experience to reach for new heights and test your abilities and strengths. Do you have a desire to experience that adventure?

Today try stepping away from the crowd. Journey out on your own and attempt something you have never done before. Do you have a special skill or aptitude that you have never really explored? Right now you must refuse to ignore it. Try it out! Take a class, join a club that focuses on the skill, or find a mentor who is willing to guide you. Aren't you curious to see if it will bring you joy and success? You will never know if you don't swallow your fear and try it.

Refuse to be average, and give your heart the opportunity to fly.

Day 84

"Nobody can do it for you."

Ralph Cordiner

For the last several days, we have been concentrating again on personal responsibility. We will continually come back to it, because it requires constant attention. It also carries more power than you realize. If you want to achieve success, you have the opportunity to do it right now, but you have to take charge of your destiny.

Go back to your journal today and write about success. Compose your own personal definition of the word. Then write down some specific ways that you imagine you will be able attain your goal. Review the ideas you write down today and any previous material you find in your journal about attaining success. Take a look at what ingredients will be needed to follow through. Make a list of those ingredients.

Now, review that list. Cross off anything that you have delegated to someone else. Nobody can do this for you. For example, if you have "get a loan from my dad" on your list, cross it off. Your dad is not responsible for your success. This is your baby. What action can you take to get the money you need? Can you get an extra part-time job? Can you cut out some of the extra expenses in your life and save some cash?

This is not one of those jobs you can hire out. If you don't like to clean, you can hire a maid (if you have the money). However, if you want to achieve success, there is no one you can call to do the dirty work. You have to roll up your sleeves and do it yourself. You can learn from others, but the effort must be all yours. Stop looking outside of yourself for the key to success. It lies within you.

"Learning to deal with setbacks, and maintaining the persistence and optimism necessary for childhood's long road to mastery are the real foundations of lasting self-esteem."

Lilian G. Katz

You will experience setbacks on the road to success, but always remember that they are only temporary. You are on this journey for the rest of your life. You must build a strong foundation using the tools of persistence and optimism, and you will succeed.

Think about how marathon runners train for a big race. They spend months conditioning. They start with a manageable distance and increase it little by little. Every step they take builds their self esteem. They set milestones and celebrate each achievement. Their success with smaller goals propels them to increase their drive and push to the next level. Sometimes injuries set them back a day or two or even longer. They attend to them through rest and rehabilitation, and then they get back on track. They are optimistic that they can achieve their goal, and they have the persistence to keep working until they do.

Are persistence and optimism words that describe how you travel on your journey through life? Compare your life path to training for a marathon. First, acknowledge your setbacks and deal with them. Then, dig up some optimism that will start to build your self-esteem. You don't have to lie to yourself. Find something that is true, even if it is not very exciting. For example, "I am healthy today" may provide you with a dose of optimism on which to build. Finally, never give up. You are not running a short race. This is a marathon, and you have the time and opportunity to build your self-esteem and reach success.

Day 86

"Success isn't how far you got, but the distance you traveled from where you started."

Proverb

For the next eight days, you are going to have a chance to take an in-depth look at success and failure and compare these two very powerful words. Let's start with the upside and dive a little deeper into what success means to you.

Read the proverb above. Does it coincide with your idea of success? Have you ever thought about success as the progress you make throughout your life instead of the end result?

Write about success as a journey instead of a finish line. You have the opportunity to be a success every single day if you take even one small step forward rather than remaining complacent or regressing. There are so many opportunities for you to thrive and to help others along their journey. Are you taking advantage of any of those opportunities right now?

The second part of your assignment today is to write about the distance you've come thus far. How are you doing? Where did you start, and where are you now? Have you gone forward or backward, or has it been a combination of both? Grab some markers and draw a graph of your journey toward success so far. What does that graph look like? Does it have huge peaks and valleys, or is it a steady climb? Maybe it was a steady climb, and then a particular event in your life caused a drop-off. Chart your success and imagine how you would like it to look from today forward.

"Success doesn't come to you, you go to it."

Marva Collins

Do you truly want to be a success? Then get moving! You will never achieve success by waiting for it complacently, like one waits for a bus or Santa Claus or the Easter Bunny. You must go and seek out success.

Think of success as a crafty little wild animal. You catch glimpses of it here and there, but for the most part it remains elusive. It will never come right to you and curl up on your lap. You must look for it in remote hiding places and eventually coax it out of its lair. You have to give success a reason to stick around by providing food to sustain it, a comfortable place to sleep, and plenty of attention.

Your assignment is to treat success like a wild — but very appealing — little animal. Do whatever you can today to find it and give it the proper environment in which to develop. What can you do right now to invite success into your life?

Consider the way you live your life today. Is it a nurturing environment for success? What does your home look like at this very moment? Is it neat, warm, and inviting, with everything pretty much in order, or does it look like a tornado roared through a few minutes ago? Do you surround yourself with interesting, fun, optimistic people who are also looking for ways to grow? Or are most of your friends complaining, negative individuals who don't take good care of themselves and tend to bring you down?

Look around the environment you've created. If you were this little animal named Success, would you drop by and stay awhile?

Day 88

"Eighty percent of success is showing up."

Woody Allen

Jessica finally worked up the nerve to look for a new job. She had been with her company for five years and had a very comfortable spot in the corporation, but she yearned for new challenges. That evening, Jessica went online to look for open positions in her line of work. She sent her résumé to ten promising enterprises and then sat back and waited. Nothing happened.

Every day she put in her usual 110 percent at her less-than-desirable job, and every night she went online to look for new job postings. Three months after she started her search, her cell phone rang. It was the human resources department of an exciting new technology firm, and they wanted her to come in for an interview.

Jessica was ecstatic. She took a day off of work for the interview and plunged forward into what was probably the most humiliating hour of her life. She was woefully underqualified for the position, and the executive interviewing her made that very clear.

Jessica returned to her ho-hum job the next day and put in her usual 110 percent only to find out at the end of the day that her office would be closing, and they were all out of a job. That's when the miracle occurred. A client of hers had been watching her performance over the past few years. When the client found out Jessica was out of a job, she immediately offered her employment at her firm. Jessica's new job included incredible opportunities, challenges, and a hefty raise.

Your assignment today is to show up. You never know what will happen.

"It took me twenty years to become an overnight success."
Eddie Cantor

How long do you think it will take you to become a success? The quote above is funny, but it holds a hidden truth. Very few people become an overnight success. It often takes years to create the life of your dreams.

Turn to a new page in your journal today and find some colored pencils or markers or even crayons. You homework is to draw your timeline to success. Feel free to include pictures and dates on the timeline that depict milestones you intend to reach along the way.

While you create this timeline, take some time to consider what you will really need to do in order to get from point A to point B. You don't just wake up one morning and find out you are success. It takes planning and actual effort. So what are you going to do to get there?

You may want to take a college course in your field of interest or lose five pounds or join a networking organization. Put those things on the timeline and give yourself a target date of completion. Think about the gradual routes to success, too, and depict them throughout your timeline. They may include spending more time with family, taking a walk every evening after dinner, meditating, or offering to help others through volunteerism. Create an appealing timeline today that you can refer to for inspiration tomorrow and every day.

Day 90

"I have not failed. I've just found 10,000 ways that won't work."

Thomas A. Edison

You've spent some time exploring success and ways in which you can attain it. Now, it is important to look at the flip side and come to terms with your observations and beliefs about failure.

Thomas Edison displayed a remarkably healthy view of failure in the quote above. When he was working on creating the electric light bulb, he dealt with thousands of roadblocks, but in the end he triumphed because he never considered failure a dead end. Instead, it was the discovery of something that didn't work! His failures provided him with valuable information in his research. Edison was one of the most productive inventors in history. He held over 1,000 patents for his inventions, and he remains a model of success today. Did you know that he also excelled in failures?

How do you react to failure? Your assignment today is to journal about how you deal with it. When something doesn't work, do you quit? Or does failure encourage you to work harder to find a better solution? Come up with three ways to change your present habits and deal with failure better.

Take a lesson from Thomas Edison today. If you want to achieve your biggest dreams, then you must practice turning failure into success. How can you use the knowledge you've gained from things that don't work? What can you do differently the next time around? What did you learn from the experience? You never fail if you learn from your mistakes.

"In Life as in Football
Fall Forward when you fall."

Arthur Guiterman

Arthur Guiterman was an American writer who was best known for his humorous poems that cut straight to the truth. In today's quote, he offers up a valuable life lesson. When you fall — and you will fall — fall forward.

Many of us fear failure. There is no way we would subject ourselves to a heavy-hitting atmosphere in life. We don't want to get hurt, so we would rather not try to reach for some of those lofty goals that will bring us success. But what would happen if we get in the game and plan to get tackled?

Think about this for a moment. Would it take a little pressure off if you just assume you will fall down and plan for how you're going to pick yourself back up? That might be less stressful than hoping and praying that you will get through life unscathed. The truth is, if you plan to reach success, you will experience failure. You will fall down. You have a choice, though. You have a choice to fall forward.

What exactly does it mean to fall forward? Write down your answer to that question in your journal. When something doesn't work, find at least one lesson you can draw from the situation that will help you move forward in life. What did you learn? What can you change? What will you remember never to do again? How can you work more effectively with others to attain your goal the next time?

Your job today is to fall forward.

Day 92

"Failure seldom stops you; what stops you is the fear of failure."

Jack Lemmon

You touched on fear a little bit yesterday. Have the courage today to take a look at your fears head on. Is it really failure that keeps you from reaching success, or is it fear? Does failure stop your progress, or does fear put on the breaks?

Failure gets a bad rap, but it is actually an integral part of success. It is essential for success. In fact, failure is the foundation of success. What do you think about that? Do you believe it?

When you learned to ride a bike, did you just hop on and take off? If you did, you are a freak of nature. Most kids experience a series of failures when they learn to ride a bike. Each failure teaches them something new about balance and coordination. They also may enlist the help of an adult or an older sibling or friend to run alongside and help them while they learn. Their fear of failure is overridden by the intense desire to ride a bike. Their failures become a foundation for their success, because they use them to learn. They modify their actions with each and every attempt, and pretty soon they're flying through the neighborhood on their own.

Failure is not something to be feared. It is a very important tool for success. Launch into new adventures today with the abandon that you had when you learned to ride a bike. Let go of the brakes and fly down that hill. Experience the rush of adrenaline you get when you go for it. Let go of your fears. They have no place on the road to success.

"Failure teaches success."

Japanese Saying

Do you consider failure and success to be opposites? That is not unusual. They are antonyms in most dictionaries. Today, you have an opportunity to look at the connection between the two. What if failure was an instructor and success the pupil? If you go with that image today, it might alter your current way of thinking.

Failure generally has quite a negative connotation, but it wouldn't be so horrible if it was thought of as a teacher. Failure provides help and insight and direction. Failure teaches success.

Pull out your journal and write for about thirty minutes on this Japanese saying. Does failure teach success in your life? Do you think this is a ridiculous statement, or are you intrigued by it? Try to come up with examples in your own life of how failure teaches success. Can you think of anything?

Failure and success may have once been opposites in your mind, black and white, good and bad. After reading the statement above, what new pictures do you think of for failure and success? Let your imagination take over and draw a few new images that emerge when you think of the idea that failure teaches success. How are these two concepts linked together?

You don't have to hold on to your traditional views of anything. Part of achieving success is being willing to change. Are you willing to change your concept of failure?

Day 94

"Never look down to test the ground before taking your next step; only he who keeps his eye fixed on the far horizon will find the right road."

Dag Hammarskjold

Do you find yourself looking down to test the ground before taking your next step? What does that mean in your day-to-day life? It may mean that you seldom make a move unless it is completely safe and you have no chance of failure. Or it may mean that you get stuck in the minutia of life and lose track of your long-term goals.

If you want to pursue success, you must take risks. You don't have to be reckless, but it's time to get off the children's rides and tackle the monster roller coaster. Fix your gaze on the far horizon and pursue those spectacular sights you see before you.

When you look back on your life, you want to be able to say, "Wow, what a ride! That was fun! I had no idea I could fly so high, and the view was incredible."

It would be pretty sad to reach the end of your life and say, "What view? Well, I never got hurt; I never failed; but I really don't know what I might have accomplished, because I was too afraid to try. I made sure I was safe on the ground at all times."

You are not going to get another chance to visit this incredible theme park called life. What do you want to do while you're here? Do you want to spend your entire time staring at the ground to make sure you don't step in gum, or do you want to look up and take in the wonders that surround you?

Your assignment today is to go back through your journal and look at some of your dreams and goals for success. Then, fix your eyes on those goals and don't look down.

"I believe life is a series of near misses. A lot of what we ascribe to luck is not luck at all. It's seizing the day and accepting responsibility for your future. It's seeing what other people don't see and pursuing that vision."

Howard Schultz

Does is seem like other people have all the luck? Are you ready for a little of that luck to come your way for a change? Well, you don't have to wait for that to happen. You're sitting on a pot of gold right now, and you don't even realize it. What makes you think other people are lucky and you're not?

You will find that when you seize control of your life, you will start to get lucky. Imagine your wildly successful future. Create a vision for yourself, and then never lose sight of it. You are responsible for what happens in your life. You deserve to have success. It has nothing to do with luck. No matter what happens today, you have an opportunity to learn and grow from your experience. No matter what your circumstances, you have an opportunity to achieve success.

Pay extreme attention to what goes on around you. You will be presented with hundreds of opportunities to do something for someone, to learn something new, to try something you've never tried before, to look at something from someone else's point of view, and to feel grateful for the life you have been given. These gold nuggets of opportunity rain down around you all day, every day. Grab them.

Seize the day, and you may suddenly start feeling like the luckiest person around.

Day 96

"Commitment unlocks the doors of imagination, allows vision, and gives us the right stuff to turn our dream into reality."

James Womack

For the last couple of days, you have been concentrating on your vision for success. It is so important to have a vision, because without it you are essentially wandering through life without any direction or goal. Today, you have the opportunity to take your vision one step further. Your ultimate goal is to turn your vision into reality, right? How do you do that? Commitment is the answer.

It's easy to come up with dreams for your life. We all like to dream. But the only way you will see your vision come true is if you back it up with commitment. You must buy in to the idea that you will actually achieve your dreams, or you are just fantasizing.

If you commit to your vision, you admit that you believe in it and you think you are capable of achieving it. You have taken an inner oath to act. When someone invites you to a party, you either commit to go, or you don't. Once you say yes, you have given a sort of promise that you will take action and attend the event. The same is true with your vision for success. When you reach a level of commitment, you promise to take action. Are you ready to commit to your vision?

You may be thinking, "Of course I am! Why do you think I bought this book?"

Are you really ready to make that commitment? Write about your honest feelings today. If you commit to your dreams, you have to act. Write an oath to yourself about the commitment you are willing to make to honor your vision.

"Your vision will become clear only when you look into your heart. Those who look outside, dream. Those who look inside, awaken."

Carl Jung

Leonard scurried around the house crossing off items on his to-do list. He was so excited about his future. He was committed to his vision and already taking action to achieve success. Suddenly, he stopped in the middle of his living room. His heart sank. Leonard was hit right between the eyes with the realization that he didn't have a clear vision.

Leonard didn't need eyeglasses; he needed inner sharpness. Here he was running all over his house getting little things done, and he wasn't entirely sure what his overall goal was — except to be a success. That really wasn't a clear picture.

How do you sharpen your vision? The general notion that you want to be a success is not really detailed enough to give you the momentum you need to achieve it. Where do you go to make your vision clear?

You look inside your heart to find your true vision. One of the best ways to do that is to sit quietly and listen. Your heart whispers clues and suggestions to you all the time, but you have to be still in order to hear it.

In a few days, we will take an in-depth look at how prayer and meditation can help you listen to your heart. Today, your job is to find some time to sit quietly and listen. Find a few minutes in the day to slow down and look inside yourself. That is the first step to your awakening.

Day 98

"When your mother is mad and asks you, 'Do I look stupid?'
it's best not to answer her."

Meghan, Age 13

Do you like kids? Some people love kids, and others try desperately
to avoid them. Whether you like them or not, kids are often our best
teachers. They're not old enough to be jaded, they look at life with fresh
eyes, they can be painfully honest, and they don't take themselves
too seriously. Over the next few days, you are going to explore the
wisdom of children and maybe even recapture some of that childlike
innocence and wonder for yourself.

Did the quote above make you laugh out loud? If it brought even
a smile to your face, take a moment to think about why. Meghan
gives you some pretty blunt advice here. It's obvious, and it's funny,
because it holds a truth that might save Meghan (and the rest of us) a
lot of pain and suffering if we follow it.

When is it a good idea to keep your mouth shut? Start a list of several
appropriate scenarios in your journal. Can you think of a time when
you spoke up recently and shouldn't have? What did you learn from
that experience?

It is a very wise person who knows when not to speak. Talk is often
overrated, and it can get you into a lot of trouble, too. What would
your day be like if you concentrated on listening and tried to avoid
talking? Give it a shot, and then write about your experience in your
journal at the end of the day. What did you learn when you cultivated
the art of keeping your mouth shut?

"Lying drives your conscience crazy."

Kyle, Age 10

Kyle just might grow up to be the next Gandhi . . . or Gandalf. He's quite the wise sage at age ten. Lying does drive your conscience crazy. So why do we do it? Is it human nature? Why do we want to step into the insanity that is created when we lie?

It might be human nature to lie, but we also have the ability to stop the madness. On a scale of one to ten, how big of a liar are you? Be honest now! Deep down you know the right answer, so it doesn't do any good to try to fool yourself. Everyone has told a lie at some point. Some do it a lot more than others. Think about the times that you've lied. How did the whole event play out? What happened? How did you feel about yourself when you lied? Did you get caught? Does it still nag on your conscience today?

Lying is cowardly, and it's also a lot easier than the alternative. It is much more difficult to tell the truth and take responsibility for our actions. If you want to become a success, however, you need to clean up your act. You must tilt the scales in the opposite direction and tell the truth much more often than you lie.

If you do lie, and it hurts someone else, you must make amends. Go to that person, tell them the truth, and offer to do whatever it takes to make things right. That's a scary thought, isn't it? The only way you can obtain real success is to clean up your own garbage and do the right thing. You have to clear away the trash in your life to make room for the light of success to shine through. Lying is the chief litter bug in your conscience, and the garbage it leaves behind blocks your true potential.

Day 100

"Just be yourself."

Jessie, Age 5

Just be yourself. What wonderful advice!

You have made it to Day 100 on your journey to become a success. What an accomplishment! How do you feel? Are you starting to feel more comfortable in your own skin? When you get into the actions that are suggested in these pages, you come closer and closer to your true self every day. You are unlocking the power that is within you. These exercises guide you toward discovering just who you are and what makes you unique.

If you want to achieve success, all you have to do is just be yourself. You have the goods. You are doing this work to uncover all of the dirt you put around yourself to cover up your true potential. You are digging up that precious diamond that is you and uncovering its brilliance. Just be yourself today. Be comfortable in your skin and thankful for your unique and brilliant gifts.

"You can't hide a piece of broccoli in a glass of milk."

Rosemary, Age 7

That is a very good point. If you want to hide broccoli, a glass of milk is not the way to go. So are you wondering why Rosemary's quote is the centerpiece of Day 101? It's amusing, but how can you learn about success from that statement?

How do you think Rosemary found out this truth? She probably tried it herself. Then what do you suppose she did? One can bet that she noted this fact and then moved on to more creative ways to hide broccoli. Rosemary learned from her mistakes, shared her experience with others, and built on her failure to find a successful solution.

This may all seem very obvious, childish, and a little trivial to you, but do you follow the same pattern in your adult life? When something doesn't work out the way you planned, do you note it, share your discovery with others so that they don't make the same mistake, and then change your tactics?

Many of us don't. Instead, we complain, blame someone else, or maybe even try to hide the whole glass of milk with the broccoli in it rather than fixing the problem. When we become adults, we have a funny way of complicating simple situations. Today, your task is to simplify your decisions. Get back to the basics. If something doesn't work, fix it. Don't worry about what others will think of your failure. Just find a better solution. Act like a child today. Be direct in finding solutions to your problems. Your ego might not want to follow the correct route, but the path is usually clear. The route to success is undeviating. Stop trying to complicate it with detours to save face.

Day 102

"It is OK to fail, but it is not OK to give up."

Kate, Age 8

Failure is no big deal. You will do it thousands of times in your life. What you cannot do is give up. Evidently, Kate learned this lesson at the ripe old age of eight. She is a bright girl. Many of us are still working on this one.

One of the most important attitudes for you to change if you truly want to achieve success is the desire to quit when you're behind. The most successful people in history failed numerous times, but the one thing they did not do is quit. They never gave up. On Day 93 you learned that failure actually teaches success. You must have that ingredient in the mix if you want to achieve your dreams. Failure is not an option; it's a given.

What you cannot ever, ever do is give up. You cannot take your ball and go home when you're losing the game. If you do, then all is lost. If you stick around even if the other team is creaming you, your luck might change. You have to stay in the game, no matter what, or you have zero chance for success.

Every time you want to quit and give up on your dreams, think about Kate's simple advice. It's not okay to give up. It's perfectly fine to fail and have setbacks and even look like an idiot sometimes. It's not okay to throw in the towel and surrender.

Read Kate's words of wisdom out loud over and over like a mantra. Then find a quiet corner somewhere and close your eyes. Breathe deeply and let your mind roll over Kate's words. Sit there quietly for as long as you have time. It might be five minutes or an hour. Feel the power inside you grow as you resolve to never give up.

"It's good to receive compliments, and it's even better to give them."

Aaron, Age 17

Aaron reminds us of another very important ingredient of success: kindness to others. You know how great it feels when someone gives you a compliment. When was the last time you gave one out? Are you stingy with praise?

Write in your journal today about how often you give out compliments to people. As you know, it is worthless to give meaningless compliments. You must be sincere. How many times this week have you given someone sincere praise? Do you remember how the person reacted when you gave them a compliment? How did you feel when you were able to brighten someone else's day? Imagine the ripple effect that occurs when you throw a positive pebble into the pond by complimenting someone.

You don't have to be stingy with praise. There's plenty of it to go around. Don't worry, you won't run out. Find the good in people today, and let them know that you appreciate them in your life. It would be a pretty lonely world without them.

The second part of your assignment is to also spend some time writing about how good you feel when you receive compliments. What does that do to your self-esteem? How does it improve your overall day? How does it change your perception of the person who gave you the compliment? Now, remember that you have the power to make someone else feel that way. What a gift! It's priceless, but it doesn't cost a penny.

Give the gift of praise every day. Remember Aaron's advice. It's good to receive compliments, and it's even better to give them.

Day 104

"Enthusiasm spells the difference between mediocrity and accomplishment."

Norman Vincent Peale

This is just great. It's not enough that you have to do stuff for other people, but now you have to turn into some kind of manic cheerleader in order to achieve success? What will be next, motivational speaking? Evangelism?

You will be exploring enthusiasm for the next few days, but have no fear. You don't have to get out the pom-poms and hop up and down like a crazy person. Enthusiasm is a little different than that.

Let's start with a definition of the word. Enthusiasm originally meant *inspiration or being in the presence of a god.* Today, having enthusiasm is defined as; *being excited, motivated, having an active or lively interest in something, or a certain intensity of feeling. Enthusiasm does not have to reach the point of fanaticism. It is a heightened interest.*

Think about the successful people you know. They do have a sort of intensity, don't they? That's why they stick out from the crowd. They are fueled to accomplish great things, because they are extremely interested in what they are doing, and they believe in their work. They are inspired.

How can you cultivate your own enthusiasm? It's not an easy thing to fake without looking completely insane. The key to finding enthusiasm is discovering what you love to do. What excites you? What do you do really well? You can't be enthusiastic about something that barely interests you. Find your passions and pursue them. Your assignment is to write down what excites you or motivates you. What are you enthusiastic about today?

"Enthusiasm is the mother of effort, and without it nothing great was ever achieved."

Ralph Waldo Emerson

What possesses some people to make heroic efforts and accomplish what no one thought possible? How do they get the strength and stamina to perform such valiant deeds? The spark is enthusiasm.

Harriet Tubman was born a slave in Maryland in 1820. She worked as a house servant as a child and in fields when she reached her teen years. Even though Harriet Tubman was a slave, she knew deep inside that she was destined to do great things. She escaped her plantation and ran away to the north in 1849, and it was then that her destiny started to be revealed. Harriet Tubman did not stay in the safety of the northern region of the United States. Instead, she risked her life and returned to the south over and over again to help other slaves escape. She was an integral part of the Underground Railroad, which was a series of safe houses where slaves could stay on their journey to freedom.

Her enthusiasm for the antislavery movement gave her the power to succeed in extremely dangerous situations. Among hundreds of other slaves, she helped her seventy-year-old parents escape and was even a spy for the north during the Civil War. Harriet Tubman had an intense belief in freedom, and that sparked her effort to achieve the impossible. Her enthusiasm helped her to become a stunning success.

Do you want to accomplish great things in your life? Then find out what you believe in, what excites you, and what sparks your intense interest. That is where you will cultivate enthusiasm and have the opportunity to achieve success.

Day 106

"Creativity is a natural extension of our enthusiasm."

Earl Nightingale

Once you begin to build enthusiasm, creativity is the natural next step. You may not think you are a creative person right now, but when you find something you are passionate about, you will be surprised at how it draws out your creativity.

When you strive for success, you are searching for that one thing that really piques your interest and makes you feel as though you have something important to contribute. Once you find it, your interest and excitement build. You start to look for ways to improve all aspects of it, and then your creativity kicks in. That is when you know you are really following your destiny. Your insides are telling you that you can add value to what you are focused on. You have an impulse to get involved and make changes for the better.

Write down the names of two or three individuals who you think are creative. What character traits do they share? What do they do that makes them creative? Is creativity a designation reserved for artistic types only, or do you know of any creative people in the business world, healthcare, construction, or other fields?

Now, take a look at your own creativity. Do you consider yourself a creative person? If not, what is stopping your creativity? Can you think of ways to make it flow more freely? What can you do to nurture your creativity?

Enthusiasm and creativity are naturally linked. When you find something you really feel enthusiastic about, you will want to study it and get involved in it. Then, your creative ability will emerge—if you let it.

"The sense of this word among the Greeks affords the noblest definition of it: enthusiasm signifies God in us."

Madame de Staël

On Day 104, we mentioned that the original Greek definition of enthusiasm is "being in the presence of a God". We haven't really touched much on spirituality yet, but how do you feel about that definition? Does enthusiasm feel like something bigger than just you?

Explore your thoughts on the word "enthusiasm" as defined as "God in us" and write in your journal about what comes up. You can have a strong religious background or be an atheist and still ponder this definition. Being in touch with your spiritual views is a very important part of your individual identity and therefore an important ingredient for your success. You don't have to adhere to a specific religious belief in order to be successful, but it is important to explore your beliefs and your values. The better you know yourself, the more capable you will be of reaching success.

Read the quote above one more time. What is your gut reaction to reading it? Is it negative, indifferent, or positive? Why?

Remember, there is no right or wrong answer here. The only thing you must do is be honest with yourself. You don't have to agree with any of the statements mentioned. Explore your thoughts and emotions on the subject honestly. Do you think of enthusiasm as God within you, or do you prefer another definition? What is your favorite definition of enthusiasm? Write it down and put it somewhere you will see it at least once a day for a week.

Day 108

"Attempt the impossible in order to improve your work."

Bette Davis

"That's impossible!" Dan cried when he looked over the business proposal his partner handed him. "There is no way I can find the money to start this new branch of the business. This will never work. You might as well forget about it."

He threw the proposal back across the desk at his partner and swiveled his chair around so that his back was to the man when he collected the loose pages and left the room in defeat. Dan cracked his knuckles and stared out the window, setting his jaw against the brilliant sunshine coming in through the blinds. There was nothing wrong with their mediocre business just the way it was. It was safe. They earned a decent living. Why did his partner always want to change things?

What do you think about Dan's reaction? Do you identify more with Dan or with his partner? Are you willing to take risks, or would you rather play it safe?

Now, consider this for a moment. How exactly does Dan know the task is impossible? Has he tried it before? That's a curious question, isn't it? You really don't know what's impossible until you try it and fail. Even then, it might be possible if you learn from your failure and alter your plan accordingly. We've already established that failure teaches success. So why not give the impossible a shot?

Maybe it's time to attempt the impossible. At the very least, you are likely to get further than you've ever gone before. Write about your thoughts on merits or insanity of attempting the impossible.

"I am always doing that which I cannot do, in order that I may learn how to do it."

Pablo Picasso

You will be considering the impossible for the next few days. Don't worry, you will not be attempting the impossible yet—just thinking about it. Yesterday, you had an opportunity to jot down your initial thoughts on the merits or the insanity of attempting the impossible. Today, you get to think about what you might get out of attempting that which you cannot do.

Picasso was quite a successful and prolific artist. According to this quote, he attempted impossible things all the time. Could that have been one of his tools for success? Why would he try to do things that he could not do? Did he enjoy defeat? He says he did them to learn.

It's a bold move to launch into something you cannot do. There is no safety or familiarity in that task, no chance to prove your knowledge and skill. It takes guts to be willing to learn something without the guarantee of success.

That is precisely why some people do it. They want to expand their knowledge, and they are willing to drop their egos and learn a new skill. In a way, they are heroic. It is a wonderful idea when you think about it. You are always armed with the potential to change and grow and learn new things. You just have to build up the nerve to make an attempt.

Your assignment is to choose three things you cannot do at this moment but you would like to do someday. You don't have to attempt the impossible; just write down your goals for future reference.

"When you have a great and difficult task, something perhaps almost impossible, if you only work a little at a time, every day a little, suddenly the work will finish itself."

Karen von Blixen-Finecke

You may not know the name Karen von Blixen-Finecke. However, you may be familiar with her pen name, Isak Dinesen. Karen von Blixen-Finecke was a Danish author who wrote in both English and Danish. Two of her most famous English works were *Out of Africa* and *Babette's Feast*, both of which were turned into stunning motion pictures. She offers very wise advice in this quote about a tactic that can be used when attempting the impossible.

When you are up against a seemingly insurmountable task, it's best to break it down into smaller, more manageable parts. Then you can chip away at it a little bit at a time, and before you know it, you'll be surprised to find that it's finished.

It is intimidating to attempt the impossible. It sounds so . . . big. But if you start with a small portion at a time, suddenly the project seems manageable. Breaking difficult tasks down into smaller parts also gives you minor victories along the road to your ultimate goal. You can celebrate each milestone and know that it is getting you closer to success.

Take a look at the three impossible tasks you wrote down yesterday. Pick one and brainstorm ways in which you can break it down into smaller sections and work on it a little bit at a time. Come up with a date for completion, and then put your smaller goals along a timeline leading to your final goal. You now have a plan to achieve the impossible. When do you start?

"The difference between the impossible and the possible lies in a man's determination."

Tommy Lasorda

Determination is the fire in the furnace of every successful person. Only you decide whether or not something is possible, because you are the only one who has the power to give up on yourself or continue on until you achieve success. You are completely in charge of your level of determination. On a scale of one to ten, how much determination do you have? What can you do to build that fire of determination inside of you?

Well, you can do a number of things. First of all, pick a task that you feel strongly about. Do something that stirs your passions and sparks your creativity. Pick something that has real meaning to you. You're not going to drum up a whole lot of determination if you're barely interested in a project.

Secondly, break it down. You learned yesterday that it's easier to achieve the impossible if you break it down into smaller chunks. Your determination to succeed will build every time you reach a milestone.

Third, be a hero and take that risk. Don't be afraid to fail, because you know that you will learn from your mistakes. Failure teaches success. You don't know what you are capable of achieving until you try.

Finally, launch into your impossible dreams with unbridled enthusiasm. Don't hold back and never, ever quit. You control the fire in the furnace. How determined are you to succeed?

Day 112

"If the only prayer you ever say in your entire life is thank you, it will be enough."

Johannes Eckhart

Over the next few days, you are going to take a look at what prayer and meditation can do to help you on the road to success. If religion of any sort makes you queasy, don't worry. Your next assignment is not to join a monastery. You will have an opportunity to take a non-denominational look at the value of each and decide for yourself if they will be useful tools in your quest for success.

Prayer is simply a form of communication. It's a chance for you to talk. For some, it is communication with their god. For others, it may be a petition that is sent out to the universe or humanity as a whole. A prayer can be a request, a petition, a thank you, or just a thought that you don't want to keep to yourself. It's really up to you who or what you address in your prayer.

A lot of prayers seem to start with, "HELP ME!"

Johannes Eckhart suggests that the most important prayer is, "Thank you."

What are you thankful for in this world? Make a list, and then find a quiet spot in your home or outside and read the list out loud. Thank God or the universe—or the doorknob if you can't think of anything suitable to pray to—for these things. Communicate your gratitude out loud.

Prayer helps you to be mindful of what is important in your life. It helps you to put words to your joys and concerns and hopes and dreams. Give prayer a try every day this week, even if all you say is, "Thank you."

"Everything can be used as an invitation to meditation. A smile, a face in the subway, the sight of a small flower growing in the crack of a cement pavement, a fall of rich cloth in a shop window, the way the sun lights up flower pots on a window sill. Be alert for any sign of beauty or grace. Offer up every joy, be awake at all moments, to the news that is always arriving out of silence (Rainer Maria Rilke)."

Sogyal Rinpoche

Cindy had heard about the benefits of meditation for years, and she finally decided to try it for herself. She bought *Meditation for Dummies* and a bunch of CDs that included chanting monks, flutes, and wind chimes. She even found a fancy animal-print pillow to sit on while she got "spiritual."

She followed all of the instructions in the book, but she felt ridiculous. Time crawled by, and she was lucky if she could sit still for two minutes, let alone a half hour. One time she sat on her fancy animal-print pillow for a full forty-five minutes, but she didn't think she could officially call it meditating. Her own snoring woke her up.

After a solid month of attempts, Cindy finally gave up in disgust. She couldn't do meditation the right way, and she hated trying and failing every day. Maybe meditation wasn't for everyone. She put away her pillow and her CDs and moved on.

Have you ever tried meditation and quit, because you got too fidgety trying to follow the rules? There is good news for you today! There are no rules to meditation. That's right. You don't have to twist your legs into a pretzel, chant words you don't understand, and listen to freaky music to reap the benefits of meditation. All you have to do is be silent and pay attention. Your assignment today is to try silence.

Day 114

"To meditate is to observe simultaneously the formation of thought and breath, and then let it go, without complicating it, without formalizing it, without identifying with it, without rejecting it, letting it follow its own way."

Allen Ginsberg

One of the great gifts of meditation is that the rewards far exceed the effort. As was mentioned before, there are really no rules for meditation. There are a few suggestions that seem to work very well for people, and they are to breathe, to be silent, and then just observe what happens. That's it. Trying meditation is one of the easiest assignments you will have in this book.

Give it a whirl today. You don't have to find a special spot in a dark room with soothing music. You can do it in the car on the way to work, on the subway, in your room, at your desk, at the gym, on your bike, in your favorite chair, wherever you want. Just take a few minutes to be silent. Feel your breathing. Then, observe the thoughts that bubble up when you have this small opportunity to be quiet for a minute.

Do not judge your thoughts. Just notice them and let them flow on by. Some people like to imagine their thoughts like clouds that pass before their eyes slowly and softly. You watch them, but you don't analyze them or reach for them or try to do something with them at this moment. You just see them float on by.

You may be surprised at what thoughts pop up in the silence. You are opening a window to your soul when you take the time to be quiet, and sometimes amazing ideas show up on one of those puffy clouds. Other times, your body might just enjoy the break. In this exercise, though, the results don't matter. It's the action of meditation that counts.

"I have never wished there was a God to call on—I have often wished there was a God to thank."

F. Scott Fitzgerald

Meditation is an exercise in listening, and prayer is an exercise in communicating. They are both opportunities for reflection. Today, you will have another occasion to see if prayer is a useful tool in your life.

You do not have to believe in a particular god in order to pray. It is primarily a form of communication, so there are no prerequisite beliefs in order for it to be useful. If you do not believe in a god, then pick anything outside of yourself, and point your prayers in that direction. The idea is that you communicate with something outside of you. This is your chance to get your grievances, concerns, hopes, dreams, or fears out into the open so that they don't weigh so heavily on your soul.

If you had an opportunity to give God or the universe (or your coffeemaker) a call, what would you say? Would you have a list of grievances several pages long? Maybe you've been saving a wish list of requests. You might also just want to say, "Hey, thanks. This has been a pretty cool ride so far."

Give prayer a try today. Just like meditation, there are no rules. Prayer is an opening for you to communicate your feelings without necessarily having to confide in another living person. Your prayer can be as short as "Please!" or "Thank you!" On the other hand, if you have a lot on your mind, you can pray for as long as you want. Communicate today through prayer and observe how you feel afterward.

Day 116

"There are no shortcuts to any place worth going."

Beverly Sills

For the next few days, you will be studying the topic of endurance. One of the most important things to consider as you strive for success is that you are in a long-distance race. The road to success is not a fifty-yard dash. There will be victories along the way, but the path stretches throughout your life.

Now that you are aware of that, take your time. Enjoy the view. Don't bother with the shortcuts, because they're not going to take you where you really want to go. Part of the joy of success is to discover the places that are worth going. Where do you want to travel in this marathon? What would you like to see?

Choose a path that will strengthen your mind, your heart, and your soul. That is not usually the easiest and shortest route, but it is always the most rewarding. Be patient with yourself as you travel. Celebrate all of your victories. Rejoice when you pass each mile marker, because you are on a path that is gradually fulfilling your dreams.

You spent some time over the last few months discovering your dreams and passions in life. Are you on a path that is leading toward them? Did you take a shortcut to obtain immediate gratification, or do you feel like you're on a road that leads to your destiny? Shortcuts might emerge in the form of frivolous pursuits, shallow relationships, greedy endeavors, or any number of distractions that send you on a detour from your true path. Look out for those shortcuts and resist taking the easier and less rewarding route. Your assignment is to journal about the path you are on today.

"Excellence is not a singular act, but a habit. You are what you repeatedly do."

Shaquille O'Neal (paraphrasing Aristotle)

Success is not a one-time deal. It's a habit. If you truly want to be successful, you have to put in the work . . . continuously. Remember, endurance is important on this road to accomplishment. If you are pursuing your passions, then the effort shouldn't bother you at all. It will be enjoyable.

Great athletes do not become successful by accident. They practice their skills over and over. They train like crazy to be the best — but they love the work, so all that sweat is worth it. Are you putting some sweat into your success? Are you practicing daily to achieve your dreams? Or do you still think success will be a one-time event that hits you over the head like a giant hammer when you least expect it?

Unfortunately, the things that sum you up are not the result of a one-time explosion of achievement. You are what you repeatedly do. If you repeatedly eat Twinkies for breakfast, lunch, and dinner, then you can call yourself a creampuff. On the other hand, if you are in the habit of reading trade journals in your field of interest and applying what you learn to your day-to-day activities, then you are practicing excellence.

Your task today is to add one thing to your routine that you can do every day to practice success. It doesn't have to be a big thing. A few options might be to get up a half hour early and practice meditation, hit the gym, take a continuing education class, or sign up for volunteer work with an organization you admire. Small steps taken continuously will get you miles ahead on the road to success.

Day 118

"A lie has speed, but truth has endurance."

Edgar J. Mohn

Another important thing to consider when focusing on your endurance is the truth. If you are about to run a marathon, you make sure you have a really good pair of shoes. You want those shoes to be made with the best material that will stand up through the continual beating they're going to take when your feet hit the road. Durability is infinitely more important than speed.

Similarly, you cannot build your journey to success on lies. A lie might provide you with a shortcut, it might look flashy and take you somewhere very fast, but it is not made of sturdy material. It will not stand the test of time, and soon it will be worthless on the road to success.

Assemble your success with sturdy materials. Make sure you have a strong foundation built in truth. That means if you don't understand how to do something or you don't have the necessary skills, the first thing you need to do is admit it. Be honest about your limitations, and be willing to learn new things and practice until you have the level of proficiency you need. That might take some time, but it is worth it. You are building a really sturdy pair of shoes for your success marathon.

Today's homework is fun. Pull out those crayons, markers, or colored pencils again, and draw your pair of shoes. You are preparing to enter the success marathon. What do you want your shoes to look like? What will they be made of? Let your imagination go crazy with this assignment.

"Endurance is not just the ability to bear a hard thing but to turn it into glory."

William Barclay

Endurance equals victory. Have you ever thought of it that way? You might equate endurance with something that is tedious, boring, and painful. Do you think if endurance is involved the event is going to be long and hard? You may be partially right. But what is the outcome? If you endure, that means you make it through. You win! You're still standing at the end of the game. Endurance will lead you to glory, so it's a trait you want to cultivate.

Another great thing about endurance is that it is a real achievement. It is never handed to you. It requires some sort of effort. If you endured something, you took it all the way to the end. You followed through, and you should be congratulated. You did not quit; you did not give up. You continued on to victory.

Is there anything going on in your life today that is unresolved? Is your endurance being tested in any area of your life right now? Write about that specific experience. How do you plan to endure? Imagine how great you will feel when you make it to the conclusion of this part of your journey. What a victory it will be! The outcome doesn't matter. What matters is that you carried through to the end. You played the game until the final buzzer. That alone makes you a success.

Consider how you can use endurance to turn the hard things in your life into glory. How can you win simply by never giving up? What can you do to make sure you go all the way to the finish line?

Day 120

"The burden becomes light that is shared by love."
Publius Ovidius Naso

All of this talk of endurance makes the road to success sound very arduous, doesn't it? Are you starting to think that maybe success is not all it's cracked up to be? Maybe you don't really want to run a marathon. You're not built for that kind of test. You prefer short walks to epic adventures.

There is good news for you today. You don't have to attack this journey in its entirety. Break it down into those short walks. Travel a little bit at a time. You can run this marathon in a series of small jaunts. Take whatever number of miles you can handle in one effort, rest a bit, and then move on. Soon, you will look behind you and realize that you've come a long, long way. The only thing you must do is continue moving forward.

There is another bit of good news: you have an opportunity to lighten the load you carry. You have already explored how important relationships are to success. Here is your opportunity to share the load through love. Love pumps air into every burden, and suddenly your cargo is as light as a feather.

Do not be stingy with love. Share your love and compassion with others. Lighten their load by giving them a hand, showing empathy, or simply offering a smile or a laugh. The more you love others, the lighter your own load will become. A race that tests your endurance is so much easier when you share the burden with those you love.

Your assignment today is to use love to lighten someone's load.

"The doctor of the future will no longer treat the human frame with drugs, but rather will cure and prevent disease with nutrition."

Thomas Edison

Health and nutrition will be the topic for the next few days, and this quote by Thomas Edison is a great way to kick it off. There are so many small steps you can take through diet and exercise that will increase your chance of success. Thomas Edison was not the first or only person to believe that nutrition can be used to treat the human frame. That is wonderful news! You don't have to invest in expensive or painful treatments to improve your health and well being. Just practice making good food choices and incorporating some type of exercise into your routine.

This subject may be stressful for some of you. Maybe food is an ongoing issue in your life; maybe it's not. Either way, you will probably pick up new and interesting information about yourself during the next week. Take an honest and non-judgmental look at what you put in your body and be willing to consider a few changes. There will not be a weigh-in later on, so don't get nervous. This is a self-assessment. It's a chance for you to get honest with yourself about your good and bad nutrition habits.

Your first assignment is to keep a food journal for one week. Get a pocket-size notebook that you can keep with you all the time, and write down every single thing you eat or drink each day. Don't try to change your habits yet; just observe them. You will have a chance to go back and analyze later. For one week, all you need to do is document what goes into your body.

Day 122

"Never eat more than you can lift."

Miss Piggy

While you are getting your food journal underway, let's go over a couple of simple rules when it comes to nutrition. Miss Piggy offers the first one. Gluttony isn't pretty. Try to avoid ridiculous food portions.

Notice the rule has nothing to do with avoiding particular foods. Instead, it suggests that you practice moderation. Most people enjoy pizza once in awhile. No problem! But a large, double cheese, stuffed crust, extra pepperoni every day fills you up with garbage that has nowhere to go but your waistline.

While you are filling out your food journal, think about your portions. Do you tend to supersize it? Or do you stick with pretty modest portions? Do you like to eat until you are so stuffed you can barely get up from the table? Or do you pick at your food and always leave a meal without feeling completely satisfied? Do you find yourself somewhere in between those two extremes?

Go back through your memory and try to remember the best meal you ever had. What did you eat that made you feel so good? Did you feel energized or sleepy, comfortable or stuffed, satisfied or wanting more?

Finally, write about your emotions as they relate to food. What do you eat when you're sad? What do you eat when you are excited? What time of day do you enjoy food the most? Does food ever make you feel guilty? Is eating enjoyable to you, or is it a necessity that doesn't provide much pleasure? Explore how you view food.

"A man too busy to take care of his health is like a mechanic too busy to take care of his tools."

Spanish Proverb

This proverb highlights another simple thought to keep in mind. Take care of yourself, because you are the instrument of your success. If you were a successful mechanic, you would take very good care of your tools, because they help you to succeed. If you were a painter, you would pay special attention to how you store your paints so they don't dry out. They are your means of expression, so you must make sure they are well cared for. If you were a computer programmer, you would constantly update your computer so it has the best software and the strongest protection from hackers.

Think about your body as a tool. It is literally the instrument of your success. Unfortunately, you can't drop off your body somewhere for repairs on the path to achievement and pick it up when it's fixed and in better working order. You're stuck with it, whether it is working well or not. Your journey will be cut short if you don't take care of yourself and make sure you are in good working condition.

In order to achieve your dreams, you want to have the best equipment you can find. You don't want rusty tools that have fallen into disrepair. You want clean and vibrant tools so that you have every opportunity to put your best effort forward.

Write about how you take care of your health. Are you too busy to eat right and exercise regularly? Is health the last thing you think of when you are striving to make a difference in this world? Do you view your body as a tool for your success?

Day 124

"The five S's of sports training are: stamina, speed, strength, skill, and spirit; but the greatest of these is spirit."

Ken Doherty

Now let's move on to the exercise side of taking care of your body. Have you ever taken part in rigorous sports training? If you have, you know that it is extremely hard work. If you have not, it sounds exciting and even a little heroic, doesn't it? Most of us have watched the Olympics and been awestruck at athletes from across the globe competing at the top of their field. We marvel at what they are able to accomplish physically.

You have an opportunity to feel the excitement and gratification of physical accomplishment on your own level. Are you willing to push yourself a little in order to experience the success of a healthy and strong body? Your goal does not have to be participation in the Olympic Games. Concentrate only on making forward progress.

You may be thinking, "I am not good at sports. This is going to be torture." It doesn't have to be. It can be a joyful and enlightening experience if you're open to it. Take a look at the quote above. The most important aspect of sports training is spirit. If you go into this project with excitement, you have already accomplished the most important part.

Imagine how great you will feel if you push yourself just a little bit harder each day. If you don't presently exercise at all, then start. If you do, then kick up the intensity. You do not have to kill yourself. Your goal is to gradually and continually increase your stamina, speed, strength, and skill. The key to your success is spirit. Launch into this like you're training for the Olympics, and enjoy witnessing how your body responds to healthy action.

"Life expectancy would grow by leaps and bounds if green vegetables smelled as good as bacon."

Doug Larson

Today you are going to give yourself a break. You have been psyching yourself up to eat healthy and exercise, but let's take a moment to get real. There are foods that you really enjoy that aren't the best for you. Do you have to give them up forever in order to be successful?

Absolutely not. You do have the opportunity to tweak your regular routine to get healthier and stronger, but nobody is perfect. Allow yourself an occasional indulgence. Give yourself a day off from exercise. The point here is not to become perfect. No one will achieve that. You want to look at the overall picture.

So you had a hot fudge sundae last night. So what? What did you do the rest of the week? If you had a hot fudge sundae every day, you might want to rethink your choices. If it was a one-time indulgence, good for you! Life is not meant to be complete drudgery. Have a little fun sometimes. Those once-in-awhile treats are a lot more pleasurable if they only happen once in awhile. Enjoy them!

Your assignment today is to either skip exercise or eat something that is not particularly healthy. Don't feel guilty. Enjoy this little delight. Tomorrow, you will go back to your regular routine and continue to progress gradually in the areas of exercise and nutrition.

Nobody is perfect. Enjoy small indulgences and then get back on track.

"Tact is the knack of making a point without making an enemy."

Isaac Newton

You have already explored the fact that you cannot reach success on your own. You need other people in your life. No one is an island, and it is important to be aware of how we are all connected. Over the next few days, you are going to further investigate ways in which you can get along with others. It is important to always be aware of how you relate to the people around you, particularly if you want to live a successful life.

Do you have tact? Do you even know what that means in your everyday life? Isaac Newton offers a great definition. Tact is the knack of making a point without making an enemy. It is truly an art.

Why do you think it might be so difficult to be tactful in various situations? Usually, the ego gets in the way. Someone says or does something particularly stupid, and you want to point it out. Your ego wants to show them that you're superior. It's even worse if they do something stupid and it affects you in some way. Then you feel superior *and* annoyed.

How do you curb those natural urges to let the person know they are a complete idiot? Try empathy first. Think about what it would be like if you were them. How embarrassed would you be if someone pointed out your shortcomings? It wouldn't feel good, would it? Another way that you can make your point without making an enemy is to identify your own flaws. Maybe you've made a similar mistake in the past. You can share your story and how you found a better solution.

Practice tact today and give your ego the day off.

"True friendship is like sound health, the value of it is seldom known until it be lost."

Charles Caleb Colton

How many friends do you have? These are not just mere acquaintances, but true friends who would be there for you no matter what. How many people would consider you a friend? Are you someone who people can come to if they need a person to confide in? Do you lift your friends up when they're down?

Human beings need friendships just as much as we need food, water, and other essentials. We have the unique capacity to share each other's burdens and help one another through life. Do you nurture your friendships? Have you utilized this rare gift to its fullest? If not, you are discarding a very important tool for success.

Take a look at your friendships today. Where do you fall short? Is there someone you haven't called in awhile? Is there a friend you can help today? When was the last time you told your friends that they are important in your life?

Write about your friendships. Have you lost a friend recently? Why? What does it feel like when you lose a friendship? There can be very legitimate reasons for ending a friendship, but it is almost always a painful process. Journal about what you can do to increase your circle of friends and take good care of the friends you have.

Friendship is a most precious gift. Do you treat it like that? Or do you tend to use your friends when you need them and discard them when you don't? These are some tough questions to ask yourself. Try to avoid feeling guilty about the current state of your friendships and instead plan concrete actions that will strengthen these ties.

Day 128

"Our prime purpose in this life is to help others. And if you can't help them, at least don't hurt them."

Tenzin Gyatso

You have been keeping a food journal for one week now. Take a few minutes today to review it. Do you see any patterns? Pick out one thing you would like to change about your diet and start today. Maybe you would like to drink less soda, stop eating late at night, or avoid snacking in the afternoon. Pick one item and change your routine for the better.

Now, back to relationships. Do you believe your primary purpose in life is to help others, or do you think others should help you? That is a pretty important distinction. Living your life in service to others is quite different from living a life where you expect others to serve you. Draw a horizontal line across the middle of one of the pages in your journal. Put "helping others" on the left end of the line and "others helping you" on the right side of the line. Where do you fall? Are you habitually helpful, or do you really require help from others much more often than you give it? Put a red dot on the line to represent where you are today. Then, put a green dot on the line to show where you would like to be a month from now.

When you think about being a success, do you imagine living in a mansion with hundreds of servants taking care of your every need? Well, that's not such a horrible image. Now you have a chance to add to your vision of success. How do you see yourself helping others — or at least not hurting them? How will you use your success for the good of someone else?

"Compassion is the keen awareness of the interdependence of all things."

Thomas Merton

Compassion carries a little more weight than empathy. When you are empathetic, you relate to how someone feels. That is a very important first step in relationships. When you are compassionate, you have a desire to help. Compassion identifies the fact of interdependence and carries with it the impulse to act. If you want to succeed in this world, then you have to take action to improve your world. It wouldn't be very satisfying to be a success on a planet that is otherwise falling apart.

Your success is inextricably related to the well being and success of those around you. Success is not a ranking system. Many of us continue to think of it as a contest that we must win and others must lose, but that is not the case at all. You will bring others with you if you are truly successful. There will not be first, second, and third place medals given out at the end of the journey. There is no limit to the number of people who reach success.

Take empathy one step further today and practice compassion. That means when you see someone suffering, take action to help that person. It's not good enough to just think, "Poor guy. It would be a bummer to be in his shoes." You've evolved beyond that now. It is your job to offer assistance.

You will reach success if you reach out to others. If you don't believe that's true, give it a try for a few weeks. Witness how your life changes when you practice compassion. Discover the rewards of helping others. You may be astonished at the results. Success has nothing to do with elbowing out the competition. You must practice compassion to reach it.

Day 130

"It's the most breathtakingly ironic things about living: the fact that we are all . . . alone. Singular. And yet what we seek — what saves us — is our connection to others."

Wally Lamb

Your connection to others is what saves you from being completely alone. It is human nature to seek out those connections. You yearn for them, and they will bring real meaning to your life. So this isn't just about learning to tolerate people or get along with them in spite of your differences. Your saving grace is the connection you have to those around you. Think about that today. People are not merely to be tolerated and occasionally helped. They are your saviors. It puts a different spin on things, doesn't it?

Conduct a little experiment. Treat the people you come across today as if you have been searching for them your whole life. They are pearls in the ocean of your existence; they are treasures that you are thrilled to discover. When you make a connection with another human being, you are winning the lottery.

Why do this? Because that's what it's all about. Your connection to others is the name of the game. Do you want success? Then strengthen your relationships and notice the value of the people around you. If you don't, it's like being offered a treasure chest full of precious jewels and not even bothering to look at them.

People are not annoyances. They are fascinating and wonderful and unique and fallible — just like you. Don't pass up the chance to experience the treasures that surround you every day. Stop and spend time with others. Add your own treasure to the chest, and become an integral part of the world in which you live.

"Have regular hours for work and play; make each day both useful and pleasant, and prove that you understand the worth of time by employing it well. Then youth will be delightful, old age will bring few regrets, and life will become a beautiful success."

Louisa May Alcott

Playtime is just as important as the hours you put into work. Isn't that great? You really must schedule time to play. Many people do not realize the importance of downtime until it's too late and they are completely burned out on work. Does that sound familiar? Do you assume that you will be a success if you keep your nose in your work and your focus only on the endless tasks ahead of you?

The truth is you will be much more productive — and happier — if you reserve time to play a little each day. When your mind has a chance to relax and follow its own whims, there is no telling what brainstorms will emerge. You just might be handed some great ideas to consider when you return to work.

Louisa May Alcott brings up another very important point in this quote. Understand the worth of time. Schedule wisely. Time is a very precious commodity, and it should not be wasted. Playtime is not a misuse of your minutes, but the time you spend in indecision, fear, or remorse is a complete waste.

Your assignment today is to look at how you spend your time. Go over your calendar from last week and point out spots where you could have used your time more wisely. What are some things you can do to exclude wasteful time and add productive minutes for work and play?

Day 132

"Necessity may be the mother of invention, but play is certainly the father."

Roger von Oech

In order to reach your full potential in life, you must draw on your fun side as well as your pragmatic side. Don't get too serious about achieving success. It will block your true talents. You are not a machine. You're a multi-faceted person, and one of the most beautiful aspects of your personality probably (hopefully) includes a little playfulness.

Think back to an assignment you did on Day 67. You started to construct a list of people you admire. Now is a great time to add to that list. Write down three or four additional people who you would like to emulate. Take some time to list all of the appealing aspects of their personalities. Are they fun people to be around? Are they inspiring? Are they smart? Do they have endless energy to accomplish the impossible? Do they seem at ease or comfortable in their own skin? Do others feel good when they are around them?

Highly successful people are rarely one-dimensional. They have a great combo of drive and frivolity in their lives, and it comes through not only in their ideas and innovations, but also in their ability to turn their dreams into reality. Successful people also share a knack of striking a great balance between necessity and play. They are almost annoyingly relaxed, and that might be because they're happy. They enjoy life every day. They didn't wait for the big payoff before they had a little fun. They realized early on that play is an important ingredient to success.

Practice your own success today by striking a balance between necessity and play.

"For the main characteristic of play — whether of child or adult — is not its content but its mode. Play is an approach to action, not a form of activity."

Jerome Bruner

Here is a great secret: play is an approach to action. That is one of the reasons why it is so important to success. The pressures of real life can paralyze you with fear, but play almost never causes that reaction. When you play, you couldn't care less about the outcome. It's not real life. It doesn't count. You can screw up as much as you want and experiment with all sorts of ideas, because you're just messing around.

The content of your play is not all that important, either. It's not a project you plan to turn in to your boss; it's not a test; it's not even something you will hold onto past the present moment. The immediacy of play is very liberating to your mind and body. You have the sense that you will not be held accountable for whatever happens, so you are willing to take a few more risks.

Play is an event that takes place almost exclusively in the present. Have you ever planned out every detail of how you will play? No. That makes no sense. Part of the idea of play is that it's unpredictable. You're just goofing around. The results are anyone's guess.

Your assignment today is to play. You can do anything you want. Go to a playground and swing on the swings; sit down and draw or color; play a sport with some friends; take in a movie; or get out a board game and invite a few people over. Just go with whatever you feel like doing. After your playtime is over, think about how play is an approach to action and consider ways that play can help you when you get stuck in real life.

Day 134

"Playing reduces stress, improves life, and increases creativity.
Who doesn't want that?"

Stevanne Auerbach

What about the guilt factor? You can't really take time out to play,
can you? You've got lots of important adult things to do. What kind
of guilt would you feel if you stopped working and sat on a swing for
a half hour? That would be ridiculous and a waste of thirty minutes.

Stop those nasty little voices in your head that are admonishing you
for taking time to play. It is not a waste of time. In fact, the opposite is
true. Play is essential. Look at the evidence Stevanne Auerbach gives
in the quote above.

Play has many advantages:

It reduces stress.

It improves the quality of life.

It increases creativity.

Seriously, who wouldn't want that? Those are all important ingredients
for a healthy, happy, and successful life. Do you feel guilty about play
because it's enjoyable? Well, here's a news flash: you don't have to
suffer mightily in order to win success. Enjoy the ride! Not all of your
tasks along the way will be difficult. If you are following your passion
in life, most of the journey will be pleasurable. Get out there and play!

"Play keeps us vital and alive. It gives us an enthusiasm for life that is irreplaceable. Without it, life just doesn't taste good."

Lucia Capocchione

Let's launch into your project first this time. You have probably already discovered that it's a good idea to keep colored pencils, crayons, or markers handy while reading this book. It's time to bring them out again. Your task today is to draw a picture of how you feel when you play. It doesn't have to be an actual picture of you, if you don't want. It can be a series of symbols or colors or scenes. Whatever you feel represents how you feel inside when you play.

Now draw another picture of how you feel when you work. What pictorial description can you make for the way you feel emotionally when you do your chores or take care of the business side of life?

When you're done, put both pictures side by side. Do they look similar, or are they drastically different? Take a close look at the differences between both drawings.

The quote above provides a perfect description of the importance of play in your life. Without play, life just doesn't taste good. You need a little hot sauce on your meal — a little spice in your life. You need more than a series of tasks to complete in order to feel fulfilled and happy. Play brings your enthusiasm out. It gives color to an otherwise black-and-white picture.

You simply cannot achieve success without play. It is the extra vitality you must have to be a notch above ordinary. Enjoy the spice that play puts into your life.

"Whenever I feel blue, I start breathing again."

L. Frank Baum

Yes, breathing is good. In fact, it's essential. But you already know that. Did you also know that it is a powerful tool in your toolbox for success — and not just because it keeps you alive? Over the next few days you will have a chance to try some exercises that will help you master breathing techniques that may become very useful as you travel the road to success.

Breathing is not only a life-giving element, but it is also a healing element. When you learn to monitor and control your breath at certain times, you can lower your heart rate, increase your ability to pay attention, relax, tap into your inner voice, and get in tune with your own body rhythms. Breath is the center of everything, and it can work for you in more ways than you may currently realize.

Your assignment for the beginning of this series on breath is to become a sort of scientist for a day. Observe your breathing as if you are observing a specimen. This may be more difficult than you think. Oftentimes, the minute you start to think about something that is as automatic as breathing you become self-conscious and uneasy with your breath. That's no excuse to quit. Continue on, and it will get easier. What do you observe about your breathing? Where do you feel it in your body? Do you breathe through your nose or your mouth? Do you feel it in your chest or your belly? Write down all of your observations. Breath is essential and transformational. Enjoy the next few days of discovery.

"Many people now are seeking organic ways to heal themselves and feel good . . . Breathwork is the ideal alternative. It is free and completely within our conscious control."

Gay Hendricks, PhD

Organic remedies are all the rage these days. Everyone is learning the benefits of ginger, pomegranate, green tea, and various other cures. The easiest and cheapest natural remedy is breathing. It is free, and you can practice its healing powers anytime you want.

Maggie wanted to change the way she reacted in stressful situations. Her biggest stressor was her boss. She got flustered whenever her boss asked her questions, and she ended up sounding like an idiot. She was a fairly intelligent person most of the time, but the minute her boss started firing questions at her, she felt her heart rate spiral and her confidence plummet.

A friend who was involved in a daily yoga class suggested that Maggie pay attention to her breathing when she got in those situations and consciously take a breath before she responded. Maggie thought she might as well give it a try, and the very next day she had an opportunity. Her boss walked into her office and launched into a series of questions about a new project. Maggie took one split second to breathe in and out, and then she answered. The result astonished her. That one second gave her a chance collect her thoughts, and instead of a reacting like she was defending herself in a dodge ball game, she came back with a calm and intelligent response.

Every time someone asks you a question today, breathe before you react. Observe the difference in your response.

Day 138

"Focusing on the act of breathing clears the mind of all daily distractions and clears our energy enabling us to better connect with the Spirit within."

Author Unknown

You know by now that you want to reach the spirit within you to tap into your true talents and unearth your unique gifts. Breathing is the express train to that place. You've studied meditation, and it is centered in breath, so you have already experienced what it's like to use your breath to slow down and listen to your inner voice.

The other great benefit of breathing is that it's like hiring a maid to tidy up your brain. If you focus on nothing but breathing, you will start to remove the chatter in your head. You will clear away the voices that are constantly saying things like: "Do I look fat in these jeans?" "Did I pay the phone bill this month?" "What should I have for supper?" "Did my son wash his hands after he played with the dog?"

That chatter is not important in the big scheme of life, and concentrating on your breath for a few minutes a day will help you brush away the small stuff to make room for your next big inspiration. You could have a great idea floating around in your head right now, but it's lost in the crowd of your minor, distracting chit-chat.

Your assignment today is to take ten minutes to concentrate on your breathing. Find a place where you will not be interrupted — even if you have to lock yourself in the bathroom. Inhale for three seconds and exhale for three seconds. Then breathe in for four seconds and exhale for three seconds and onward until you get to ten. Then reverse the numbers and exhale longer than you inhale. Don't assess; just practice.

"Watch breath, soften belly, open heart, has become a wake-up call for mindfulness and mercy, which takes people beyond the mind-body of suffering into the deep peace of their healing."

Stephen Levine

Breathing exercises, when practiced regularly, will give you the gift of peace. Measured breathing helps you to slow down and sets up an environment of mindfulness that automatically invites peace, healing, and a feeling of centeredness. You deserve to take the time to practice breathing and connect to your inner self.

You've already had some practice watching your breath and counting your inhalations and exhalations. Now add a soft belly to the exercise. That's right, a soft belly. You may have spent your whole life trying to suck in your tummy. Now is your chance to let it relax a little. Nobody's watching. Try it!

A relaxed belly allows you to breathe more deeply. Let the muscles of your belly relax, and then take in a nice, slow breath. A breath that goes down into the belly is much fuller and more relaxing than one that goes into the chest. Try both so that you can experience the difference for yourself. First, take a deep breath high in your chest. Raise your shoulders, too, if you want. Then, let it out. It's a relief to let that breath go, isn't it? It promotes tension rather than relieving it.

Now take a long, slow breath into your belly. It's as if you are a round jug filling with water. Exhale. You should be feeling even more grounded and relaxed. Let your breath fill downward into your body instead of up around your chest and neck when you practice your ten minutes of breathing today.

"Fear less, hope more; eat less, chew more; whine less, breathe more; talk less, say more; hate less, love more; and all good things are yours."

Swedish Proverb

Leave it to the Swedish to sum it all up. Evidently, they are a practical bunch! Write this proverb down on a piece of paper and post it on your bathroom mirror, the cupboard where you keep your coffee cups, or anywhere you will see it daily. It sums up many of the topics you have been studying so far in order to achieve success. Concentrate on "whine less, breathe more" today.

Doug had an excuse for everything. He whined and complained nonstop. When he thought about it, he wasn't even sure why he did it. At some point it had become a bad habit. He took a breath in, and he exhaled a litany of complaints, even if no one was listening. His constant complaining was blocking his opportunity for success.

Doug talked to a counselor about his problem, and the counselor suggested that he exhale without words. He had gotten used to whining when he exhaled. He needed to replace that with silence. For the next couple of weeks he practiced a different habit. He inhaled and exhaled twice before he let himself say anything. By that time he usually forgot what he was going to complain about. It broke him of his habit.

The truth is Doug wasn't all that upset about any of those little things. He just got used to complaining. He needed to change his automatic reaction. By simply breathing, he changed his bad habit and made room for inspiration to replace his complaints. Follow Doug's lead and whine less, breathe more today.

"The healthiest competition occurs when average people win by putting above average effort."

Colin Powell

Success doesn't necessarily have anything to do with how brilliant you are in a given field. It has much more to do with your passion and your purpose. Average people accomplish extraordinary things every single day. They are able to do it, because they put in above-average effort.

Do you want to win this game, or are you just along for the ride? There is nothing standing in the way of you achieving success except you. If you really want this, then put in the effort. You can't fake passion or purpose in life. Most people do not stumble into success through halfhearted efforts. They put everything they have into their dreams, because they believe they were meant to win. They are single-minded about their goals, and they believe without a doubt that they must be achieved.

Have you found something you are passionate about yet, or did you get bored and stop looking for it? If you have not done so, now is the time to find that one thing that really fires you up and makes you want to put forth a herculean effort. It is so much easier to achieve success when you believe strongly in what you are doing. It is also the healthiest way to compete. When you feel that you have a true purpose in what you are doing, you will be willing to do whatever it takes to make it happen.

Find that special purpose in your life today. If you have discovered your passion, then plot out ways that you can put an above-average effort into following it.

Day 142

"Great minds have purposes, others have wishes."
                                        Washington Irving

What's the difference between a purpose and a wish? Write down your own definition of each in your journal before you read further.

Everyone has wishes. You might wish you were taller . . . or shorter. Maybe you wish you could sing. You might even wish you had something nicer to wear to a party you plan to attend this evening. Wishes are often dreams that will not come true without divine intervention or a fairy godmother. They are things that you want, but you don't have the power to get on your own. There is very little chance that you can make your own wish come true. You might have the power to make someone else's wish come true, but not your own.

A purpose is different. If you have a purpose, you are going to make it happen. You have a clear goal, and you're drawn to it like a magnet. There is power in purpose. You follow your purpose in life, because it's what you were meant to do. It's your destiny. You are compelled to accomplish it. Wishes don't have that kind of power.

Turn to a new page in your journal and make two columns. In one column write your purposes. What are you compelled or destined to do? In the other column write your wishes. These are the things you wish for on a star. Once you've finished, you can rip off the wishes side and throw it away. It's fun to think about your wishes, but you personally can't do much about them. Concentrate on your purposes. Focus in on them and direct all your talents to achieving those goals. You have the power to do it.

"Spirit . . . has fifty times the strength and staying power of brawn and muscle."

Unknown

You had an opportunity to think about spirit on Day 124 when you were studying the advantages of sports training. Today you will look at how it can add strength to other areas of your life.

Jackie Robinson broke the color barrier in 1947 when he took his position at first base for the Brooklyn Dodgers. He was the first African-American to play for major-league baseball. That in itself was a success, but Jackie Robinson had to prove that he had staying power. His spirit in the face of hate mail, death threats, and physical violence was a testament to the passion and the purpose he possessed. He paved the road for change and showed an entire country how to move toward integration and understanding.

Jackie Robinson knew his purpose. He never fought back when he was hit with pitches or insults. Instead, he let his spirit shine. He played in 151 out of 154 games, batted .297, and stole twice as many bases as any other player in the league. Jackie Robinson became the major league's first Rookie of the Year.

How did he accomplish so much when so many people wanted to see him fail? He had spirit on his side. He didn't need to use brawn. He had no use for ugly words and fighting. He had a purpose and a passion for baseball. Jackie Robinson knew he had a right to play in the major leagues, and he proved it beyond a shadow of a doubt in his very first year. How can you follow his lead and use your spirit instead of brawn to accomplish great things?

Day 144

> "The human race may be compared to a writer. At the outset a writer has often only a vague general notion of the plan of his work, and of the thought he intends to elaborate. As he proceeds, penetrating his material, laboring to express himself fitly, he lays a firmer grasp on his thought; he finds himself. So the human race is writing its story, finding itself, discovering its own underlying purpose, revising, recasting a tale pathetic often, yet none the less sublime."
>
> Felix Adler

You have been working very hard to discover your passion and purpose. If you feel like you are not quite there yet, do not despair. Keep searching. Consider this quote by Felix Adler and compare yourself to a writer. As you write your own history, you do not know for sure how it will turn out. You follow various leads, and the plot unfolds through time.

You don't have to know exactly how you will achieve success. If you put in the work and continually search for your true passion and purpose, you will be on the right road. Everyone reaches milestones of achievement at different times. No one takes exactly the same path. Stay true to yourself and constantly explore your talents and your ability to contribute in a positive way to the world. You don't know how the book will turn out, but you can take action to make sure it is an interesting story.

Some people know their purpose in life practically from the moment they are born. They are lucky ones. Wolfgang Amadeus Mozart knew he was an exceptional musician when he was still a kid. He wrote his first symphonies at around age eight or nine. But you don't have to be a child prodigy to have a successful life. Follow your passions, do things for others, and search for your purpose. Write a chapter in your own history today. Find yourself.

"I'm doing what I think I was put on this earth to do. And I'm really grateful to have something that I'm passionate about and that I think is profoundly important."

Marian Wright Edelman

Finding something that you are passionate about is not just a vehicle for success. It is a gift and something for which to be profoundly grateful. This book stresses that you continue to search for your purpose and passion in life, because it is an incredible feeling to know that you are doing what you were put on this earth to do. Have you experienced that feeling yet? If you have not, then keep searching like your life depends on it. If you have, then continue on that road and give everything you have to the things you believe are important.

Marian Wright Edelman established the Children's Defense Fund in 1973. It is a vibrant voice for poor, minority, and handicapped children, and the organization has made an impact on innumerable lives. She is grateful to have something that she is passionate about, and her purpose is fulfilled every day when children are given help and hope. Marian Wright Edelman's résumé is filled with purpose and passion, and the Children's Defense Fund is one of many contributions she has made to this world.

Are you doing what you were put on earth to do? Do you feel happy and proud of what you have done to influence the world around you? Spend some time writing in your journal today about your purpose and passion. Ask yourself if you are doing everything to pursue your purpose in life, or if you have gotten a little lazy. You are not going to get a second chance. Start doing what you were meant to do today.

Day 146

" . . . When it's over, I want to say all my life
I was a bride married to amazement.
I was the bridegroom, taking the world into my arms.
When it's over, I don't want to wonder

if I have made of my life something particular, and real.
I don't want to find myself sighing and frightened,
or full of argument.

I don't want to end up simply having visited this world."

Mary Oliver

None of us wants to think about death. If your life ended today, would you be satisfied with how you spent your time here, or would you be wondering if you could have done more?

Your assignment on Day 146 is to write your obituary. That might sound slightly morbid, but it is actually an opportunity for you to think about how to get the most out of life right now. It's a dangerous move to put off your success and procrastinate participating in life. You have no idea how much time you have left to embrace it.

Don't get too depressed about this assignment. You are not going to imagine that you kick the bucket today. Write about what they will say after you've lived a long, full life. What do you want people to remember about you? What do you hope they will say at your funeral? If you have a chance for assessment in an afterlife, will you give yourself a good grade? Imagine how it will feel to know you were an active participant in the world, rather than a visitor. What can you do today to make sure that happens?

"Our days are numbered. One of the primary goals in our lives should be to prepare for our last day. The legacy we leave is not just in our possessions, but in the quality of our lives. What preparations should we be making now? The greatest waste in all of our earth, which cannot be recycled or reclaimed, is our waste of the time that God has given us each day."

Billy Graham

Yesterday you wrote your obituary. It was probably a sobering exercise and maybe not that much fun, but it's important to look at the big picture. Have you thought about your legacy? As Billy Graham says in this quote, it's not just about the possessions you leave behind. You have an opportunity to contribute to the world in so many ways that have nothing to do with money or things. You will live forever if you touch the heart of someone else while you are here.

Kathy's grandmother died five years ago, but she left a rich legacy. She was not a wealthy woman. In fact, she was quite poor. But Kathy thinks about her every day, and in some ways she models her life after her grandma. Kathy has a beautiful, clean home where family and friends are always welcome. Her grandma taught her that it is an act of love to clean your house until it shines. It shows everyone who enters that you care about yourself and about them. She also taught Kathy that it's important to leave the light on and welcome family and friends whenever they need a safe haven or a place to feel loved. Kathy's grandmother lives on in Kathy's actions. She didn't waste her time on earth. She filled her days with joy and love and gave that wealth away every day.

Write about a person in your life who left you a rich legacy. How would you like to emulate that person?

Day 148

"The legacy of heroes is the memory of a great name and the inheritance of a great example."

Benjamin Disraeli

Who are you heroes? Everyone has at least a handful of people who are heroes to them. What traits make someone a hero?

The most common response people give when describing their heroes is that they offer a great example. Heroes are larger-than-life examples of how to be a success. They are legendary, because they had the tenacity to live life to the fullest and seemed to make all of the right decisions when faced with adversity.

Heroes also live by a code. They have a high standard for themselves, and they follow that standard in all of their affairs. They set the bar way up in the stratosphere, and they achieve success because they are willing to adhere to their higher standards.

Your assignment today is to become a hero. This is not a joke. Today you will become a hero. There is no reason you cannot be one. The first thing you need is a mission statement. This will be your code to live by. It states clearly what your overall goals are in life. It says who you want to be. Write your mission statement today and live by it from now on. How would you like to define your purpose in life? Here is your chance to get it down on paper. You can't ignore your aspirations. They are part of your innermost self. Now, what you must do is attempt to live up to those aspirations.

Be a hero today. Set your standards high in your mission statement and live by your own code of success.

"Here is the test to find whether your mission on earth is finished. If you're alive, it isn't."

Richard Bach

You became a hero yesterday. How does it feel? Are you a little uncomfortable with that title? Do you think you already messed it up and don't deserve to be a hero anymore? Here's the good news: you get a chance to start over every day — every minute if you choose.

It is admirable to set lofty goals and try to live up to them, but you will fail sometimes. Even heroes fail. The beauty of life is that as long as you're breathing, you get a do-over. You have an opportunity to change the way things are every single day and every single moment.

You don't live in a static world. Your mission continues as long as you are alive, and you will be presented with a ton of new opportunities for change and growth throughout your journey. You have absolutely no idea what today holds, but there is one thing you can do to make it a good day. Participate!

Dive into your mission today, and remember the code you wrote yesterday describing your standards for how you want to live your life. You aren't done yet. In fact, you're just getting started. Enjoy your mission. It is completely, uniquely yours. At the end of the day, write in your journal about how the mission went on Day 149. List at least three things that were a success, and then list a few things that you could improve next time around. Then reset, recharge, and get ready to continue your mission tomorrow.

Day 150

"Life without a purpose is a languid, drifting thing; every day we ought to review our purpose, saying to ourselves, "This day let me make a sound beginning, for what we have hitherto done is naught!"

Thomas Kempis

You have done some pretty amazing things in the first 150 days of this book. Look back through your journal and review all of the work you've done. You are laying a very solid foundation for success, and chances are you are already starting to see a change in yourself.

Today you have a chance to review and reflect on the last fifty days in particular. Write about how you are changing and what it feels like to find your purpose in life and reveal the gifts you have to offer.

In a few short days you have practiced personal responsibility and kindness to others. You found out that failure is no big deal. You learned that you can actually cultivate enthusiasm without acting like a crazed lunatic. You have been a hero and attempted the impossible. You gave prayer and meditation a shot, and either or both of those might be part of your daily routine now. You have also gotten used to the fact that achieving success is a long-distance race. You will need to develop endurance to continue on this journey. You nourished your mind and body through health and fitness work and breathing exercises, and you even got to play a little. Finally, you discovered just how important relationships are in your life and you resolved to improve your ability to interact with those around you in a positive way.

You have done amazing work. Rest today and enjoy your accomplishments.

"You can't wait for inspiration. You have to go after it with a club."

Jack London

Barry was ready for success. He had his goals in mind; he could envision a future full of achievement. He was just waiting for inspiration to hit him. Well, here's a news flash for Barry: nothing is going to happen if you sit back and wait. You have to go after inspiration with a club.

Many people think inspiration is the ticket to success, but they don't believe they have any control over how and when inspiration hits them. That is simply not true. Inspiration is nothing more than a great original idea, and it has very little to do with chance. In addition, it can't be your ticket to success unless you follow it up with some leg work to turn your great idea into a reality.

So how do you get an inspiration? Can you force it? You can practice making conditions right for inspiration, and the more you practice, the better your ideas will be. Your assignment today is to list things that inspire you. Does music inspire you? Maybe art does the trick. Some people get inspired by getting out into nature — taking a hike in the woods or sitting by the ocean or skiing in the mountains. What gives you a sense of awe and wonder? What perks up your senses and makes you feel grateful to be alive?

Find out what inspires you. If you don't know yet, then try things until you hit on a particularly inspiring event. Practice putting yourself in a place of wonder. It will get your mind in gear and help you tap into that innermost spot where your unique talents are waiting to be discovered. Don't sit around waiting for inspiration. Go after it right now.

Day 152

"Wait a minute. Maybe I can do anything."

Janis Joplin

You have done a lot of great work over the last 151 days. Are you starting to feel a little brazen? Can you sense the power you have within yourself to change your life and reach for success? It has always been there, and through this work you are uncovering layers of dirt that have been covering it up. How does it feel to know you've got the goods?

It can be an epiphany when you realize you have every right to be successful. It's not just that you deserve to be successful; you have the talent to do it. You are not mediocre. You are not undeserving. You are actually entitled to be successful. There is absolutely nothing holding you back. Maybe you can do anything.

Today you get to have an ego the size of an elephant. (That doesn't give you license to be mean to anyone, by the way.) You are all that—and a bag of chips. It doesn't matter if you recently gained twenty pounds, lost your job, and got a gigantic zit on the end of your nose. Who cares? Even when you're a complete mess, you are beautiful in the eyes of creation. You might be a beautiful mess, but you're still lovely. And you deserve success, so get back in the game and prove to yourself that you can do anything.

No one else has your unique talents and gifts, and it's about time you unleash them on the world. What do you want to do today? What goals do you want to strive for next? Pretend you have a huge ego today and zero doubts about your capabilities. Now write in your journal about everything you are going to accomplish. You can do anything . . . anything. So what's it going to be?

"So-called inspiration is no more than an extreme example of a process which constantly goes on in the minds of all of us."

Anthony Storr

Inspiration is a process. It's not a one-time sledgehammer over-the-head kind of deal. It's constantly going on, and it gets really intense when you make the conditions just right for it to grow.

Dana started to practice inspiration. She went to museums, wrote in her journal often, and went for jogs in the park by her home. Most importantly, she spent some time alone each day. She had three kids and a host of commitments between work and family activities, but she still spent at least fifteen minutes of quiet time each day, just to give her mind a break. Before Dana practiced inspiration, she was constantly ticking off a to-do list in her head of things she needed to do each day. She was preoccupied with the minutia of her life and never got a look at the big picture. She was often overwhelmed, and there didn't seem to be enough hours in the day to get things done.

Finally, Dana made a commitment to practice inspiration. She took that fifteen minutes of quiet time each day, and she scheduled a date with herself at least once a week to do something that inspired her. Within weeks she noticed a change. She was no longer preoccupied with the little things. Suddenly, her mind was working overtime in other areas. Out of the blue she would get a great idea for a project at work or think of something she wanted to do to help a friend in need. Inspiration came at her from all angles and when she least expected it. Are you willing to make a similar commitment for a week?

"You are the embodiment of the information you choose to accept and act upon. To change your circumstances you need to change your thinking and subsequent actions."

Adlin Sinclair

You may remember way back on Day 2 you considered the fact that you are not a victim of circumstances. Your choices landed you right where you are at this moment. Personal responsibility is not the easiest road, but it is the most rewarding. Take responsibility for your actions, and your chances for success will multiply exponentially.

You have no control over what people say or do, so you can stop worrying about trying to change others. You have absolute control over what information you choose to accept and act upon. If someone tells you that you are stupid, you can choose to accept that information, or you can choose to throw it away as useless and false. It is not the fault of the person who uttered those ridiculous words. It is your fault if you believe them.

Think about what information you accept and what information you discard today. Dig deep and ask yourself if you have bought into any statements that are blatantly false. Don't feel bad if you have. You have the opportunity to discard those untrue statements right now and collect information that is more conducive to your success.

On the other hand, sometimes the truth hurts. If someone tells you that you are not qualified for a particular job, do they have a point? Maybe it's time to take a class and get qualified. Remember that you are the one who gets to decide what is true and what is false. You pick the information you will act upon. What information will you choose to collect and act on today?

"Just don't give up on trying to do what you really want to do. Where there is love and inspiration, I don't think you can go wrong."

Ella Fitzgerald

Are you afraid to do what you really want to do? Why? Do you think if you fail you will have nothing left? Consider this: if you don't do what you really want to do in life, what kind of life are you living?

Ella Fitzgerald provides a wonderful message in the quote for today. The final results really don't matter. If you do what you really want to do, if you follow your heart's desire, then there is love and inspiration involved in your actions. When you have those two things, you can't possibly go wrong. The process is just as important as the end result. Life is short. Do what you really want to do.

Let's say you really want to be a singer. You've been listening to Ella your whole life, and you want more than anything to sing like she does. But you're afraid. What if you find out you're no good? That doesn't matter. Do you love to sing? Then give it a shot. Take voice lessons, join a choir, or go to karaoke night at your local tavern. Experience what it feels like to let your pipes make a joyful noise.

You might be a horrible singer. The people at karaoke night might start throwing pretzels at you and boo you off the stage. Who cares? You did it. You did something you really wanted to do. Check it off the list and sing in the shower from now on. Maybe you'll discover that you're pretty good, and months later you find yourself on TV in front of millions of people on *American Idol*. You won't know the answer unless you do it.

Day 156

"Procrastination is the art of keeping up with yesterday."
Don Marquis

Ann was the queen of procrastination. She actually thought it was a good strategy. She let herself believe that if she put things off long enough, either someone else would do them for her, or she would find a way to get them done in a shorter amount of time because she was under the gun. She enjoyed the adrenaline rush she got when a deadline was looming. Never mind the fact that half the time Ann had to ask for an extension. She was happy with her strategy, but her boss was not thrilled at all with her performance.

Ann may have been comfortable with her plan, but it was not a good one. She spent all of her time catching up, and therefore she had no opportunity to get ahead in life. When she was constantly working on yesterday's tasks, she never had the opportunity to reach forward for success.

If you want to have a successful life, you should be so far ahead of the pack that you are making news rather than reading yesterday's news. Success comes with responsibility, and you have to be willing to work a little harder to get to the front of the line. Keeping up with yesterday is worthless. To achieve success you have to create the future.

Your assignment today is to stop procrastinating. If there is any part of your life right now where you are behind, take the extra time you need to catch up. Don't start anything new until you complete old business. You will get a huge amount of satisfaction out of tying up your loose ends and taking responsibility for completing your jobs. Then you can move forward and focus on the future uninhibited.

"Never forget: This very moment, we can change our lives. There never was a moment, and never will be, when we are without the power to alter our destiny."

Steven Pressfield

Do you think that you'll change your life after something else happens? You want success, but you envision it happening down the road a ways. The conditions need to be just right. You'll start that new business after the kids go off to college. You'll talk to your boss about a raise right after you complete a project. You plan to start dating again . . . after you lose ten pounds.

Stop waiting. This is the moment for change, and you have the power to do it. You control your destiny. Thousands of choices are made every day — by you — that lead you toward success or away from it. It is true that you are completely powerless over other people, places, and things, but you do have the power to alter your own destiny, and there is no point in waiting. Work with or around or over or under the circumstances that you face, but never lose sight of your destiny.

Your job today is to do something. You have no excuse to wait until tomorrow. Take this moment to change your life. Don't even open your journal today. Your assignment is not to write about your goals and dreams. Your job is to get out there and start working toward them. What can you do to use the power you have within you to change your destiny today? There are a number of actions to take. Pick one and take action. You have done a lot of writing about things you can do to achieve success. Now you have to stop dreaming and start doing.

Day 158

"Tomorrow, every Fault is to be amended; but that Tomorrow never comes."

Benjamin Franklin

Tomorrow I'll eat better; tomorrow I'll go to the gym; tomorrow I'll sign up for that computer class; tomorrow I'll apologize to my spouse for the way I treated him or her; tomorrow I'll work more and surf the Internet less. Sound familiar?

Tomorrow never comes.

Today is your reality check. You almost never do all those things you plan to do "tomorrow." Procrastination is a trickster. It helps you feel comfortable with complacency. It lets you be lazy. Procrastination is a liar, too. It talks you into thinking that you are taking action by planning to take action on a future date. Not true. That date will never come. Planning is not doing. You are no closer to your goals if you say you will do something tomorrow. Your intentions don't carry any weight at all in the real world. If you have a heart attack today, it doesn't matter that you intended to get to the gym and eat better "tomorrow" for years.

You have to fight your impulse to procrastinate with everything you've got if you want to move forward in life. If you want to stay right where you are, then feel free to put off the actions that might bring you success. It's your choice. Remember, you have the power and no one else.

Watch yourself today. What are you putting off until tomorrow? What are you actually getting done? Evaluate whether you are moving forward or standing still. Don't forget that tomorrow never comes.

"Procrastination is the thief of time."

Edward Young

Yesterday you read that procrastination is a trickster and a liar. Well, it's a thief, too. In other words, you don't want to hang around with procrastination for very long. It's a shady character in a bad neighborhood.

How is procrastination a thief? Think about what happens when you procrastinate. When you plan to put something off, you have to come up with a reason why, to make yourself feel better. You could spend all afternoon talking yourself into procrastination.

Tomorrow will be better, because I'll have more time. Wait. I won't have more time tomorrow. I've got three major appointments. Well, next week will be really ideal, because I'll be done with one project by then, and I think I don't have to take the kids to soccer practice that week and . . . oh, wait. I do have to take them to soccer. Okay, well, maybe I should start the whole thing next month. That's a great idea! Start fresh next month. I'm not going to let myself feel guilty about this. I'm a very busy person. Life just gets in the way sometimes . . .

In the time that you took to have that conversation with yourself you could have gotten several things done. Procrastination is the thief of time. It takes planning, and the ridiculous thing is you are planning to *not* do something. It's a complete waste of time. Spend today not procrastinating.

Day 160

"If it weren't for the last minute, nothing would get done."

Anonymous

You've been reading about procrastination for the last several days, but today you will get a chance for rebuttal if you are a chronic procrastinator. There is a very slight difference between procrastination and doing things at the last minute. Ann kind of had a good point on Day 156 when she admitted that she enjoyed the adrenaline rush of working with a deadline looming. Some people actually do their best work that way. Are you one of those adrenaline junkies? That's not all bad.

The important distinction is that you have to meet your deadlines. If you wait until the last minute to do something, that's fine if you produce great work on time. But you must complete the job using all of your talents to the fullest. Pay attention to the results. If you're churning out fabulous ideas and contributing everything you have, it doesn't matter if you wait until the last minute. The point is that you did it, and you did it well.

Ask yourself if you are one of those people who enjoys the rush of doing things at the last minute. If the answer is yes, then take a close look at your results. Are you really showing the world everything you've got when you get things done at the last minute? If the answer is yes again, great! Knock yourself out. Have fun with the drama of sweating out last-minute deadlines. If the answer is no, maybe you should rethink your strategy. You have an incredible amount of talent within you. Everyone lets their gifts emerge in different ways. If you need more time to give your unique talents a chance to work their magic, don't wait until the last minute. If you don't, more power to you. Do it at the eleventh hour.

"I was irrevocably betrothed to laughter, the sound of which has always seemed to me to be the most civilized music in the world."

Peter Ustinov

Laughter is music. It is a delight to the soul and a wonderful way to tap into your inner self. You have read about many quiet and meditative ways to reach inside and draw out your unique talents, but the music of laughter has that same ability. It's hard to fake laughter if you're not really amused, so it comes from a place of truth and pure joy. When you really start to laugh it is like a song that bubbles up from a very deep place inside of you. It taps into your soul and opens you up. Laughter has the power to remove barriers and let you to enjoy the moment.

Laughter is a very present activity. It takes place right now. You laugh in immediate reaction to something you see or hear or do. Laughter will take you right out of regrets of the past or worries over what the future holds. It happens now, and then it's gone. You have to enjoy it while you've got it.

Your assignment today is to take part in something that makes you laugh. Watch a funny movie, hang out with a friend who makes you giggle, or go to a comedy club. Or you could even try something that you haven't done in a long time. When was the last time you went roller skating? That might give you a chuckle or two if you try it again.

Put yourself in situations where you might break out into hysterical laughter. Laughter is great medicine. It has the power to heal you emotionally and even physically. Stop taking yourself so seriously and have a little fun today.

"The more you find out about the world, the more opportunities there are to laugh at it."

Peter Nye

Life is funny. If you stop and take a good, long look at all the crazy things going on in this world, you will have ample opportunity to laugh. Have you noticed what a mixed-up group of weirdoes we are? It's pretty hilarious when you think about it.

Go find a public place today and sit down and observe the human species in action. You can choose to go to a park, the library, a coffeehouse, or a mall, whatever makes you happy. Pick a place where you will have an opportunity to observe a lot of people. Bring your journal with you and jot down some of the things about this world that are really funny to you when you look at them. Study the way people interact with each other. Observe how they dress and talk and the kinds of gadgets they use when they're out and about. Take apart every facet of our civilization and look at it as if it you have never seen it before.

Ask yourself what you have learned about life in the last twenty years that makes you laugh when you think about the absurdity of it. You may draw a blank at first, but think about this question for awhile, and soon you will probably come up with quite a few answers.

Life is wonderful and funny and crazy . . . and a little absurd. Enjoy it. Laugh at it. When you stop thinking of the world as a place that's doomed and start thinking about it as a beautiful, unique, and very funny mix of opportunities, then the door is open for change.

"Laughter gives us distance. It allows us to step back from an event, deal with it and then move on."

Bob Newhart

Laughter provides a great buffer. If you completely mess something up, but you are able to stop and laugh at yourself, then you are in great shape. Have you ever tried it as a response to failure? It works beautifully. Laugh first, and then think about what to do to make it right.

Laughter gives you distance. It takes away the personal sting of falling short. Everyone screws up sometime, and it doesn't feel very good when it happens. For some reason when we fail we think that no one else in the entire world has ever done so. That's simply not true. If you want to prove your success, then don't bother trying to be perfect. A sign of a successful person is how he or she deals with the aftermath of a mistake. Try laughter this week as a first step in dealing with failure. You will be pleasantly surprised at how quickly you are able to recover from disappointment.

Laughter puts that cushion between you and the event. It lets you drop your ego and pick up the pieces and move on. When you put a little distance between yourself and your failure, you can see more clearly what needs to be done to make things right. On the other hand, if you are not able to laugh at yourself and you take failure very personally, you will dig a pretty deep hole of disappointment, and change won't happen anytime soon.

Laughter is a wonderful — and efficient — coping mechanism. Practice using it whenever you face a disappointing outcome.

Day 164

"Always laugh when you can. It is cheap medicine."

Lord Byron

Never pass up a chance for a good laugh. The healing effects of laughter are no joke. Laughter triggers the release of endorphins, and those are your body's own natural painkillers. Recent studies have found that laughter can actually help prevent heart disease. It can also relieve stress, restore hope, and enhance your immune system. It keeps the cognitive function of elderly individuals in shape and lowers blood pressure. It's even a good exercise for deep breathing techniques.

So why not laugh whenever you get a chance?

Maybe you're thinking, "I'm just not that funny."

You don't have to be. There are loads of comedians out there. They need an audience. You can add humor to your life just by reacting to funny people or situations—or laughing at yourself in funny situations. Don't worry; you don't have to come up with your own material. Day-to-day circumstances will provide more than enough opportunities to laugh.

Maybe you're afraid that you don't really see the humorous side of things. Do you take life more seriously than everyone else most of the time? That's okay. You can practice humor. Watch what other people find funny and observe their joy. Soon you may be able to identify with their humor and let go of your serious side a little. It's not healthy to be serious all the time. It's not going to make you successful faster. Learn to laugh, and then take advantage of this free medicine whenever you get the opportunity.

"Among those whom I like or admire, I can find no common denominator, but among those whom I love, I can: all of them make me laugh."

W.H. Auden

For the last several days, you've learned about a number of positive reasons to have laughter in your life. One of the biggest advantages of laughter is its ability to draw people together. Laughter is a way to relate to each other that is purely positive. It is a shared experience in the present, and there is nothing serious or judgmental or sad or depressing about it.

Think about the five people that you enjoy spending time with the most. They may each have very different personalities and interests, and you've probably shared a number of positive and negative events with them. Is it safe to bet that most or all of them share one trait – the ability to make you laugh?

Laughter is a terrific tool for friendship. If you want to be a good friend to others, laugh with them. You know that you are not an island. You need other people in your life to share your joys and your sorrows. Humor is a way for you to be a really good and healthy and healing friend.

Your assignment today is to journal about what kind of friend you are. What characteristics do you have that make you a good friend? Then write about what characteristics your friends have that you really love. Can you learn anything from your best friends? How can you be a better friend? Spend some time with your friends over the next few days and watch how laughter draws you together.

> "Almost anything is easier to get into than to get out of."
>
> Agnes Allen

"What have I done?" Eli muttered to himself as he stared at the pile of bills on his desk.

Six months ago Eli launched a new business, and now he had nothing but debt to show for it. He had been so sure that he had the right stuff to pull it off. He had a great idea, and he took action. Soon he was buying office furniture, ordering materials, and building his website. It was so easy to get started. But then nothing happened.

Eli didn't get clients as quickly as he had hoped. He sat in his office staring at his brand-new furnishings and high-tech website, but there was nothing much to do without customers. It had been so easy to launch this endeavor, but in six short months he had managed to fail. How was he going to get out of this mess?

Have you been in a similar situation? Have you felt like quitting when you were barely out of the starting gate? It's easy to get excited and then end up in so deep that you have no idea how to get out. Eli found himself in that spot, but he did climb out of the hole. He took it one step at a time. First, he got a part-time job to help pay down his current debt. Then, he researched strategies to build his audience. He knew he had a great idea, but he hadn't yet reached his audience. He became a master of network marketing, and six months later his business started to see a trickle of customers. One year later, he was making some real money. You can find your way out of any mess one step at a time, just like you found your way in. It might take longer, but be patient and keep moving forward.

"All things are difficult before they are easy."

Thomas Fuller

Another excuse we have for giving up before we find success is to say that the job is too difficult.

It's too hard.

I'm not smart enough.

I'll never learn this.

I'm just not cut out for this job.

Have you used those phrases? Think about the endeavors that you quit before you were successful. Were you really not smart enough, or did you give up too soon? Journal about your experiences with dashed dreams or projects that you gave up on in the past. What stopped you from trudging forward?

Things are almost always difficult before they are easy. There is a learning curve, and you have to be patient enough to get through it. Impatience is a big offender when it comes to ruining an opportunity for success. We all want success, and most of us want it right now. We're not willing to wait.

If you want a true and lasting success, you have to be patient, and you have to be willing to learn new things. No one is immediately an expert. Embrace the opportunity to learn. It will eventually get easier, and you will find success if you are willing to be patient.

"To overcome difficulties is to experience the full delight of existence."

Arthur Schopenhauer

That's right. The difficulties you face are gifts. When you face a roadblock on your journey and you find a way around it, that is when you get to experience the full delight of existence. Every difficulty you overcome is a small dose of success. It feels great. You have not really lived until you have had an opportunity to face a problem head on and find a way to resolve it.

Look at your difficulties in a different light today. Change them into opportunities to really live life to the fullest. No one gets through life without facing some challenges. How are you going to react to them when they show up? What would happen if you decided to welcome your difficulties?

You can whine and moan and wish that you didn't have the problems you have, or you can choose a different route. Practice walking through your difficulties today knowing that they are offering you the chance to experience the full delight of existence. Find out what you can learn from your situation and how you can change. Come to the problem like a student who is eager and willing to discover new solutions.

Your reaction to difficulties is completely up to you. You will either choose to cause yourself more suffering by procrastinating, complaining, and wishing circumstances were different, or you will take steps to overcome your difficulties. You have the power to choose delight or misery. What will it be?

"The harder the nut, the sweeter the kernel."

Saying

Pam is a novelist. Her latest book caused her more problems than she could ever have imagined. None of her previous books had been so difficult to write. She almost threw it in the trash numerous times before it was complete. She gritted her teeth and pushed forward every day, even if she didn't have much to show for her efforts sometimes. Eventually Pam finished the manuscript, and a big-time publisher snatched it up almost immediately. It was her sweetest victory.

When Pam was interviewed a year and a half later, she talked about how the book was her hardest project ever and her greatest reward. It was not just because it made it to *The New York Times* Best Seller list. It was because she struggled and wrestled with it from the day she started writing it. The entire project was "like pulling teeth," as Pam liked to say. She would go for days without feeling like she made any progress at all, and then she would get a small glimmer of hope that gave her the strength to continue.

This was a victory for Pam, because she stuck it out. She ran the entire marathon, and that made her a success long before the publisher accepted her manuscript, long before the reviews, and years before she sold her millionth copy. She had an intense feeling of satisfaction, because she cracked that nut. She stuck out the hard days, and she finished.

How do you want to feel when you look back on your achievements? Do you want the satisfaction of having done everything you could do to finish the race? Or do you want to wonder if you quit before getting to the sweet kernel of success?

Day 170

"No tree becomes rooted and sturdy unless many a wind assails it. For by its very tossing it tightens its grip and plants its roots more securely; the fragile trees are those that have grown in a sunny valley."

Seneca the Younger

Your fortitude develops through the storms you face in life. You don't need to build character and spirit and drive if you will never be tested. But in this world you will most likely face a few tempests if you hang around long enough. Growing up in a sunny spot where nothing ever threatens you sounds nice, but it won't give you the chance to build sturdy roots and find out exactly how strong you are. You must face difficult times and prove that you can weather the storm.

If you are at a place right now where you feel as though the winds are assailing you from all directions and you are battered and broken, don't lose hope. The storms of life will strengthen you and allow you to grow firm in your convictions and the knowledge that you have the ability to endure and thrive.

If you were a tree, what kind of tree would you be?

That question is asked by psychologists, reporters, and even potential bosses in interviews. What's your answer? Your assignment today is to once again put your artists' tools to work. Get out those colored pencils, crayons, or markers and draw yourself if you were a tree. Have you developed strong roots that allow you to stand firm against the wind, or are you frail and easily bent? What kind of tree do you want to be?

"The two great springs of life, Hope and Fear."

William Hazlitt

Hope and fear are two highly motivating factors. Which one rules your life?

Does fear motivate most of your decisions? It is an instinctual response to certain situations. If you are in a physically dangerous situation, then fear is a great natural response. For example, if a mugger tries to attack you, your fear instinct might help you to fight back or run faster than you ever have before. That primal intuition is valuable in fight or flight situations.

What about internal fears? Do you allow your mental fears to motivate your actions? Fear is useful if you're being chased by a bear, but it might cause you to lapse into inaction when less-obvious factors are involved. What are your fears? List them in your journal today. Do you fear being promoted to a job where you have more responsibility? Do you fear talking in front of other people? Name your fears today.

Now let's turn to hope. How does hope work in your life? Does it motivate you? What are you hopeful about today? Some people think of hope as a sort of vague idea, but it can be a very concrete reason to take action. What are your hopes? Do you hope you can find a new job? Do you hope that your kids will grow up safe and happy?

Look at your lists of hopes and fears, and work on crossing fears off your list and adding to your list of hopes. Hope has amazing power to motivate people. It is a positive force in this world that should not be underestimated. Fear is useful at times, too, but it should not be overestimated.

Day 172

"We should often blush at our noblest deeds if the world were to see all their underlying motives."

La Rochefoucauld

Yesterday you considered fear and hope as motivating factors in your life. What are your other motives? A motive is anything that causes you to take action. Motives can be noble; they can be pure; they can also be sneaky, underhanded, or selfish. Someone may have questionable motives, and that means that they probably aren't taking action for the right reasons.

What are your motives for obtaining success? Are your motives selfish, or are they noble? When you complimented your boss on his tie this morning, what were your motives? When you got up to grab a midnight snack after everyone else in the house went to sleep, what were your motives then? Sometimes very noble actions come out of very underhanded motives. It might not matter what the original motives were if the result is a positive contribution to the world.

What are your thoughts on motives? Do you strive to have pure motives, or do you want to get things done any way you can? Do you care if greed, selfishness, or fame is a motivating factor in achieving success? Or do you think impure motives somehow taint the final prize?

Motives are very interesting, because they are not always clear even to the person taking action. Think about your motives behind achieving success. Try to be as truthful as possible when you write in your journal about motives today.

"All actions are judged by the motive prompting them."

Muhammad

Anita didn't care if she lied, cheated, or stole to get to the top. She was completely focused on achieving success at any cost. Her single-mindedness left many broken relationships in its wake, but she didn't care. Anita knew that once she was a success, no one would remember her motives. She would have everything, and she would be loved for her achievements.

She was wrong. Anita did achieve success, but when she reached the top of the mountain, she was all alone. People didn't want to come anywhere near her, because she had turned into a pretty hateful person as she clawed her way to the top. Anita's motives had not been the least bit honorable. She forgot that she could not use the people around her as opportunities for advancement. She needed to cultivate relationships and find ways to contribute positively to the lives of others rather than only taking what she could get from them.

It was lonely at the top for Anita. She had riches and power, but she had no friends. People judged her motives and decided they wanted no part of her. She was wealthy on the outside but bankrupt on the inside. Anita sat in a house filled with every luxury, but it wasn't a home. She couldn't even buy friends, because they were afraid she would unleash her ruthless behavior on them eventually. She learned too late that the most precious treasures are human relationships.

What are your motives? You will be judged by them.

"Kindness can become its own motive. We are made kind
by being kind."

Eric Hoffer

Yesterday you viewed the downside of having impure motives. Today
you will have a chance to look at what might happen if your motives
tend toward the positive side. You don't have to be like Gandhi, but
you can practice having good motives, and it could change your life.

According to Eric Hoffer, kindness can become its own motive. If
you are kind to others, you will become a kind person by default.
That makes sense when you think about it. It would be impossible to
consistently offer kindness to others and remain an ugly person on the
inside. You cannot put your life in compartments like that. Eventually,
the real motives shine through, ugly or beautiful. You are the sum of
your actions and your motives, and it's very difficult to separate them
and only show one or the other to the world.

Think about the intuitive feelings you get when you are around a
genuinely nice person. You immediately feel at ease and happy and
important in their life. On the other hand, you probably can spot a
faker a mile away. How do you feel when you deal with someone
who is outwardly nice to you, but you can tell it's only because they
want something?

Practice having good motives today. You might be a selfish person
most of the time, but you can change that. Practice acts of kindness
and you will become kind. There is no way around it.

"Had it been merely vanity that had made him do his one good deed? Or the desire for a new sensation? . . . Or that passion to act a part that sometimes makes us do things finer than we are ourselves?"

Oscar Wilde

What happens if you just don't feel like a "good" person? Do you wish people thought you were? Well, that's a good start. If you would like to have pure motives and do good things in the world, but you are still drawn to the dark side, you have to practice changing your motives. That starts with actions.

Let's say you are a liar, a cheat, and a thief. You can change. The first step is to pretend. No kidding. You can act as if you are full of good motives. Do things that you think a nice person might do and try to stop thinking about what you will get out of it. That's all you have to do. You don't have to suddenly change your stripes. Just act like the person you want to be, and eventually your actions will change who you are.

Are you skeptical? Give it a try. You don't have to believe. Get proof. Give yourself a month and start practicing. This doesn't work if you do one good deed and then forget about it the rest of the month. You have to continue to act the part. Perform as many good acts as you can for thirty days and then take a look at your results. Are people nicer to you in return? How do you feel on the inside? Has your self-image improved at all?

By the way, this works if you are basically a good person, too. You can be even better just by pretending for awhile. Let your actions dictate who you are for a period of time, and then evaluate the changes you see in yourself.

Day 176

"It's choice—not chance—that determines your destiny."

Jean Nidetch

Your destiny is not in any way related to chance. People who fulfill their destinies are not merely lucky. They choose success. They go after what they want, and they achieved it. It has nothing to do with chance. You're not playing a card game here or rolling the dice to find out the outcome. This is real life. You determine what happens next.

You create your destiny every day through the choices you make. It's not necessarily just the big choices, either, like what you decide to major in if you go to college, where you plan to live, or if you want to get married or remain single. Your destiny is determined by all of the millions of little choices you make, too. They may seem insignificant when you make them, but they add up like change in your pocket, and pretty soon you're looking at substantial life choices.

If you choose to go to the gym today, you are shaping your destiny of becoming a healthy and strong individual. If you choose to help a friend in need, you are also fulfilling your destiny. You are creating a perception in their mind that you are a caring and loving friend they can count on. Let's say you choose to go to a one-day job fair just to check out your options. It may only be a couple of hours out of your entire life, but it could change your destiny.

Refuse to let chance rule your destiny. Be aware of your choices today and remember that the small decisions have just as much power to shape your destiny as the big ones.

"Tomorrow is the most important thing in life. Comes into us at midnight very clean. It's perfect when it arrives and puts itself in our hands. It hopes we've learned something from yesterday."

John Wayne

What will you do with the gift of a brand new day? Think about the way John Wayne describes it in the quote above. It is brand new when it arrives, and it is placed right in the palms of your hands. You can do whatever you want with a new day. What's it going to be?

The pristine nature of a perfect new day is exciting. It is brimming with potential. When you wake in the morning, absolutely anything can happen to shape your destiny. You might discover something you never knew about yourself, or you could get the satisfaction of conquering a big problem at work or at home. Maybe you will spend some quality time with your family and remember how important those people are in your life and how much they add color and vibrancy to your days.

Your assignment today is to write down some of the things you learned from yesterday. It's so important not to waste the gift of a new day by repeating old mistakes. Life is too short to play reruns of the less than perfect parts of your life. Write down the lessons you've learned, and apply them to this new day.

The universe wants you to learn from life and take each new morning in your hands like the precious gift that it is and mold it into your destiny. Be prepared to shape today into a beautiful day, no matter what outside forces blow through your life. Today is perfect, and tomorrow will be, too. They are in your hands. Have you learned from yesterday?

Day 178

"What we call the secret of happiness is no more a secret than our willingness to choose life."

Leo Buscaglia

Dawn was miserable 99 percent of the time. She was a beautiful, smart woman brimming with potential, but she refused to step up and try something new or change the way she had always lived her life. She sat over coffee with her friends and complained about her weight, her job, and her relationships at least once a week. They offered ideas and advice from their own life experiences, but she looked at them skeptically as if to say, "well, you're lucky. I'm not. This is just the way my life is."

As a direct result of her actions (or inaction), Dawn was completely unhappy with the direction her life was headed. She had been in a string of mediocre relationships, never meeting anyone who was captivating enough to consider marrying. Her job was reliable but boring. At work her own clients told her she could do better, but their comments fell on deaf ears.

One day when Dawn returned from work to her small apartment, she sank to the floor like a wilted flower. "Will I ever know happiness?" she sighed to herself through tears of frustration.

Dawn held the secret of happiness within her all along, but she had to get up off the floor and be willing to choose life.

What do you do to choose life today? Are you happy? If the answer is no, you now have the secret of happiness. Choose life.

"In every single thing you do, you are choosing a direction. Your life is a product of choices."

Dr. Kathleen Hall

You have been considering your choices in life for several days now. If you've actively participated in the exercises of the last 178 days, you realize by now that this book will offer you no chance to pass the buck. You can't blame anyone but yourself for your present circumstances. That can be a slightly depressing thought, but it is also liberating. It doesn't mean that everything is your fault. It means that you have the power to change anything you want from here on out.

It is exhilarating to find out that life is a product of your choices. Think about the alternative. How disheartening would it be to find out life is the product of other people's choices? You would be tempted to give up on the whole journey if you had no say in the direction. Lucky for you, that is not the case.

Your assignment is to look back on the last seven days of your life. Write down all the choices you made over the last week in your journal. That's a pretty daunting task, isn't it? You most likely made thousands of choices, but just come up with the highlights. Next to each choice write a few words about the direction you took as a result of that choice. Now sit back and examine the results of your week. How does it look as a whole? Did you make good choices for the most part? If your plotted your direction on a chart, would it be all over the place, would it be all downhill, or would you be steadily climbing toward success? Your life is a product of your choices. Take them seriously.

"I believe that we are solely responsible for our choices, and we have to accept the consequences of every deed, word, and thought throughout our lifetime."

Elisabeth Kübler-Ross

It is extremely liberating to know that you always get to choose the direction you take in life. You are in complete control. Unfortunately, that also comes with some responsibility. If you want to accept the glory when you achieve success, you also must be willing to accept the consequences when you screw up.

Do you believe there are consequences to every deed, word, and thought you have throughout your lifetime? Write in your journal for at least fifteen minutes to answer to that question. Are there always consequences, or do you feel like you probably get away with some things in life unscathed? Can there be consequences to your thoughts if you don't follow through and act on them?

Consider this brain teaser: if you really can't stand someone at work, but you never say anything mean to them or do anything harmful to that person, are there any consequences to your thoughts?

Do you think about consequences much? It can be debilitating to worry too much about consequences and never have the guts to move forward and take action. But it can also be damaging if you forge ahead without regard to the potential penalties. There must be a balance. Your choices can bring you success, but there will be good or bad consequences to all of your actions. You have to take responsibility for it all if you want to take credit for any of it.

"Uncertainty is the refuge of hope."

Henri Frederic Amiel

Uncertainty doesn't have a very good connotation, especially when you think about it in relation to your life. It brings up thoughts of doubt, mistrust, and skepticism. You would probably rather have guarantees. If you use uncertainty to describe your situation, it sounds like you don't believe in yourself.

You assignment on Day 181 is to consider an alternate definition of uncertainty. What if uncertainty means that there are no limits to the possibilities before you? Your future is uncertain, because it hasn't been decided yet whether it's going to be really good, great, or over-the-top fantastic. The sky is the limit to what you can achieve if your future is uncertain. If it's guaranteed, then you're stuck with what you've got.

Write down in your journal all of the things that have not yet been determined in your life. What is uncertain? Make a list of everything you can think of that's still up for grabs.

What you have just done is create a list of opportunities. You can do anything you want with that list. Go for it, because nothing is set in stone. You can be wildly successful in any of those areas if you choose to chase the opportunities.

What steps can you take to turn even one uncertainty on that list into a huge opportunity for success? You can use the ambiguity it represents to break all the rules and go for it. Uncertainty is the refuge of hope. The fact that the future is yet to be decided means that you still have an opportunity to shape your success.

Day 182

"Doubt is not a pleasant condition, but certainty is absurd."

Voltaire

It is unpleasant to be doubtful, but doubt occupies some part of any thinking person's life. The fact that you have doubts shows that you are considering situations from every angle. You realize that you might not have all the right answers, and you seek further confirmation. There is nothing wrong with that. Doubt often leads to striving for knowledge, and that can ultimately bring you success.

Certainty, on the other hand, is completely absurd. There is almost nothing that you can claim with absolute certainty. For example, you do not know what will happen in the future. You might have a pretty good hunch about things, but you cannot predict any of it without a doubt. If someone is certain about their future, be very wary of this individual. They are either delusional, or they're pulling your leg.

A feeling of certainty about things can also bring with it a position of close-mindedness. Tina's grandmother was certain that all people in the acting profession had loose morals, but that was not reality. It was what she guessed to be true, and she refused to think about whether or not she could be wrong. She wouldn't let doubt concerning her convictions lead her to search for the truth. She wanted to be right, and she didn't want to think about it too much, so she fabricated a certainty in her mind.

Pay attention to where and when you have doubts today. Let your doubts lead you to new knowledge, and don't worry if they make you feel uncomfortable for a brief period.

"Without a measureless and perpetual uncertainty, the drama of human life would be destroyed."

Winston Churchill

Winston Churchill was right. There would be no drama in life if we didn't have uncertainty. We don't know how this book ends, and that's part of the fun. Can you imagine how boring your life would be if everything was certain? Not only would you miss the surprises in life, but you also wouldn't have an opportunity to change your destiny.

A few days ago you pondered the idea that your days include thousands of choices, and each one of those choices shapes your destiny. Everyone else in this world is doing the same thing, and that is why our collective future is uncertain. There are billions of variables. The drama of human life unfolds before us moment by moment in all its beauty and tragedy. Do you really want to know how it turns out? You are a lead character in this drama. How is your plot developing?

Uncertainty is something you can count on every day for the rest of your life. You can choose to fret about it and rail against it and wish it wasn't so, or you can choose to revel in its possibilities and take advantage of the perpetual uncertainty. Have fun with the drama of life. Take healthy risks and see what happens. Try something new and find out where it takes you. Run a little bit longer on the treadmill or get on one of those weird-looking machines that you've never used before at the gym and find out which muscles will be sore tomorrow.

Embrace the drama of human life in all of its uncertainty. It is your story.

Day 184

"The only thing that makes life possible is permanent, intolerable uncertainty; not knowing what comes next."

Ursula K. Le Guin

Don was a terrific businessperson. He had great instincts and quite a bit of knowledge in his field, but unfortunately he also had a high level of fear. He couldn't stand the uncertainty of not knowing how a new job opportunity would turn out. Therefore, Don often passed up new opportunities. He waited for a sure thing to come along, and it never did.

Years later, Don was still in about the same place he started with the firm. He had all of the skills he needed to be promoted, but he found the uncertainty intolerable. When he refused to take risks, he forfeited his chance to reach the level of success that he was capable of obtaining. Don wanted to feel as though he was in control of the outcome at all times, and that severely limited him.

How are you at tolerating uncertainty in your life? Write about your feelings in your journal today. If you can't stand uncertainty, there are a few things you can do to combat your feelings. First of all, list your fears. What are you afraid of when you don't know what comes next? Write down your worst fears and get them out in the open. Another thing you can do is take action. You have the power to shape your future by taking positive steps to make the conditions right for a successful outcome. You don't know what comes next, but you do know how to actively chase your future. Uncertainty is what makes life possible. Learn to embrace uncertainty with wonder and excitement, not dread and fear.

"Uncertainty and mystery are energies of life. Don't let them scare you unduly, for they keep boredom at bay and spark creativity."

R.I. Fitzhenry

Do you like a good mystery? You're living one right now. Your life does not have to be a horror film, though. It can be an exciting mystery, where the twists and turns lead to a successful conclusion. Don't be scared of uncertainty. You know that the person who freezes with fear in a scary movie usually bites the dust. You don't want to be that character. Anything can happen. Uncertainty might not lead to your destruction. It might be just the inspiration you are seeking to get to your happy ending.

Have you ever considered the idea that uncertainty and mystery are the energy that fuels your life? They can be your muses and propel you to follow your creative impulse. Not knowing what is going to happen sparks the question "what if." That draws out your unique talents. You don't know what the right answer is, so you are free to wonder about the possibilities.

List the ten best movies you have ever seen. Then take a look at your list and put those movies in categories. Are they love stories, mysteries, scary movies, adventure films, or something else? How do you think the movies you enjoy reflect your real life? Are they parallel to your life, or are they completely opposite? Do you like heart-pounding thrillers, but in real life you rarely leave the house after dark?

Is the movie of your life a boring remake of an old, predictable theme? Or is your movie filled with excitement and surprises at every turn?

Day 186

"We are drowning in information but starved for knowledge."
John Naisbitt

Unless you have been living in a cave for the last few years, you know that we are lucky enough to exist in a time when technology makes massive amounts of information easily accessible. You can Google just about anything and instantly receive hundreds of reports, articles, blogs, websites, and the like describing the topic of interest. In many ways, that is a huge advantage. You have access to information now that would have been difficult to find a few short years ago. The opportunity for you to collect hoards of information without ever leaving your home is infinite.

That is an incredibly exciting prospect, because it levels the playing field. You have an equal opportunity today. You can access much of the same information that other people use to obtain success. If you are willing to do the work, you can gather up all sorts of facts and figures that will help you achieve your dreams.

On the other hand, information means nothing if it is not verified or applicable to your life. What you are ultimately striving for is knowledge. What's the difference? Journal for a few minutes today about what you believe the difference is between information and knowledge.

Here are a few more questions to consider while you are writing in your journal: When you look something up on the Internet, how do you know it's true? What information do you look for, and how do you use it? Are you drowning in information but starved for knowledge today?

"Trust yourself. You know more than you think you do."
Benjamin Spock

Another interesting side effect of this "information age" is that many people stop trusting their instincts. They want to check their ideas with an expert before making any sudden moves.

Brenda was tired of her children spending too much time on the computer. When she was a kid, she was always outside playing with the other children in the neighborhood. She fondly remembers the forts they made and the elaborate games they cooked up in each other's backyards. Their parents had to yell at them to come inside when it was dinnertime, because they were having such a great time together.

Brenda wanted to encourage her own children to get out of the house and into some physical activity, too. She herded them out of their rooms where they were isolated on their laptops, chatting with friends online and playing video games.

"Why don't you go outside and play for awhile?" Brenda suggested. "It's a beautiful day."

The kids agreed, but all three of them momentarily ducked back into their rooms to prepare. When she followed them, she found out they were looking up ideas online for games to play outside.

This might sound like a ridiculous story to you, but it happens all the time. How often do you check online to see if your instincts fit in with what the general population is doing? Are there ways you can trust yourself more?

Day 188

"Knowledge is power. Information is liberating. Education is the premise of progress, in every society, in every family."

Kofi Annan

Kofi Annan was the seventh Secretary-General of the United Nations, serving from 1997 to 2006, and he won the Nobel Prize for Peace in 2001 jointly with the United Nations. He speaks English, French, and several African languages fluently. Kofi Annan has used his education as a powerful tool to become a global leader and work diligently on important issues from human rights to the world economy. One of his strengths is his knowledge. He has the ability to look at problems individually and also globally and highlight the point that personal issues affect the entire world.

The biography of Kofi Annan is a powerful testament to the fact that knowledge is power, whether you agree with his policies and decisions or not. Information is liberating, and education is the premise of progress.

You have no excuse to remain in the dark today. You have access to the tools that will bring you knowledge and aid your progress in this world. How are you building your knowledge right now? What are you doing to liberate yourself from the bonds of ignorance? No one is going to take those steps for you. You cannot blame your lack of education for your failure. You can obtain knowledge in so many ways today, and you do not have to pay a heavy tuition to get it.

What are you doing to obtain the knowledge you need to achieve success in your life?

"Everybody gets so much information all day long that they lose their common sense."

Gertrude Stein

Paul had a flat tire one morning. He went online immediately to find the tire shops closest to his house. None of them were open yet, so he called in to work and told his boss he would be a bit late. In the meantime, Paul spent an hour on the Internet. By the time the shop opened at eight o'clock in the morning, Paul had checked out the bus and train routes online, used MapQuest to find out how many miles it was to his office, and used another site calculate the time it would take to ride a bike there, joined an online carpooling network, and submitted a down payment for an electric-assist bicycle.

Paul could have done some work from home, but instead he got sucked into the black hole of information that is available to him through any number of technological devices. He started looking for answers, and his common sense went right out the window.

Has this ever happened to you on some level? You are on the receiving end of a lot of information every day through TV, radio, and the Internet, not to mention other human beings who have also picked up tidbits they would like to share. What do you do to stop the noise and maintain your common sense?

Information isn't everything. It is also important to have face-to-face communication, relationships, wonder, and peace and quiet, among other things. What can you practice in your everyday life to make sure that you don't lose your common sense when you go searching for information?

"Technology is so much fun but we can drown in our technology. The fog of information can drive out knowledge."

Daniel J. Boorstin

You have been thinking and writing in your journal about the difference between information and knowledge for several days now. What are some of the conclusions you have drawn?

Information is merely a collection of data. Knowledge is what you have when you are able to turn information into understanding. It usually comes through experiencing whatever you are learning about. A blind person could be given a stack of information on paper, but it would mean nothing to them, because they have no way of turning that information into understanding. A person who is born and raised at the North Pole could hear stories about what it's like to live in Florida, but they don't have real knowledge of what it feels like to sit in the blazing sun and sweat on a sandy beach in Ft. Meyers in July until they are able to experience it themselves.

Information can be a tool for success, but it is important to build your skills at picking out only the information that is important to you and then utilizing that information to develop your knowledge. If you are greedy with information and grab a hold of everything you can get, you will be swimming in data, and it will be difficult to figure out what is important to your ultimate success and what isn't. Technology is a lot of fun, and it can certainly help you get ahead in life. Just make sure that you are not drowning in information.

"One of the hardest things in life is having words in your heart that you can't utter."

James Earl Jones

James Earl Jones is an extraordinary American actor, who is probably most widely known for his portrayal of Darth Vader in the popular Star Wars movies. Did you know he is also a stutterer? He said in an interview that he practically gave up talking until high school when an English teacher found out he secretly wrote poetry.

The teacher said, "No one will believe you wrote this, Jim. You should get up in front of the class and read it."

The mere idea must have struck terror into the heart of James Earl Jones, but it was a big compliment coming from his teacher. He wanted very badly to prove that the poem was his, so he overcame his fear and got up in front of the class. He was able to read the entire poem without stuttering.

The teacher's response was, "Now we have something to work with."

It's hard to believe that someone with the big, booming, confident voice of James Earl Jones was afraid to speak in public when he was a young man. What an amazing talent emerged when he was able to overcome his obstacle and continue to move toward his destiny.

What obstacles do you face today? List them in your journal. Then write about ways you can overcome them. No one on earth is without challenges. The trick is to conquer them and continue on toward your goal. Success will be so much sweeter after you've overcome difficulty to get to the rewards.

Day 192

"We do on stage things that are supposed to happen off.
Which is a kind of integrity, if you look on every exit as
being an entrance somewhere else."

Tom Stoppard

Theatre is not real. Sometimes it imitates real life, but it is a fantasy world. However, there is a very important real-life lesson that can be learned from life on the stage. Every exit is an entrance somewhere else.

What would happen if you treated your real life that way? Often an exit seems like the end of something in the real world. If you are fired from a job, you may think you will never find such a great position in another firm. You feel like you are at a dead end, or at least a brick wall. Change that thinking. The end of your job is actually the first day of a new adventure, and you have no idea where that new entrance will take you. You suddenly have opportunities that you never had before. You can try your hand at a completely different profession if you want. Maybe you left an accounting firm, but you've always secretly wanted to be a chef. Now's your chance! What a terrific twist of fate!

You are the one who chooses whether an event is labeled as an obstacle or an opportunity. You are writing this script. A change in plans is only devastating if you make it so. Pick one of the obstacles you listed yesterday and work on some concrete ways you can turn the obstacle into an opportunity. How can you make that exit and entrance to a whole new world? Don't come up with a superficial answer to this assignment. Really get into some tangible ways that you can change your circumstances. You are in control of this play, and you can choose where this entrance will lead you.

"Obstacles are those frightful things you see when you take your eyes off your goal."

Henry Ford

Chad was only five years old when he was captured in a fire in his apartment building. His mother rushed to retrieve his baby brother from a crib in the bedroom, and when she returned, Chad was gone. He had been too scared to stay put and retreated to the roof to escape the smoke and flames.

A firefighter found him coughing on a ledge twenty-five stories above the ground, and he coached Chad along the narrow ridge and into the safety of a cherry picker where the he was waiting with open arms.

After a tearful reunion with his mother, Chad was interviewed by one of the local TV news crews. They asked him how he was able to have the courage to balance along that thin ledge to safety.

Chad replied simply, "I walked to the fireman."

Sometimes it's best not to even look at obstacles. They can be a frightening sight. If you keep your eyes fixed on your goal and continue moving forward, you may never know about some of the close calls you had along the way.

What are some ways that you can concentrate on your goals for success and avoid wasting time and energy worrying about the obstacles along your path? That doesn't mean that you remain ignorant of the problems you face. The suggestion here is that you give more time and attention to your goals. Obstacles can be frightening, and the more you pay attention to them, the stronger they become. Don't give them an audience.

Day 194

"If you can find a path with no obstacles, it probably doesn't lead anywhere."

Frank A. Clark

That is an interesting quote, isn't it? What was your initial reaction when you read those words by Frank A. Clark? Your assignment today is to journal for twenty minutes using that quote as a topic. Try to keep your hand moving the entire time. Don't stop writing, no matter what. One enlightening form of journaling is to keep the pen moving even if you are writing "I don't know what to write" across the page. Eventually, your honest feelings will emerge if you keep practicing putting pen to paper and don't give your mind any time off to rest or distract you.

You choose your path in life. Did you pick an easy hike? Did you try to find a route that had few or no obstacles? If the answer is yes, how do you like the journey so far? Are you bored out of your mind? Maybe you feel like you're walking in circles, because the view never really changes.

You can change your path right now. You can opt for more treacherous terrain if you're up for the challenge. The bigger the challenge, the greater the rewards. Would you like to travel along an interesting road that is sometimes laced with failure but leads to spectacular views, or would you rather take an easy path that leads nowhere? It's completely up to you. You are the tour guide on this excursion.

Just remember, if you are not happy with where you are you have the power to alter your trip itinerary. Do you want to travel to new heights, or do you want to go nowhere?

"There seemed to be endless obstacles . . . it seemed that the root cause of them all was fear."

Joanna Field

You have been journaling about overcoming obstacles for the last several days. Obstacles do come up in life. That's something you can count on. How many of them did you create yourself?

Some of the obstacles you face in life are just there. You didn't put them there. They are a byproduct of living in an unpredictable world. Your challenge is to find a way to overcome them when you encounter them.

But what about the obstacles you create?

You may be thinking, "What? I don't create obstacles. Why would I sabotage myself?"

Are you sure about that? You might be doubling the obstructions you face by creating obstacles that aren't really there. Those obstacles are trickier to deal with, because they change shape. They get bigger when your fear grows, and they show up when you feel the most vulnerable. Those are also the obstacles that you have the power to obliterate completely. You don't have to deal with them. You can zap them out of your life.

Look back at the list of obstacles you made in your journal several days ago. Take a close look at them and try to ascertain whether they are real or a fabrication you created in your mind. If you find out some of those obstacles are a product of your imagination, you can cross them right off your list. Zap their power. They can't hurt you. You can walk right through them.

Day 196

"Around here, however, we don't look backwards for very long. We keep moving forward, opening up new doors and doing new things, because we're curious . . . and curiosity keeps leading us down new paths."

Walt Disney

It's not very productive to look backwards. You can't do anything about your past. On the other hand, you can do anything you want with your future. Walt Disney was a stunning example of success because he was always moving forward.

Curiosity is a great tool for moving forward, because it lacks judgment. You don't ask if something is correct or perfect. You ask yourself questions like:

What does that do?

Where does that path lead?

What would happen if I do this?

What would that look like?

What if I looked at it this way?

I know what's behind door number one. Now what's behind door number two?

When was the last time you used the tool of curiosity to lead you toward success? Have you asked any of these questions or similar ones lately? Make time to be curious today. Don't worry about past mistakes. They don't matter anymore. Keep moving forward. You've got an endless supply of doors to open and paths to walk down.

"The most important thing to remember is this: To be ready at any moment to give up what you are for what you might become."

W. E. B. Du Bois

It's hard to give up things. Watch any TV game show, and you will see people struggling with it. They can keep the one thousand dollars, or they can go for the big money. What will it be? They sweat and stammer and look back at their loved ones in the audience for guidance. Gosh, a thousand dollars would be nice, but I could become a millionaire if I let go of this cash and take one more risk!

You have to be ready to give up things if you want to make progress. It's like taking a trip. You can't bring your entire closet full of clothes with you when you go on vacation. Just take what you need and leave the rest. It's a good rule to go by on your journey toward success, too. You don't have to take everything with you. You don't need it all. There are items that make up what you are today that you can leave behind to make room for what you might become.

What are some of the things you can give up? Well, you certainly have no need for fear. Leave that at home. What about the beliefs you have about yourself that are no longer true? Those are great things to ditch, and your load will be much lighter. Maybe you used to think you were not smart, but recent experience has taught you otherwise. Drop that old belief. Did you use to think you weren't worthy of success? Well, that's completely untrue now. Give up that dusty old thing and make room for your new image. Write about what you are willing to give up today for what you might become.

Day 198

"The great thing in the world is not so much where we stand, as in what direction we are moving."

Oliver Wendell Holmes

Steven had an ultimate goal in mind, and when he made it to that spot, to that X on the map he had drawn for himself, he would consider himself a success. He did make it to the X, and he stood there admiring his achievements with a grand feeling of satisfaction. Steven had a great job, a huge house, and three sports cars in the garage. That was his goal, and he achieved it.

Now what?

The one thing Steven didn't learn on his journey to achieve his dreams was that it doesn't matter where he stands today. What matters is the direction he is moving. The game isn't over until you're six feet under. He will be faced with the same question today as he was yesterday: what are you doing to move forward in life?

The truth is you are not striving for a gold star or a first place ribbon. You are looking for the fulfillment that comes every day when you learn something new or help another individual on their journey or triumph over an obstacle that stands in your way. Knowledge and love and compassion are signs of success, not obtaining the coolest toys on the block. Material things are nice, but personal fulfillment is even better.

Are you standing still or moving? What direction are you moving today? Are you following your destiny, or are you on a detour somewhere lost in a forest of superficial desires and looking for an X on the map?

"Discontent is the first step in the progress of a man or a nation."

Oscar Wilde

Think back to the times when you've made a lot of progress in your life. What brought on the impulse to move forward? Write about a few instances in your journal and try to remember exactly what initiated your progress. Did you have an inspiration? Were you solving a problem? What was the catalyst that caused your growth spurt?

Sometimes progress does not come out of a positive feeling of wanting to move forward. It more often comes from feelings of discontent. Even though moving forward is a good thing, it's much easier and more comfortable to stay in the same spot. Therefore, it takes a strong feeling of discomfort to get in gear. Things have to get pretty bad before most people are willing to change.

The formation of the United States came out of the massive discontent of British colonies in America. Their situation finally got so bad that they were willing to fight for independence. Apartheid, a system that institutionalized racial discrimination in South Africa, caused years of discontent, and ultimately it was dismantled in 1994 as a result of the combined discontent represented by demonstrations, riots, and international pressure. In 1980, Gdańsk , Poland, was the site of a labor strike that resulted in the recognition of the first non-Communist trade union in the Soviet Eastern Bloc. The discontent of those 17,000 shipbuilders was one of the first steps toward the collapse of Communism in Eastern Europe. Discontent cannot be underestimated as a powerful tool for progress. It has been the first step for change throughout time.

Day 200

"We all want progress, but if you're on the wrong road, progress means doing an about-turn and walking back to the right road; in that case, the man who turns back soonest is the most progressive."

C. S. Lewis

Welcome to Day 200! You have made a huge accomplishment by coming this far in your work to achieve your dreams. You are more than halfway through the year, and if you are diligently working on the exercises presented in this book, change is starting to occur in your life whether you recognize it yet or not.

Progress doesn't happen all at once. It is a gradual transformation that becomes more and more visible over a period of time. You should take time to congratulate yourself today for the hard work you have put into achieving success. You have more to learn, greater opportunities for growth, and thousands of new chances for progress ahead.

Do you feel like you are on the right road today? This moment of reflection on Day 200 should give you an opportunity to make sure you are traveling down the correct path. It's easy to get off and end up on the wrong road. Actually, it's not that terrible if you think that's what you've done. You learn from your mistakes just as much as your triumphs. Maybe you tried your hand at a new job opportunity, and it just doesn't seem right for you. That's okay. Admit when you've made a mistake and change. As C. S. Lewis mentions in the quote above, the guy who turns back the soonest when he realizes he is on the wrong road is the most progressive. Notice it doesn't say the guy who never makes any mistakes is the most progressive.

"Sometimes questions are more important than answers."
Nancy Willard

What? How can questions be more important than answers? You are striving for success, and that means you should be finding the answers. You should be getting to the truth, reaching your destiny, and making things work. You want conclusions, not questions.

Not true! Questions will lead you down new and inspiring roads. Where do answers lead you? If you already have a conclusion, why would you go exploring?

When you start really asking questions and pondering the things you don't know, that is when you have the ability to reach beyond your current abilities. Questions open doors and give you choices. Answers tie everything up in a neat bow and close things up. Been there, done that, bought the T-shirt. End of discussion.

Are you asking enough questions? Do you prefer to be the know-it-all in the group, or would you rather be the one with the least experience who is willing to learn new things? Maybe you fall somewhere in the middle of those two extremes.

Ask questions today. That's not just a general idea, it's a directive. Try to ask more questions than provide answers today and see where it takes you. At the end of the day, journal about your experience as a result of this assignment. Did the questions open any doors for you? Did they change your current way of thinking? Did you gain any valuable knowledge from the questions you asked? Make it a daily practice to ask questions and actively search for new information. The more you seek, the more you'll find.

Day 202

"Millions saw the apple fall, but Newton asked why."

Bernard Baruch

Sometimes asking questions is not the most popular thing to do. People around you might think you're a troublemaker . . . or just plain stupid. Are you willing to go out on a limb—just like Newton did—and ask why?

Asking questions is a character-building experience, and that's a good thing. The more you can be true to yourself and not worry about what the rest of the crowd is doing, the better. It doesn't matter if your co-workers are snickering behind your back. You have an honest motive when you ask why. You are gaining knowledge and increasing your chances of success. You might also ask a question they've been wondering about for months and were too afraid to voice.

If you don't understand something, ask. It's much better to admit you need help and learn something new than it is to pretend you know what you're doing and then get caught in your ignorance. It's okay to be curious. In fact, it's the sure sign of someone on the road to success.

Trust that every single question you ask will lead you to a greater understanding of the world you live in. Find something today that you don't know everything about. Ask questions and find some answers so that you have a deeper understanding of that subject by the end of the day.

"Be curious always! For knowledge will not acquire you; you must acquire it."

Sudie Back

Jennifer worked in a bookstore, and she was complaining one day to her coworker that she had nothing new to look forward to in her life.

"It's the same old thing, day in and day out. I come here, I sell books, I go home. How am I ever going to learn anything new and interesting?"

Her coworker was a high school junior at least fifteen years younger than Jennifer. He glanced around the store and then looked at her blankly, unsure of how to respond. You see, the high school student couldn't wait to get to work at the bookstore three times a week, because he was surrounded by shelves and shelves of undiscovered territory. He could work there for years and never fully take advantage of all of the information at his fingertips.

The young man had no idea what to say to Jennifer. The books weren't going to jump off the shelves and into her brain. She needed to have enough curiosity to wonder what was on all of those beautifully bound pages.

Are you waiting for knowledge to acquire you? It's not going to happen while you are sitting there doing nothing. Get into action and go after knowledge. Go to a bookstore today and stroll along the shelves. What subjects interest you? Grab a book or two and take them home with you (after paying, of course). You can do the same exercise in the library if you don't want to spend any money. Acquire a little knowledge today. Read something new and find out how it feels to increase your depth of knowledge.

Day 204

"There are no foolish questions, and no man becomes a fool until he has stopped asking questions."

Charles Proteus Steinmetz

What happens when curiosity dies?

Nothing.

That is not good.

You should be curious about things always. Curiosity is the centerpiece of progress. Think about how many great men and women achieved incredible success because they were curious. Can you name a few people who are in our history books today because they asked questions and went after the answers? Open up your journal and brainstorm the names of individuals who are famous in our world today because of their curiosity.

Take one or two of those historical people and learn a little bit more about them today. Go online and pull up their biographies or stop by your local library and do a little research. What did you find out about them? How were they treated by their peers when they first started to find the answers to the questions they asked? How exactly did they achieve success through their discoveries? What can you learn from them and apply to your own life?

Don't let anyone make you feel like a fool for asking questions. You can relax in the awareness that you can never possibly have too much knowledge. You are the smart one to indulge your curiosity. It is a fool who stops asking questions.

"The cure for boredom is curiosity. There is no cure for curiosity."

Ellen Parr

Curiosity is a gift. It's a gift and a cure, and it should be accepted with the joy and reverence it deserves. Curiosity relieves you of boredom. It gives meaning to your life. When you are searching for answers you have hope and optimism about how your life (and maybe even the lives of others) will change as a result of the knowledge you pick up to satisfy your curiosity.

On the other hand, curiosity can drive you crazy! Have you ever been so completely wrapped up in something that you can't eat or sleep? Curiosity can very easily turn into obsession.

Thomas Edison kept a cot in his lab, because he never got much sleep. He had to take catnaps during the day to catch up. His mind was constantly turning over new ideas and asking questions that kept him up at night as he pondered them and looked for solutions.

You don't have to become an insomniac to be successful, but it isn't so terrible if curiosity cuts into your quality snooze time every once in a while. It's a better alternative than complete boredom. The next morning you may be sleepy, but you will also be satisfied.

Sometimes people talk about curiosity as a disease for which there is no cure, but they say that with a twinkle in their eye. They know how exhilarating it is to pursue knowledge. Let your curiosity get a little out of control this week and enjoy the rewards.

"I like nonsense, it wakes up the brain cells. Fantasy is a necessary ingredient in living, it's a way of looking at life through the wrong end of a telescope. Which is what I do, and that enables you to laugh at life's realities."

Theodor Seuss Geisel (Dr. Seuss)

The next few days will be spent exploring the benefits of fantasy. Dr. Seuss says in the quote above that fantasy is a necessary ingredient in living. Do you agree? Or do you consider fantasy a waste of valuable time? Write about your thoughts.

Fantasy has to do with complete creative play. When you fantasize, you allow yourself to ponder improbable or impractical events. It doesn't matter if what you are thinking about is totally unrealistic. Fantasy removes all limits to your imagination.

Why would you spend your time dreaming about stuff that has no basis in reality? Well, there are lots of reasons. Fantasy gives you permission to go so far outside the box that you may come up with real-life solutions that you never considered before. Another reason is that you honestly don't know what is realistic and what is not realistic until you give your ideas a try.

One final reason is exemplified in Dr. Seuss himself. When Dr. Seuss first tried to get his children's books published, he was rejected by twenty-seven publishers before one of them accepted his first book. It took a long time for the rest of the world to recognize Dr. Seuss' creative genius, but he knew his fantasy could become a reality, and he never lost hope. At the time of his death in 1991, Dr. Seuss had published over forty-four children's books in more than fifteen differently languages. There are more than two hundred million copies of Dr. Seuss' fantasy world floating around the world today. Fantasy became reality.

"Fantasy is an exercise bicycle for the mind. It might not take you anywhere, but it tones up the muscles that can. Of course, I could be wrong."

Terry Pratchett

Fantasy does not have to ever turn into reality. Think of it like an exercise bike. When you ride the bike at the gym, you don't actually go anywhere. You stay right in front of the big TVs watching CNN or ESPN SportsCenter or whatever you choose. You don't have to get from Point A to Point B as a result of your effort. You stay right where you are, but you have stronger legs, fewer calories in your body, and maybe a little more information on why they fired your favorite football coach when you're finished. That half hour on the stationary bicycle doesn't complete a journey, but it is very useful.

The same is true of fantasy. When you engage in fantasy, you are exercising your brain. You are letting your mind come up with things that no one has ever considered before. You don't have to walk away with something at the end of the exercise. It is simply engaging your brain in a new way, so that in the future your mind will be open to greater possibilities.

Your assignment today is to fantasize. If you're not sure how to get started, pick three unrelated objects and write them down on a piece of paper. Now create a story that uses those three objects. It should not be in any way realistic. Let your imagination go crazy. You will not be turning this exercise in to a teacher. You can even burn it when you're finished so that no one ever uses it as evidence against you. What you get out of it is the opportunity to remove the rules and exercise your brain without any limits.

"Fantasies are more than substitutes for unpleasant reality; they are also dress rehearsals, plans. All acts performed in the world begin in the imagination."

Barbara Grizzuti Harrison

Judith was not in the job she wanted, but she was not the least bit discouraged. She continued to show up at work and did a great job, but every time Judith had the chance she fantasized about the real career she wanted. She daydreamed about what her office would look like and what kind of clients she would have. Judith even fantasized about where she would eat lunch in the city when she was fabulously successful. She had her wardrobe, her office furniture, and her client list all picked out—in her mind.

Is Judith a silly dreamer, or is she cleverly planning her destiny? You be the judge. It might be important to get a little more information before you make that call. Judith might be a silly dreamer if she does nothing but fantasize. On the other hand, if she is backing up her fantasies with solid work in the real world to obtain her goals, then she is brilliant.

Behind every successful person is an out-of-control imagination. It's true! You have at least to be willing to live a little on the edge in your dreams if you ever hope to take risks in real life. If you want it all, you've got to imagine it first. Are fantasies a part of your preparation for success? If not, you need to add them into the mix right now.

Spend at least a half hour today writing down your fantasies for a successful life. What does it look like? What are you doing? Who are your friends? Where is your office? What are you wearing? (That last question sounds like a more sordid fantasy, but try to keep it clean.) Fantasize about your success. It will open unseen doors in reality.

"It is in our idleness, in our dreams, that the submerged truth sometimes comes to the top."

Virginia Woolf

The other reason fantasy is a useful tool for success is that it allows you to get to the truth. When you practice fantasy and use your creative mind to remove the barriers you have attached to your real-world persona, you are sometimes able to see the truth about yourself.

In the real world, you may see your identity as a blue-collar worker who doodles a little on the side. In your dreams, you are an artist, and that truth might continually emerge in different forms when you fantasize. There is truth in fantasy. Do you have the courage to recognize it?

Your inner soul talks to you through your fantasies. That is one of the reasons they are so important to incorporate into your routine for achieving success. Your job today is to set aside thirty minutes to go in a room by yourself and listen to your favorite music. You can put on ear plugs to listen or crank up the volume on your computer or stereo (if it won't bother anyone else in the vicinity). Pick music that makes you happy. It doesn't matter what genre it is. It could be rock, pop, country, classical, reggae, new age, whatever pleases you today. Close your eyes and let the music wash over you. As you listen, allow your mind to wander in the direction of your fantasies. No fair thinking about real-world concerns.

Remember, your fantasies can be as unrealistic as you desire. Unleash your mind for thirty minutes and see where it takes you.

"The dream of reason produces monsters. Imagination deserted by reason creates impossible, useless thoughts. United with reason, imagination is the mother of all art and the source of all its beauty."

Francisco Jose De Goya y Lucientes

Goya was an extraordinary Spanish painter who lived from 1746 to 1828. He was on the cusp of change in the world of art, so he is often considered one of the "old masters" and also one of the first "modern" painters. His work influenced such greats as Pablo Picasso and Edouard Manet in the next generation of artistic giants, and he was well-known for making a very bold statement with his brush strokes.

In this quote, Goya makes an important point. Imagination is a wonderful tool, but it is useless without reason. Your fantasies fuel what is unique about you. They tap into your soul and allow your mind to blossom in a way that is uninhibited. You must take it another step, though. You cannot obtain success without incorporating a dose of reason into your fantasy world. When the two unite, you will come up with a truly rare jewel.

Look back at the fantasies you wrote about in your journal a few days ago. Think also about the fantasies that your mind came up with when you listened to music. How can you infuse those fantasies with a dose of reason and create something truly unique? This is going to take some thought and planning on your part. Take the time over the next week or so to write in your journal about how you can combine imagination and reason to further your journey toward success. You are the inventor. What are you capable of accomplishing when you unite these two very potent powers?

"During adult-hood, along with the earning of wealth and involvement in the improvement of Society, attention must be paid to the promotion and preservation of virtues and to the observance of moral codes."

Sri Sathya Sai Baba

A moral code is a set of rules that is accepted by a person or a group of people that explains acceptable behavior. Moral codes define the difference between right and wrong according to that group or individual. It's important for any society to be governed by the observance of certain moral codes, or the result would be chaos.

What are some moral codes by which your society is governed? "Do not kill" is probably one. What are others?

What about a personal code? Do you have your own moral code? If you haven't stopped to define what you individually believe is right and wrong and the rules you choose to follow in your life, then you may be living in individual chaos.

What is your moral code? Create one today in your journal. Write down all the rules you think you should live by in order to be a productive member of society and a successful person. For example, one of your rules may be to be helpful to others. Also think about individual activities. You might want to write down something like, "It's good to meditate daily," if that is a rule you value. Create your own list of laws, or code, today, and you will have a chance to go back and look at it again in a few days.

"Men make the moral code and they expect women to accept it."

Emmeline Pankhurst

Emmeline Pankhurst was a British woman born in 1858 who spent most of her life working to get equal voting rights for women in Great Britain. This right came to many societies around the world at different times, and Great Britain was one of the last countries in the western world to embrace equal voting rights for men and woman in 1928, just a few weeks before Emmeline Pankhurst died.

What do you do when the moral code of the society you live in does not match your own moral code? Emmeline Pankhurst spoke out. She was jailed many times for protesting the fact that she was not allowed to vote on the moral codes of her society.

How far are you willing to go? Would you break one moral code in order to establish another? What are your priorities when you find that the code of your society needs to be revised? Write about your code for dealing with the revising of moral codes. What is acceptable behavior? What is brave, and what is arrogant or dangerous? How can you honor your moral code but also have the ability to revise it if it can be improved upon?

This exercise is asking you to go down a very philosophical road, but it's worth it. It can be extremely difficult to look at long-held beliefs under a microscope and consider altering them. Change is difficult. Changing a code that has long been part of your life is harder still.

"Property is not the sacred right. When a rich man becomes poor it is a misfortune, it is not a moral evil. When a poor man becomes destitute, it is a moral evil, teeming with consequences and injurious to society and morality."

Lord Acton

What is your moral responsibility in this world? Do you have any responsibility to reach out and contribute to the society you live in, or is it your duty simply to be a good individual and not cause any harm to anyone else?

Lord Acton brings up an interesting contrast in the quote above. It is not really a moral dilemma if a rich man becomes poor. It is unfortunate, but it is not a moral evil. This man is not completely in dire straits. He still has something to work with. He may have the capacity and good luck to build his fortune once again.

On the other hand, if a poor man becomes destitute — meaning he may die as a result of his lack of basic necessities like food, clothing, or a roof over his head — then it is the moral obligation of the society in which he lives to lend a hand.

Some people believe this to be true, and some do not. Where do you fall on the spectrum? Do you have an every-man-for-himself moral code? Or do you feel that it is the obligation of society and you individually to help those in need?

Consider the actions you take today that reflect your moral code. Do you help those in need? Do you donate to any causes? Do you spend time volunteering? What are the ways that you contribute in a positive way to your society? How much do you take from your society, and how much to you give back to it? Draw a picture that reflects your answers.

Day 214

"Moral codes adjust themselves to environmental conditions."

Will Durant

Every society is different, and it evolves when the environmental conditions change. Therefore, moral codes tend also to adjust themselves to be responsive to changing conditions in society. That can be a good thing or a bad thing.

If greed becomes increasingly important in a society because economic times are good and many people are prosperous, there may be a loosening of the business code of ethics. That in turn can result in an increase in fraud, theft, or simple dishonesty within the group. A society can just as easily make a negative adjustment to environmental conditions as a positive one.

Let's look at a different scenario. Famine is an issue in parts of the world, and other countries where food is plentiful respond to that famine by sending food to those who need it. That is an example of a positive adjustment to a moral code. There was no need to share their food before the development of this environmental condition, but when the famine occurred, they adjusted their moral code to environmental conditions and chose to lend a hand.

What are the environmental conditions that surround you now? Take a few hours and look through at least three popular newspapers in your country. What are the top stories? How do those stories relate to you? Do you see the moral codes in your society adjusting in reaction to the environmental conditions? What part do you play in that? Are you proud of your moral code in relation to the present environmental conditions?

"Change before you have to."

Jack Welch

Rob was the last person on the block to get a computer; he held out and didn't buy a cell phone until his boss forced him to do so; and Rob is still trying to find a way around the move to HDTV. He resists change, and that resistance wastes a lot of time in his life. If Rob added up all the hours he spent refusing to change and evolve with society, he would be mortified to see the days and years that have been shaved off of his life.

Are you like Rob? Do you resist change? If you want to achieve success, you need to always be on the front end of change. That means you should constantly be asking yourself questions to check in with where you stand in relation to the rest of society. One of the best ways to do that is to have the courage to question your own moral code.

Go back and look at the moral code you wrote down on Day 211. Has anything changed in the last few days? Have you read anything or considered any new ideas that might cause you to want to edit your moral code?

Today you have an opportunity to go back and edit your code. Add anything you didn't think of a few days ago and delete items that don't seem as important now that you have had several days to consider them. Your moral code should be a constant work in progress. It is not set in stone. It will change as you grow and mature, and it will also adjust as a result of the changes in your environment. Be willing to always improve your moral code. Change before you have to.

Day 216

"If I had influence with the good fairy who is supposed to preside over the christening of all children, I should ask that her gift to each child in the world be a sense of wonder so indestructible that it would last throughout life."

Rachel Carson

It certainly would be a wonderful gift if the good fairy could instill in each of us an indestructible sense of wonder. Then all of the doors that slammed shut as we became older and "wiser" would automatically reopen.

Do you remember what it was like to have a childlike sense of wonder? Think back to when you were a small child. What gave you a sense of wonder? Can you remember a specific memory of when you experienced something that was completely new? Draw up one of those memories and write about what it felt like to see, touch, hear, taste, or smell something for the very first time. Maybe it was the first time you rode a ferris wheel, or the very first time you held a garter snake in your backyard. Do you have a special memory of your experience the first time you tasted your grandma's homemade pie or cookies? What did it feel like when you were introduced to a brand new family pet?

You can recapture a childlike sense of wonder by recalling these memories and remembering what it was like to experience the world for the very first time. When you were a child, the world was open to you. You had very few limitations, and you were eager to learn about how things work. Practice bringing that innocence back into your life, first by re-experiencing your childhood and drawing out the memories of a sense of wonder. Remember what that felt like, and imagine what it would be like to experience the world from that childlike perspective again.

"The great man is he who does not lose his child's-heart."

Mencius

There! Mencius said it! You have permission to never grow up.

That may not be entirely true, but it is very important as you travel on the road to success that you keep a child's heart.

What does that mean? Your assignment today is to write about what you think it means to have a child's heart. What are some of the traits children possess that would be helpful for you to incorporate into your life today? Why is it so important not to lose your child's heart?

Notice that this quote does not say it's nice to have a child's heart. It says the great man is he who does not lose his child's heart. You are working through this book because you want to be a great person. You want to live a successful life on a number of levels. Does it seem odd to you that a great person should be childlike?

You do not have to come along willingly here. If you don't see why you would want to recapture a child's heart, then write about that. Get your feelings out on paper. Why would you rather maintain your adult status and not go back to childish ways? Is this thought process a little unsettling for you?

On the other hand, you may be excited to have the chance to reach back to your childhood. Maybe you miss that childlike sense of wonder that you had when you were innocent and had not yet become jaded by the ways of the world. There is an idealistic side to having a child's heart. Is that something you can embrace?

"I wish I didn't know now what I didn't know then."

Bob Seger

On Day 210 you were asked to start brainstorming ways in which you could combine fantasy and reason to achieve success. How is that going? Are you coming up with some great ideas? What are you doing to incorporate those ideas into your life? Here's the bad news: the assignment you started on day 210 is going to last a bit longer than a week. It should continue throughout your lifetime. Never stop finding ways to unite these powerful devices. They will guide you on the road to success — and maybe that's good news!

Now for today's lesson. Bob Seger incorporated the quote above into his song "Against the Wind," and it exemplifies the transition from innocence to experience. The longer you hang around in this world, the more life experiences you accumulate. At some point you will most likely wish you didn't know now what you didn't know when you were a child full of optimism and wonder.

How do you combat the sadness, regret, and cynical feelings that come with adult knowledge of the world? What can you do to maintain a bit of your childhood sense of wonder at the beauty that surrounds you? It's hard not to become jaded, especially if life has dealt you some serious blows. The trick is to continually look for the good. There is something redeemable in every situation you face. You can choose to concentrate on the negative, or you can instead decide to pay attention to the positive aspects of life. You don't have to pretend you don't know now what you didn't know then. Instead, you might try to use your knowledge to grow and extend your sense of wonder into a larger arena.

"The reluctance to put away childish things may be a requirement of genius."

Rebecca Pepper Sinkler

Did you ever think that being immature would be a requirement of success? Isn't that great news? If you were a late bloomer in life, one of the last to put away your toys and transition to more grown-up activities, your reluctance to move on may be a sign of genius.

There are numerous reasons that it's not a good idea to put away all of your childish things. Those toys and games you took part in as a child allowed you to make leaps and bounds in development. They helped you practice a sense of wonder and expand your mind. They also instilled an idea that anything was possible.

It still is. If you don't believe that, you have set up too many adult-size barriers in your life, and it's time to remove them and return to your childish ways. Your assignment today is to bring back childish things. Return to games that you enjoyed as a youngster. Read a book that transports you into a fantasy world; spend some time coloring or drawing; go to see a movie that has very little basis in reality; eat an ice cream sundae and savor every spoonful; roll down a grassy hill; or make angels in the snow.

Returning to childish things helps you to not take yourself too seriously. It removes a lot of the judgment that adults like to attach to everything we do. When you are just playing, you don't care about the results. You are in a constant state of experimentation and wonder. Let yourself go back there. It will open your mind and give the judge who resides in your head the day off. The best way to release your genius is to remove anything standing in its way.

"Maybe we should develop a Crayola bomb as our next secret weapon. A happiness weapon. A beauty bomb. And every time a crisis developed, we would launch one. It would explode high in the air—explode softly—and send thousands, millions, of little parachutes into the air. Floating down to earth—boxes of Crayolas. And we wouldn't go cheap, either—not little boxes of eight. Boxes of sixty-four, with the sharpener built right in. With silver and gold and copper, magenta and peach and lime, amber and umber and all the rest. And people would smile and get a little funny look on their faces and cover the world with imagination."

Robert Fulghum

Read the passage above several times. Imagine the world Robert Fulghum created when he suggested that the next secret weapon be a Crayola bomb. Does that sound completely ridiculous to you? Did you turn off this image the minute you were halfway through the paragraph because it was silly and fanciful? Did you question why it was included in a book about achieving success?

Table your misgivings for a moment and go with this exercise anyway. Find a quiet corner sometime today and give yourself permission to experience this world where we solve crises with Crayolas. Draw your own picture of how the earth would look after a beauty bomb is released. Write about how your personal life would change if something like this actually happened.

You don't have to be a slave to your cynicism. Absolutely anything can happen. You make choices to go with enlightenment or obscurity every single day. It's not fair to blame anyone else for the state of world affairs, because you are a member of this team. You choose how active you will be in your society. Are you going to cover the world with imagination and a sense of wonder, or are you going to close doors on the future?

"I always wondered why somebody didn't do something about that. Then I realized I was somebody."

Lily Tomlin

Yes, you are the somebody who has the power to do something about that. A very big part of achieving success is taking responsibility. If you want to excel, you no longer get the luxury of blaming your circumstances on anyone or anything else. You have to get into action and do something about the things that bother you.

So what exactly does bother you? What do you come across during the day that causes you to think, "Hey, I wonder why somebody hasn't done something about that?" Make a list of items that you think need to change in this world. Nothing is too big or too small. What gets on your nerves? What do you think is just plain wrong? What are you surprised that no one has fixed yet?

Once you have a healthy list going, pick three of the items on the list. Now you are that somebody. What are you going to do to remedy those issues on your list? What actions can you take as an active member of your society that will create change?

You may not be able to fix the entire problem on your own, but you can probably take steps in the right direction that will help to solve it. You can be a catalyst that will inspire others to join your cause and take action. You are more than halfway through this year. The time for reflection and waiting is long gone. Now you must act in order to create a better future for yourself.

Day 222

"The human contribution is the essential ingredient. It is only in the giving of oneself to others that we truly live."

Ethel Percy Andrus

Do you give of yourself? Do you make a human contribution to your society? It sounds like you have to donate a kidney or something, doesn't it? That's not the case. The human contribution described in this quote is when you personally help another human being. It's face-to-face, one-on-one giving. Donating a kidney is one way to do it, but there are many other opportunities, and not all of them require surgery.

Part of your destiny is to be helpful to others. It is not to always take and never give back. You may not see a direct correlation between giving of yourself and achieving success, but there is a very strong relationship. If you want to get into the game of success, then you have to participate in the overall game of humanity. That requires a human contribution.

Make a list of the things you do today to help others. Once you have completed this assignment, take a look at your list. Are you proud of it? Is there more you can do?

There are thousands of ways you can lend a hand to those who need help. You can tutor someone who is learning to read, work in a soup kitchen, or collect clothing and food for an organization that serves the homeless population. When was the last time you called a friend just to see how they are doing? Have you hugged your child recently? The only requirement is that you pay attention to someone else. Don't just write a check this time. Give a human contribution.

"No act of kindness, no matter how small, is ever wasted."

Aesop

How do you know when you're wasting your time? Sometimes you go down a road you probably shouldn't have taken, and you end up having to backtrack. You try a new technology that doesn't quite work for your business; you court a potentially lucrative client for several months only to lose them to your competitor; you move to a new town hoping to find work but ending up further in debt. Valuable time is wasted. Often, you don't figure out you're on the wrong path until you've gone too far. The road back to where you started is full of regret.

Life is full of good and bad choices, victory and regret. However, there is good news: you will never regret an act of kindness. There is always something positive to be gained through lending a hand to another person, no matter what the outcome. An act of kindness is never wasted.

Let's say you give a warm coat and a new pair of shoes to a homeless person. Is your act of kindness wasted if they turn around and sell those items for drugs? The answer is no. You cannot control what others do, but you are in complete control of your own actions. If you choose to act kindly toward someone else, you are honoring that person and contributing in a positive way to the world around you. You are creating positive energy for yourself and your community. The choices they make afterward are none of your business. Most often your act of kindness will send a positive ripple effect throughout the world that is extremely influential. Choose acts of kindness today, big and small.

Day 224

"Service to others is the rent you pay for your room here on Earth."

Muhammad Ali

Your assignment today is to make a list of all of the things you have been given just because you showed up here on earth. What are your natural talents? Are you healthy today? What interesting and wonderful people have you met so far on your stay here? What has given you joy? If life is a giant party just for you, what are some of the best presents you have received so far?

Now here's the catch: all of the wonderful things you listed are technically not free. There is a price you must pay for your room here on earth. It can't be settled by cash, check, or credit card. This world wants a part of you.

Your service to others is direct payment for your life on earth, and it should not be paid unwillingly. It is a privilege to make this contribution. You have been given a huge number of gifts just for showing up at this party, and it's time to write your thank-you notes.

Before you get started, here's another secret to keep in mind: service to others is a payment that comes back to you with interest. If you want to really get the ball rolling, be abundant in your thankfulness. Pay your rent in advance—and double and triple the payment. The more you give back to the world through your service to others, the more you will receive in return by ways you have yet to imagine. The entire process is cyclical. In a way, you are the renter and the landlord. You have received so much just by being here. What are you willing to give?

"If you want to lift yourself up, lift up someone else."

Booker T. Washington

Have you ever been a teacher? If you think about it, you probably have taken on that role at some point in your life. Whether you are teaching a child to tie her shoes, offering to help a tourist find the right subway line, or explaining an algebra problem to a classroom full of students, you are a teacher.

When you bring new and useful information to someone who needs it, you are lifting them up. How does that feel? Maybe one of the reasons it happens so often is because it benefits the teacher as much as the student. It is not a purely selfless act. Think about the last time you helped someone or taught them something new. When the light bulb went on and you saw it in their eyes, didn't you feel great?

Scott went to the county jail once a week to talk to men there about his experience with alcoholism and his recovery through the program of Alcoholics Anonymous. Every time he left that dingy, sad place he felt almost overwhelmed with happiness. It wasn't just because he was relieved not to be one of the prisoners. It was because by simply telling his story he could offer hope to people who had lost it. It wasn't much. It never caused him pain, and it was hardly an inconvenience. He took one hour a week to lift someone up, and in turn his own soul soared.

Try lifting someone up today and observe how it makes you feel. Every time you teach, every time you offer compassion and understanding, every time you reach out your hand to lift someone up, you are doing the same for yourself.

"First comes thought; then organization of that thought, into ideas and plans; then transformation of those plans into reality. The beginning, as you will observe, is in your imagination."

Napoleon Hill

For the next few days we will be talking about the transition from innovation to organization. It's important to cultivate creativity, but that creative thought is meaningless if it never moves from your head into the real world. Many of us are geniuses in our minds, but that doesn't count for much if the thoughts in your head never see the light of day. So what's the process? The quote above explains it very well. There are a number of steps:

1. Have an innovative thought.

2. Organize that thought.

3. Make plans.

4. Transform the plans into reality.

First your imagination gives you a unique thought. Then, you have to organize that crazy idea into something that makes sense. The best way to do that is to spit that idea out of your head by drawing pictures, writing about it, or recording your thoughts. Once you have it on paper, your next move is to create plans around making it happen. Build your blueprints. Finally, when you are satisfied that you've completed the preparation, turn your plans into reality. Success is taking steps to craft your crazy innovative thoughts into real, tangible items.

"The five essential entrepreneurial skills for success are concentration, discrimination, organization, innovation and communication."

Michael Faraday

There are thousands of gurus out there who will tell you about the essential skills you need to achieve success. You get to choose which of their ideas will help you the most as you organize your innovations into actionable items. Take a look at the quote above and the quote from Day 226 as two examples of suggestions to help you turn your ideas into realities.

Now you get to practice being the guru. How can you organize your life so that you are better at turning your ideas into real actions that will help you achieve success? Come up with your own unique game plan using these quotes as templates. Write your own steps for success.

Your assignment does not end there. You have to try out your new plan to see if it works. Take one of your crazy ideas, and walk through the steps you have created to turn it into reality. Give yourself at least a month to make this happen, but make sure your deadline, whatever it is, is clear. What milestones can you set along the way that will help you gauge whether or not you are on track?

You are now getting into the nitty gritty of achieving success. You may not get this process right the first time, but don't be discouraged. This is extremely rewarding work if you are up for the challenge. Be willing to tweak your process when you find parts that do not quite work, and you will be rewarded for your continual improvements. Good luck!

Day 228

"Don't agonize, organize."

Jim Hightower

If you want to achieve, you must do. Don't spend too much time in the dreaming stages. Taking action is a high priority. In the quote above, Jim Hightower says it perfectly. Don't agonize, organize. Don't worry if you're doing everything perfectly. You'll never know how things are going to work out until you get organized and do something.

Agonizing over your plans leaves you with nothing. If you spend all of your time fretting over your decisions, what product do you have to show for your worries at the end of the day? Maybe the beginning of an ulcer, but that's about it. Drop the worrying. It is useless.

Instead, spend your time on something you can hold on to. Organize your thoughts. Plan out how you are going to achieve your goals. You will be surprised at how exhilarating it is to see the process laid out. It will prove to you that you can achieve success. You can attain your dreams. You just need to organize a set of steps to get there.

Organize and get into action. If something doesn't work, then re-organize and take action again. Concrete steps will give you concrete achievement. Ideas without organization are like dreams. They eventually fade, and you have nothing to prove they ever existed. Don't be afraid to take this next and very important step in achieving success. You are done dreaming. It's time to organize and attack.

"We give our lives to that which we give our time. I have learned that it is very difficult, if not impossible, to unclutter one's life by starting at the top of the pile with the idea that the solution is to just get things sorted and better organized. It is nice to get better organized, but that is not enough. Much has to be discarded. We must actually get rid of it. To do this we need to develop a list of basics . . . . [This list] must be the product of inspiration and prayerful judgment between the things we really need and things we just want. It should separate need from greed. It must be our best understanding of those things that are important as opposed to those things that are just interesting."

William R. Bradford

Is your life cluttered? It is much harder to reach success if you allow yourself too many distractions. In order to remove the clutter from your life, you need to do more than organize. You must streamline your life.

Your assignment today is to sit down with a large piece of paper and map out what you did last week. Go through your calendar if that helps you remember, but divide the page into seven days and try, as accurately as possible, to account for all of your time.

How much time did you spend watching TV? How many hours (or minutes) did you dedicate to family? What percentage of your time was spent at work? Did you spend a lot of time surfing the Internet? You can record the events in your seven-day calendar any way you want, but find a clear way to identify the amount of time you spend on various activities throughout the day.

After you have completed this task, take a look at the entire week. Where do you see wasted time? Are there tasks you can cut from your routine to give you more time for creative growth? Part of organization is trimming off the excess. What can you do without?

> "The trouble with organizing a thing is that pretty soon folks get to paying more attention to the organization than to what they're organized for."
>
> Laura Ingalls Wilder

Laura Ingalls Wilder offers one final piece of advice for this section on organization: Make sure you do not lose sight of the big picture.

It's a great idea to get organized. It will prepare the path for success and also help you get there faster than you would if your life was cluttered. However, sometimes you get so wrapped up in the organization that you forget why you're organizing in the first place.

This problem is most plainly seen in a corporate setting. Have you ever been a member of a council, a board, or a club that is so wrapped up in the rules of the group that nothing is ever accomplished? It's extremely frustrating to those members who joined the assembly to make a difference.

You can fall into the same trap personally. Your ultimate goal is to achieve success. Don't get stuck picking out the right colors for the file folders in your new office or deciding which laptop to buy to record all of your latest creative brainstorms. Those are insignificant pieces of the whole picture.

Do you think you've lost sight of the big picture? Take a look at the seven-day map you made on Day 229. How much of that time was spent working directly on achieving success? If it's less than 50 percent, then you may have detoured away from your true goals. It's not too late to change your routine. Organization is not the ultimate goal. Success is your objective.

"Let us rise up and be thankful, for if we didn't learn a lot today, at least we learned a little, and if we didn't learn a little, at least we didn't get sick, and if we got sick, at least we didn't die; so, let us all be thankful."

Buddha

Gratitude is an important attitude no matter what is going on in your life. Even if your current situation sounds like a bad country song — you lost your job, your truck, your significant other, and your dog all in one day — find at least one thing, no matter how insignificant, to be thankful for. It's important to practice being grateful, even in the bad times, because if you are able to lift up the good things in your life, you open the door for more of the same. On the other hand, if you keep pointing out the rotten stuff and the disappointments, you might become a magnet for even more bad news.

Your assignment today is slightly challenging. Are you up for it? This may take more than one day to complete, but don't let it run on forever. Try to complete it within a week. Make a list in your journal of 100 things you are grateful for. They can run the gamut from being thankful for the love of family to something as simple as being thankful you woke up that morning. Duplications don't count. You must come up with 100 different items. This list will be very helpful in the future. It will become a reference for you on bad days.

The quote above says it brilliantly. If you can't be thankful you learned a lot today, be thankful you learned a little. If you can't be thankful for your health, be thankful you're still breathing. There's always something positive to put on your gratitude list. Some days it's more difficult to find than others, but it's always there. Capitalize on the positive aspects of your life, and you will continue to move forward toward success.

Day 232

Terri could feel the light within her slowly going out, but she didn't have any idea what to do about it. She had always loved horses and had been a successful competitor in national horse shows since her teen years. But it was a costly hobby, and she just didn't have the money to continue in her mid-twenties. She now had young children who came first. There was no way she could justify spending thousands of dollars on horses and leave her daughters wanting. So she sold her horses. It was an easy decision at the time, but now she felt unfulfilled. She missed the time she spent riding. The light of inspiration was getting dimmer.

Then a miracle occurred. Terri's own cousin started a therapeutic riding school, and he was in need of more trainers. He casually mentioned it to Terri at a family Christmas party, and her eyes lit up. She immediately offered herself as a volunteer twice a week. In the months that followed, Terri blossomed. She was able to ride again without the expense, and she had the additional joy of helping special-needs students. The spark her cousin offered through his own new venture rekindled the light in her soul, and she was filled with gratitude.

Who has been a light in your life? Who gave you hope when you were in despair? Write about your experience when someone reached out and helped you. Then journal about ways in which you can become the spark in someone else's life.

"Gratefulness is the key to a happy life that we hold in our hands, because if we are not grateful, then no matter how much we have we will not be happy — because we will always want to have something else or something more."

Brother David Steindl-Rast

How do you feel today? Do you feel happy? Or do you have a gnawing feeling in your gut that signals how much you yearn for more than you have right now?

Practicing gratitude will help you to feed that need in your soul. It is important to strive for more — especially when you are on the road to success but you have to stop on the path to achievement and be grateful for all of the wonderful things that are part of your life right now. Are you aware of the good things in your life? Some people will never be satisfied until their ultimate goals are achieved, but that kind of tunnel vision robs them of a host of events that happen every day in real time that should be celebrated. They don't even notice them.

If you are too focused on the finish line, you might miss the best parts of life.

Work on increasing your awareness. Stop reaching for ultimate happiness and concentrate instead on awareness. What do you notice? What surprises you? Be aware of people, places, and things. Pay attention to the mood of your co-worker. Maybe there is something you can do to help them if they're having a bad day. Take a look at the progress of that construction site near your office. How is it going? Awareness is your assignment today.

Day 234

"As we express our gratitude, we must never forget that the highest appreciation is not to utter words, but to live by them."

John F. Kennedy

To this point, you have shown your gratitude by writing lists. There are other ways in which you can express gratitude, and John F. Kennedy mentions one very important one in this quote. The highest form of appreciation is to live a life that is full of gratitude. That is even more important than saying thank you or writing down a gratitude list. It is the final step.

How exactly do you live by words of gratitude? It makes sense to say, "I'm grateful for my family." But how do you live by that? Think about ways you might live your gratitude.

You can start by telling your family members you love them. Here are a few other ideas: hug your kids; call your mother or father just to see how they are doing; complete a chore for your significant other that you know they don't enjoy, like cleaning out the cat box or straightening up the garage; or drop your over-competitive compulsion to win every time you get together with your brother on the basketball court. All of those things are fairly easy to do, but they put words into action. They show the people in your life that they are important to you, and you love them. Anyone can utter words of gratitude. The words take on greater significance when they become actions.

"Tests build our testimony."

Nicole Johnson

Nicole Johnson was crowned Miss America in 1999. If you knew nothing except that one fact about her, what would you assume? She's probably got a lot going for her—looks, education, a really white smile. She must live a charmed life, don't you think? It's hard to be beautiful.

Ms. Johnson also suffers from diabetes. Does that change your image of her?

Her quote here reveals a lot about her character. The tests she has faced so far in life don't limit her. They are the bricks and mortar that build her testimony. What a unique attitude. She is putting her gratitude into action.

You have two choices when you face difficulties in life. You can learn from them and overcome them, or you can let them limit you. It is completely up to you which route you decide to take.

You are wasting your time if you try to find someone or something to blame for your circumstances. That will provide you with nothing in the way of good materials to build a happy life. Let's say you're right. There is someone to blame. Once you put the responsibility on them, what do you have left? You have just given all of your power away.

Let your tests build your testimony. Forge through the difficult times and learn how to conquer your problems without passing the responsibility on to someone else. That will build the story of your life. It can be a heroic tale if you want it to be. You're the author.

Day 236

"Anger is a momentary madness, so control your passion or it will control you."

Horace

A pastor was standing in line at the local grocery store. He was in a hurry to get home, and the person in front of him had about thirty items in the ten-items-or-less aisle. After making several sighing noises and glaring at the back of this person's head, he finally muttered under his breath, "Boy, some people sure can't read the signs!"

The person in line finally turned around, and it was one of his parishioners.

Why don't we treat the people we don't know with the same respect as the people we know? When did road rage (or grocery store rage) become okay? Why do we lose all sense of decorum when we get mad? Anger is a momentary madness. It causes people to do and say things they normally would never do. This pastor would never speak that way to his parishioner at church, but in an anonymous situation, his anger built up, and he said something he regretted.

It is important when striving for success to learn to control your anger. Anger management is essential to success. You have to be able to diffuse the momentary madness that occurs when you let anger control you.

During the next few days you will read about methods for effective anger management in your life. Everyone deals with anger — some to a larger extent than others. The goal is to learn how to diffuse that anger and not let it block your path to success.

Your assignment today is to recall an incident when you got angry. Write about what happened and detail the results of your angry moment.

"No man can think clearly when his fists are clenched."
George Jean Nathan

Today's task is going to center around awareness. What happens to you when you get angry? Recall the moment you wrote about yesterday or another time when anger got the better of you. Try to remember what anger felt like physically. Did it feel a little bit good to get boiling mad? Be honest. Is there some sort of satisfaction you draw from getting your blood boiling over an issue that is important to you?

Experts say that a number of things happen to people when they get angry. Their blood pressure goes up, their face gets red, they clench their fists, and their body tenses up. Another very important thing happens. The brain moves from logical thinking to more primal instincts. In other words, you lose your ability to reason or think clearly. Instead, you turn to more of a fight or flight mentality.

Wait a minute. That doesn't sound like that much fun. So basically when you get mad, you're out of your mind. There is no way you can think clearly when you're angry. The emotion takes over, and your actions are up for grabs. Do you want that?

Spend today thinking about times that you've acted uncharacteristically when you get mad. Write about them whenever you get a chance throughout the day. The short-term satisfaction you feel when you get angry may not be worth it if the consequence is doing something you will regret later.

Day 238

"I don't have to attend every argument I'm invited to."

Author Unknown

On day 231, you were asked to write down one hundred things you are grateful for. How is that going? Have you completed the list yet? If not, keep going until you come up with at least one hundred different things.

Today you are going to begin to look at solutions to anger issues. You will explore several different ideas over the next few days that will give you tools for anger management. The first solution is to walk away. The quote above says it very clearly. You are not required to attend every argument you're invited to. Walk away.

That is often easier said than done, but it is a terrific reaction. Practice it in your daily life. If someone at work tries to bait you into starting an argument, let it go. Let them think they won. Just simply walk away. The more you do it, the easier it will be.

It can be pretty hard at first not to attend every argument you're invited to, especially if you think you're right (and we all do). It's important to realize that the person on the other side of the argument is equally passionate, and it isn't likely in most situations that you are going to change their mind. You can keep your power and your self-respect if you refuse to be drawn in to the conflict.

There are times, of course, when it is important to stand up for what you believe in and take part in an argument. However, nine times out of ten nothing is accomplished through bickering. Pick your battles very carefully and reserve your wits for the issues that mean the most to you. Practice self-control today and don't accept the invitation to argue.

"The best remedy for a short temper is a long walk."
                                                    Jacqueline Schiff

When a pot of water comes to a boil on the stove, you take it off the heat. You need to do the same thing when your temper starts to boil. Remove yourself from a heated situation.

One great way to diffuse your anger is to take a walk. It's healthy, and it helps you get away from conditions that are making you angry. Get out into the fresh air and breathe. Remember your priorities in life and gauge where this incident ranks in the big scheme of things. Also, when you go on a long walk you will have time to calm down a bit and think through the reasons for your anger. Are they justified? Or are you angry because your pride is just a little hurt?

Anger boils up quickly, but it often takes time to cool down. Give yourself that time. You don't want to lose your right to rational thought. If you let your anger get the better of you and take action when your temper flares, you give away your power. Unleashing your anger may feel powerful at the time, but displaying a temper is never truly powerful. It usually comes across as reckless, irresponsible, and childish. Do you want to use those adjectives to describe yourself?

Your assignment is to practice positive remedies for anger. When your temper boils over, take a walk. Also, start keeping a list of other actions you can take to detour your anger. Keep that list close by. You never know when you'll need it!

"Always write angry letters to your enemies. Never mail them."

James Fallows

Cliff was a top-level executive at an insurance firm. To say that he often had to deal with personality issues, particularly with his own employees, was an understatement. Nevertheless, Cliff never lost his cool. How did he do it?

He did not succumb to the "I'm running a daycare, not an office" theory that many top executives in large corporations admit to believing. Instead, he maintained his composure and found ways to help people come together, build on their strengths, and act like adults. He was a very successful leader.

You may be surprised to find out that part of Cliff's success was due to one very simple practice. He wrote letters and emails that he never mailed. In fact, he didn't even save them. When an employee did something that really sent Cliff's blood pressure through the roof, he sat down at his computer and fired off an angry letter. Then he hit the delete key. Cliff found a way to release his anger without imposing it on other people. It's just not helpful in most cases, and he knew that. On the other hand, he had to find some way to release the tension. After he unleashed his anger in a way that did not offend, he was able to look at the problem rationally and find a better solution.

Your assignment today is to add this tactic to your list of remedies for anger. Give it a try if the opportunity presents itself sometime during the day. Just remember never to send that letter, because if you do, you'll have a lot of cleaning up to do later. Hurt feelings take a very long time to mend.

"The first and most basic habit of a highly effective person in any environment is the habit of proactivity. Being proactive means that as human beings, we are responsible for our own lives. Our behavior is a function of our decisions, not our conditions. We can subordinate feelings to values. We have the initiative and the responsibility to make things happen."

Stephen R. Covey

We often talk about habits in a negative way. You want to get rid of a smoking habit; you need to change the habit of eating fast food for lunch every day; or you have a bad habit of biting your nails. For the next few days we're going to turn that around and talk about forming good habits. These are routines you can sink into — even get stuck in — that will actually help you on the road to success rather than impede your progress.

The best place to start is with one of the biggest gurus of forming good habits, the author of *The Seven Habits of Highly Effective People*, Dr. Stephen R. Covey. He points out that the first and most basic habit of highly effective people is proactivity. He also says that it is true in any environment. So it doesn't matter if you are a construction worker or an artist or a florist or an administrator. Action is the key.

One of the biggest issues anyone faces on the road to success is how they react to the conditions that surround them. Behavior is not a function of conditions. It's a function of the decision you make every day to be proactive or not. Practice proactivity today. Take the initiative and be responsible for your own destiny. You are not a victim of circumstances. You hold the power to change your life through your actions.

Day 242

"We first make our habits, and then our habits make us."

John Dryden

How do you form good habits? First of all, don't complicate the task. It's really not that hard. Just do it today, and then do it tomorrow, and then do it the next day. Don't worry about the future. Just practice today. Pretty soon you will find you have strung a lot of todays together, and suddenly you're forming a habit.

To build on Dr. Covey's point in Day 241, proactivity is the first and most important habit for success—so get in gear. You can use that advice right now. Be proactive by starting another good habit. Make the habit first, and then the habit makes you.

Your assignment is to come up with a good habit you would like to form. Don't think about this all day. You can probably come up with something in five or ten minutes. Do you want to incorporate meditation into your routine? Would you like to go for a daily walk? What about setting aside thirty minutes to read? Pick something now, and do it today. No excuses.

When you wake up tomorrow, resolve to do it again, and so on until it becomes a habit. You don't have to think wishful thoughts anymore. Wistful phrases like "I wish I was in better shape" do not need to escape your lips. Make something (like exercise, for example) a habit starting today. In a few months your habit will make you. There is no doubt you will be in better shape if you proactively go after your goal each day.

"Stop the habit of wishful thinking and start the habit of thoughtful wishes."

Mary Martin

Wishes aren't bad at all. However, wishful thinking is awful. It breeds inactivity. It sounds like you've already lost the game. Are you a wishful thinker? Do you catch yourself saying things like the following:

I sure wish I hadn't gone to Whatever University. It wasn't a very good school.

I wish I didn't have so many commitments today. Oh well.

I wish I was smarter and better looking.

I wish I had a million dollars.

You can't do anything with any of those kinds of statements. You don't have a million dollars; you're not Einstein; you created the schedule you're stuck with today; and you already completed the degree at the school you didn't like that much. Those things are over. You can't change them. Move on to thoughtful wishes.

Thoughtful wishes are dreams that can actually come true. Start a list of thoughtful wishes today. The important thing to remember about a thoughtful wish is that it has to be attainable. You can't talk about past regrets or completely ridiculous goals. Sit down and really think about this (hence the word thoughtful). Write down what you wish would come true in your life. Now, of those wishes, what do you have a shot at achieving? Highlight attainable wishes. Those are your thoughtful wishes. Pick one and pursue it.

"Live out of your imagination instead of out of your memory."

Fortune Cookie

Janis had an incredible imagination. She had dreams that were so full of color and beauty that others would be stunned to witness them. She wondered what it would be like to live her imagination out loud. It was a scary proposition. What if people thought she was weird? The ideas that sprang from her imagination were incredibly unique, and Janis knew it. What if the rest of the world didn't like them?

There was one memory that held Janis back. In grade school she did let her imagination emerge into the real world. She drew a fantastic picture for a school project. It was beautiful and brilliant and uniquely her. But her fourth-grade teacher didn't have much of an imagination. She couldn't see the beauty in Janis' work, and she chastised her for not "coloring in the lines."

That one memory held Janis back for a long time. She was afraid of letting her brilliance emerge again. One day she decided to take a risk. She would not limit her imagination to her dream world. Her creativity was keeping her up nights, and she had to do something to share it with others. Janis started writing and illustrating a series of children's books that night. She lived out of her imagination; she got her thoughts onto a page and dared to share them with the rest of the world. Within months, a major publisher accepted her first couple of books and gave her a hefty advance to produce more.

Janis finally had the nerve to live out of her imagination instead of her memory. Are you that brave?

"Long-range goals keep you from being frustrated by short-term failures."

James Cash Penney

It's great to have long-term goals. They help you remember that there is a bigger picture. Life is a series of ups and downs, but the overall trend is what should really command your attention.

It probably doesn't matter in the larger scheme of things if you flub a presentation at work. Is anyone going to remember that a year from now? Probably not. It's not the end of the world if you got a rejection letter from a college you really wanted to attend. That is only one aspect of your life, and there are a lot of other options for you to get a great education. No matter what happens to you today in the negative column, things are bound to get better tomorrow. You just have to learn to ride out the storms and keep moving in the right direction.

Look at your overall progress. Is the red line on the chart moving upward despite occasional dips? Then you are in great shape! Failures are very frustrating, but they really don't mean much if you resolve to keep moving forward. Everyone has failures. Do you still have your ultimate goal in sight?

Your assignment today is to make a line graph of your progress over the last year. Pinpoint specific victories and failures along a timeline and then connect the dots. How does it look? Is there a trend upward or downward? What can you do today to keep the overall direction moving up?

Day 246

"Life isn't about waiting for the storm to pass — it's about learning to dance in the rain."

Anonymous

There will be storms in life. You can be absolutely sure of that. Will you choose to hide in a corner and wait for the storm to pass, or will you dance in the rain?

This is a great quote, but it's a lot harder to put into practice than it sounds. When life is going badly, it's difficult to find positive actions to take. It's much easier to hide and wait out the storm. If you really want to move along the road to success, though, you need to get out there in the rain. Launch yourself into the eye of the storm. When you're in the center of the action, you have a much better chance of changing the outcome for the better.

Paula was the CEO of a small factory, and she was facing economic crisis and potential layoffs. Instead of hiding behind false reports and fake smiles, she told the truth. Paula went to her employees directly by holding a company meeting. She told them exactly what was going on and let them know that she was open for suggestions that would save the company money and increase profitability. Paula was shocked at how her employees responded to her plea. They came up with terrific ideas for saving money and increasing efficiency. By the end of the year, sales were looking up, and Paula offered an across-the-board raise to her employees as well as several bonuses to the workers with the most effective contributions. They came together as a corporation during a time of crisis rather than scattering and hiding in the corners. Paula and her employees learned to dance in the rain.

How can you practice dancing in the rain rather than hiding from storms?

"When I go to farms or little towns, I am always surprised at
the discontent I find. And New York, too often, has looked
across the sea toward Europe. And all of us who turn our
eyes away from what we have are missing life."

Norman Rockwell

Do you find yourself constantly turning your eyes away from what
you have? Do you spend a lot of time comparing and ranking yourself
against your co-workers, friends, and family members? Why do you
do that?

Discontented people have a very difficult time getting ahead. That
attitude of wanting what you don't have is a little like getting stuck
in the mud. You can't move forward, and you can't move backward.
Instead, you spend your time watching everyone pass you by.

It takes a considerable amount of energy to be discontent with life.
You can spend a lot of time wishing you were anyone but you, in
any location other than where you are, doing anything but what
you are presently doing. Does that sound productive? When you
look elsewhere for satisfaction, you often miss the great things that
surround you every day. You put your life on hold, and in a way you
stop living and start watching other people live. Life is priceless, but
you throw it away when you succumb to feelings of discontent.

When you start getting that itchy feeling of dissatisfaction, what can
you do? Start by looking around you and making a quick list of the
things for which you are grateful. Then take a mental inventory of
where you can make immediate improvements. Is there more you can
do to get the most out of your present situation? Take advantage of
who you are today, and stop being envious of who you are not.

Day 248

"The splendid discontent of God with Chaos, made the world; And from the discontent of man the world's best progress springs."

Ella Wheeler Wilcox

You read yesterday about how discontent can slow you down and keep you from achieving success. Today you are going to study a different interpretation. The quote above by Ella Wheeler Wilcox suggests that discontent breeds progress.

Sometimes that itchy, unhappy feeling of restlessness makes you just uncomfortable enough to get into action. When you are content, you may not have a reason to change for the better. You're happy right where you are. But if you are nursing feelings of discontent, you want out. You want to be somewhere else—you are just disgruntled enough to work for something better. Some of the greatest achievements in history were direct results of someone's discontent.

Compare the quote today to Norman Rockwell's quote from Day 247. Write in your journal about the word discontent. What role does it play in your life? Does it help you to move forward and get things done, or does discontent give you a feeling of being stuck? You have to come up with your own unique answer to this question. Only you know the truth.

It's important to know how you personally deal with your feelings. Discontent may be a terrific motivator for you, or on the other hand it could be a huge roadblock. When you are in tune with how you react to feelings of dissatisfaction, you can start to use those emotions as a tool for success rather than a hindrance.

"We love in others what we lack ourselves, and would be everything but what we are."

Richard Henry Stoddard

How big a role does envy play in your life? Do you look at others and see traits that you wish you had?

Today you are going to tackle a personal issue. Are you content or are you discontent—with yourself? Sometimes the source of your dissatisfaction is you. Now that would be a bummer, wouldn't it? You are the one thing you can't escape! On the other hand, you are a unique and beautiful gift to the world. Stop trying to be what you are not, and start enjoying what you are.

Sometimes you see gifts that others possess, and it's easy to forget that you have a treasure chest of your own. Mark was often envious of his younger sister's singing ability. He could barely carry a tune. When he got stuck in that jealous place, he forgot that he was a genius with numbers. Maybe his younger sister was a songbird, but he had a different and equally beautiful gift.

It's hard to be content with yourself sometimes. You might feel like you're not quite good enough to stand up to the rest of the world. You long to experience the riches of someone else's life. Practice celebrating your gifts rather than being envious of the talents of others. You're stuck with you, whether you like it or not. You might as well look around and check out your own aptitudes. Pretty soon you may be surprised to discover you aren't lacking at all. In fact, you are rich with talent.

Day 250

"I used to think I had ambition . . . but now I'm not so sure.
It may have been only discontent. They're easily confused."
Rachel Field

Congratulations! You have arrived at day 250! How do you feel? You are more than two-thirds of the way through the year, and your life is changing—maybe drastically. This is the point where you are probably feeling one of two things: either you are gaining confidence, or you are completely confused. Don't worry. Either way you are right on track.

Spend at least thirty minutes writing in your journal today. Try to capture the emotions that have come up over the last 250 days. What has the journey been like so far? Has it been a vacation, or has it been hard work? Maybe it has been a little of both. Specifically how have you changed?

You have been asked to complete a lot of exercises in the last couple of months. You are continuing to increase your awareness, but now you are adding concrete actions to back up your newfound knowledge. Has that been difficult? Sometimes transformation is painful. Have you been willing to change?

Secondly, take some time today to meditate about the extent to which you are completing the exercises in this book. Have you really been getting into the work, or have you turned in a half-hearted effort? Are you waiting to see if you notice any minor changes before you really go for it?

Finally, do something really nice for yourself today. You've come a long way since Day 1, and you have an interesting road ahead. Stop and appreciate this moment.

"A man wrapped up in himself makes a very small bundle."
Benjamin Franklin

It is important to have confidence in yourself, but there is a line you shouldn't cross: the line into self-absorbed thinking. If you are all wrapped up in yourself you do make a pretty small package.

Today you are going to look at an alternative to being wrapped up in yourself. What if you took a genuine interest in other people? It is important to be in tune with your own thoughts and feelings, but you are not all there is in this world. Look around and see who else is out there. Make friends, help others, and learn from those around you. If you do so, you are latching on to a wealth of knowledge, camaraderie, and love that will nourish you in ways you cannot even begin to imagine.

Your assignment today is to make a new friend. You may decide to talk to someone at work that you've never interacted with before. You could also strike up a conversation with someone in a waiting room. Age doesn't matter. You might find one of your children's friends fascinating if you spend a few minutes talking with them.

The object of this exercise is not to turn you into a creepy stalker or a nosy neighbor. Just take an interest in someone else when the opportunity arises. People really do enjoy talking about themselves when given a chance. You probably won't have trouble starting a conversation. Make it your goal to find out something new and interesting about another human being. Pay attention to others for a day and see how it enriches your life.

"Treat your friends as you do your pictures, and place them in their best light."

Jennie Jerome Churchill

You will be studying friendships for the next few days, and one of the most important aspects of a good friendship is highlighted in the quote above, attributed to Winston Churchill's mother. Treat your friends like your pictures. Place them in their best light.

Friends are valuable. It's important to lift them up and show off their strengths rather than cut them down and point out their flaws. Friendship is an opportunity to celebrate another person. The goal is not to keep them in your shadow.

Who are your best friends? Why do you like them? How do they treat you? Do they make you feel good about yourself? Write about the characteristics of the best friends you've had in your life. Then journal for awhile about what kind of friend you think you are to others. Are you a good friend? What do you do to put your friends in their best light? Do you stick up for your friends, or are you really only around if there is something they can do for you?

Some people are takers in friendships and some are givers. You want to lean toward the giving side. Don't worry about ending up with nothing. When you give yourself to others you very seldom end up bankrupt. Kindness has a way of multiplying and enriching your life, not taking away from it. It isn't a chore to be a friend. It's a gift. Put your friends in their best light, and you will be surrounded by beautiful images.

"You got a lotta nerve
To say you are my friend
When I was down
You just stood there grinning

You got a lotta nerve
To say you gotta helping hand to lend
You just want to be on
The side that's winning . . . "

Bob Dylan

Bob Dylan is not depicting an ideal friendship in this excerpt from the song "Positively 4th Street," released in 1965. Do you know someone like this? Do you see yourself in this song?

Loyalty is a much sought-after trait for friendships, and it is not that easy to find. On a scale of one to ten, how would your friends rate you in the loyalty department? It's actually more important to be loyal than it is to be on the winning side all the time. Do you agree with that statement?

You don't become a good friend by accident. You have to practice it just like you practice many other aspects that build your character. Get in the habit of helping your friends when they are down or if they need a hand. If your friend is moving into a new home, put on your work clothes and offer to pitch in and help him. When your friend goes to the hospital for surgery, visit her and keep her company.

You are well into the action phase of this book, so it's time to get to work. Make a list of things you can do during the next week that would be helpful to your friends. Follow through with at least five items on your list before the week is over.

Day 254

" . . . Winter, spring, summer or fall,
All you have to do is call
And I'll be there, yeah, yeah, yeah.
You've got a friend . . . "

Carole King

There is a reason why the last two days have highlighted song lyrics as quotes. Millions of composers have used friendship as a subject to inspire their music. Poets, novelists, dancers, and painters have also depicted friendships. Relationships with others, both good and bad, are a common thread that holds humanity together. You choose whether you will create a strong and lasting strand or whether you will be a corrosive and withering cord that could snap at any moment.

Today you get to be the poet. Write a set of song lyrics, draw a picture, or find another artistic way to depict the kind of friend you would like to be. If you have some musical talent, you might want to compose a tune. Try to find an inspiring way to describe how you view friendship in your life. After you have completed this exercise, keep the end result nearby and refer to it often. You don't ever have to share it with another person, but you should use it as a reminder to live up to that goal.

Strive to be the kind of friend Carole King describes in the quote above. Be a beacon of light when your friends find themselves in darkness. Be a source of hope and peace rather than discord and distain. Let your friendship be a happy tune, not a dismal picture. Let it be a rousing dance, not a mournful ode.

"Best friend, my wellspring in the wilderness!"

George Eliot

How much do you value your friendships? Do you agree with George Eliot? Do you think of friends like a wellspring in the wilderness? Or do you consider the duties of friendship more like a muddy puddle you would rather avoid?

Today you will have a chance to write about your honest feelings regarding friendships. Think about how they affect your life. Journal your positive and negative thoughts on the subject. One person will consider friendship a chore, while another individual thinks of friendship as a precious gift. Once you get your thoughts down on paper, try to link instances in your life to your conclusions about friendship.

Some people have not had good luck with friendships. They are mistrustful of confiding in a new friend because they have been ill treated in the past. Others have used friendships like money in exchange for things they want. Their lack of consideration for the feelings of others soon causes people to avoid friendships with them.

After you have given a thorough report on your assessment of friendships, the next thing you should do is consider ways you might improve or change your views. Is there anything you can do that might increase the value of friendships in your life? Write down actions you can take to change. You are not allowed to consider how others might change. This is up to you. What can you do to improve how you handle friendships?

"It takes courage to push yourself to places that you have never been before . . . to test your limits . . . to break through barriers."

Anaïs Nin

Who do you think of when you see the word courage? Do you think of daring explorers like Ferdinand Magellan or Neil Armstrong? Maybe you think of people in history who had the courage to stand up for their beliefs like Chief Sitting Bull or Joan of Arc. You are just as courageous as those giants of history. All you have to do is give yourself a little push.

Your assignment today is not to become a superhero in world history. Your assignment is to give yourself a little nudge. Go somewhere you haven't gone before. Do something that you're not entirely sure you can do. Test your limits. You have the ability right now to be great. You can do that by stretching yourself just a little bit today. Then tomorrow you will do the same thing.

Heroes don't often break through barriers in one push. They tap away at a roadblock until it crumbles. There are often numerous small failures before there is one huge victory. You have to be willing to put in the effort and continue tapping away at that wall.

Your assignment today is to push yourself. Don't be happy with where you are. Test your limits, even if you do it timidly. Rewrite your big presentation one more time to make it even better. Spend an extra fifteen minutes at the gym. Interview for a new job that will really push your limits. Go just a little bit too far out on the ledge and see what the view is like.

"None of us really pushes hard enough."

Fran Tarkenton

Dave was a successful entrepreneur. Within three short years he built his business from a workshop in his basement to a million-dollar enterprise. When asked about the methods he used to rocket to success, Dave smiled and gave a three-word answer:

"Reality Check Day."

The interviewer looked at him suspiciously, but Dave went on to explain that he chose one day a week as Reality Check Day. He spent thirty minutes first thing in the morning on Reality Check Day (usually Monday), and he went through his calendar for the previous week. He wrote in his journal about his victories and also made a list of where he didn't push hard enough. Then he took five minutes to close his eyes and concentrate on his breathing. He came up with short mantras, like "come hope," "come innovation," and "come God" to accompany his breathing technique. When Dave was finished with this exercise, he launched into the week with renewed energy and a resolve to push harder. It was an extremely successful technique and easy to do.

You may have already guessed your assignment. It is to give Reality Check Day a try for at least two months. Every Monday practice what Dave suggested and see if, at the end of the second month, you find you pushed a little harder and created a little more success in your life. Almost no one pushes hard enough, but you can become the exception one week at a time by incorporating this new habit.

Day 258

"Every morning I wake up saying, I'm still alive; a miracle. And so I keep on pushing."

Jacques Cousteau

If you are reading this, you were successful in at least one thing today: you're still alive. Congratulations! Now, what are you going to do with that miracle you were just handed? Are you going to waste it, or are you going to use it up and find out about its full potential?

You are a living, breathing miracle every day you spend on this earth. It's time to celebrate that fact. Take your life and seize its potential today. It is a tragedy to let the hours of your life slip by without incorporating some effort into the gift you have been given. If someone handed you a brand new invention, something that is so unique that you are the only one in the world who gets to use it, would you leave it on your couch untouched?

Are you even a little bit curious about what you are capable of doing? Think of yourself as that brand new invention. What can you discover about your talents and strengths? How can you test your limits? Are there any things you can do to improve your efficiency and productivity? Use up this life you've been given right now. Test it. There's no reason to save up your efforts for another day. That day may never come. Keep pushing, and you will be surprised by the capabilities of the invention you were given.

"If you ask me what I came to do in this world, I, an artist, will answer you: I am here to live out loud."

Emile Zola

Why are you here? What did you come to this world to do? Some people say they didn't ask to be born into this world. It's not their fault they're here. They take a "just visiting" attitude and the stance of a bored teenager on a family trip who refuses to enjoy the scenery. Are you like that?

You can certainly choose that route in life. What will it get you at the end of the day? Probably a healthy dose of resentment, boredom, wishful thinking, sadness, and maybe a little anger. You have every right to choose that, but it's not your only option.

What would it be like if you took on Emile Zola's idea and decided that you are here on earth to live out loud? What does that mean to you? What would that get you? Most likely it would provide you with a heavy helping of contentment, joy, exhilaration, intrigue, and wonder.

You get to make the choices about what you are going to do in this world. Your choices create your path. Describe what you will do if you choose to live out loud. Draw a picture of your life if you refuse to apologize for who you are and if you openly pursue your dreams. What would happen if you didn't whisper your dreams in dark rooms? Instead, choose to bring your desire for achievement into the sunlight and actively live it and work it. Live out loud today. Don't be afraid.

"I long to accomplish great and noble tasks, but it is my chief duty to accomplish humble tasks as though they were great and noble. The world is moved along, not only by the mighty shoves of its heroes, but also by the aggregate of the tiny pushes of each honest worker."

Helen Keller

Helen Keller reveals a very big secret in these few sentences. It's an exciting revelation if you give yourself a moment to think about it. The world is really moved along by lots of tiny pushes from ordinary people. If you want to accomplish great things, you have to take on humble tasks like they were the most important jobs in the world. Great people do not do one big and wonderful thing and then call it a day. If you take a microscope to the lives of your heroes, you will find that they actually did thousands of little things very well in order to achieve success.

Pick one of your heroes and look closely at their life. Read a biography about them or collect as much information as you can find on the Internet. Make a list of all of the smaller goals they accomplished in order to reach great heights of success. No one made a single big shove to greatness. Noble achievements are the results of numerous tiny pushes up the mountain.

Draw a picture of a mountain and write one of your biggest goals for success at the top. Next, write down as many smaller goals as you can think of that will push you up that mountain toward your highest achievement. This is your new check list. Feel free to gaze up at the summit often, but concentrate your work on the smaller tasks along the way. You will get there if you accomplish the humble tasks as if they were great and noble.

"You are the only person on earth who can use your ability."
Zig Ziglar

It's difficult to get into the mode of thinking like a successful person if you are unsure of the unique abilities you have to offer. You begin to sabotage your success when you start thinking thoughts like, "I'm not that unique" or "I don't really have anything new to contribute."

Are you acutely aware of your abilities? You've worked through a number of exercises in this book to discover the things that interest you and draw your attention. You have also done some work to unearth your unique talents. Now is the time for you to get really specific. What precise endeavors do you want to pursue? Where will your abilities be used to the fullest?

As this quote suggests, you are the only person who can use your ability. If you don't take advantage of your particular gifts, they will go to waste. Look at your current profession or the vocation you intend to pursue. Is it the best use of your ability? Very often people choose a job that is safe or easy, and they only use a small portion of their abilities each day. Are you willing to let your talents be wasted in that way?

Write down everything you did yesterday, and then write down what percentage of your overall talents were used during that day. If it's below 50 percent, you need to make a change. To be successful you must spend at least half of your day on tasks that show off your natural ability and allow you to grow and excel and contribute your unique gifts.

"Knowing what you cannot do is more important than knowing what you can do. In fact, that's good taste."

Lucille Ball

It's painful to watch someone relentlessly pursue something for which they have no talent. Sandy had a romantic notion from the age of about thirteen of being a wedding planner. She loved weddings. Unfortunately, Sandy did not have the right set of talents for the job. She was not organized; she wasn't a very social person; her personal skills were lacking; and she was a horrible negotiator. After numerous failed attempts to start a business, Sandy finally realized this was not her forte. Quite by accident, she found out that where she really excelled was in designing wedding invitations. She transferred her efforts to something she did well, and her new business took off.

Knowing what you cannot do is more important than knowing what you can do. Make sure you're not wasting valuable time trying to break into an area that isn't right for you. Ask yourself the following questions:

Does this always seem difficult, like I'm fighting upstream?

Am I having fun?

Do I look forward to going to work to pursue this area of success?

If your answers give you pause, you might be in the wrong field. Don't waste your time on what you can't do. It's good taste to go with your strengths.

"Ability without ambition is like kindling wood without the spark."

Anonymous

Let's say you found out without a doubt where your talents lie. You know exactly what you should pursue in order to achieve success. The only problem: your get up and go got up and left. You feel lethargic, and you don't have any ambition. You're lacking the fuel to propel you to success. You are thinking maybe it would be better to wait for a moment when you are ready.

What should you do?

Snap out of it!

You're wasting valuable time trying to work up the energy to grab onto opportunity. It's like being in the same room with a priceless treasure but not having the energy to cross the floor to get it. It's that ridiculous. Success is just sitting there waiting for you. Who cares whether or not you "feel like" going for it? If you wait around to be in the right mood, someone else will steal your opportunity while you're putting off achievement.

As the quote suggests, you may be standing in front of a huge stack of firewood. Without a spark it doesn't have much of a chance to turn into a roaring fire. It doesn't matter how talented you are; you have to follow ability with hard work. So get out there and stack up that kindling — and then light the match. You can turn opportunity into a blazing fire in a very short time if you are willing to do the work.

Day 264

"We all have ability. The difference is how we use it."

Stevie Wonder

Everyone has ability. We have that in common. If you want to be uncommon, you have to find a great way to use your ability. Are you starting to formulate some good ideas on how you can do that?

List your abilities again in your journal. Look over your list and let yourself be a little smug. You are one cool individual. Are you ready to turn your ability into success? Scoop up those abilities and put them to work. Are you good with numbers? How can you capitalize on that talent? Are you artistic? What can you do to build on your artistic nature and come up with something really unique? Do you excel in the sciences? How can you get into a position where you have more of a chance to pursue your talents in that area?

You understand by now that it is not good enough simply to be talented. You need follow-through to make this work. No one can tell you exactly what route to take to reach success. You have to find your own opportunities.

Singer, songwriter, and instrumentalist Stevie Wonder has been blind since birth, but he has not centered his life on his physical challenges. He recognized that he had talent as a musician at a very early age, and by the time he was eleven years old he signed his first contract with Motown Records. Now he boasts a pile of top-ten hits and awards that reflect his success. Stevie Wonder knew how to use his ability. He followed through by working hard to expose his talents to their full extent, and now he is without question a success. There is nothing stopping you from doing the exactly the same.

"I've had smarter people around me all my life, but I haven't run into one yet that can outwork me. And if they can't outwork you, then smarts aren't going to do them much good. That's just the way it is. And if you believe that and live by it, you'd be surprised at how much fun you can have."

Woody Hayes

If you are suffering from a feeling of inferiority in the smarts department, don't worry about it. It won't keep you from achieving your dreams. You have a weapon, and that is hard work. You don't have to be brilliant to be successful. History is littered with people who had mediocre talents but excelled through their extraordinary ability to outwork everyone around them.

Do you know what this means? (This may be unfortunate if you have a lazy side.) You have no excuse not to be a success. You deserve to achieve your dreams every bit as much as anyone else. It all comes back to effort. Are you willing to put in the effort you need in order to achieve success?

Woody Hayes was right. You can have a lot of fun with life when you start believing that you deserve success. When you believe that all you need to do is outwork those around you to get ahead, you no longer spend your time worrying *if* it's going to happen. Instead you start planning for *when* it's going to happen. When a competitor scoffs at your talents, just smile and keep on working. You will come out the winner no matter what they think of you. This is a life-long race, and you've got plenty of time to make up the distance.

What can you change in your routine to increase your efforts to achieve success?

"Unless you try to do something beyond what you have already mastered, you will never grow."

Ronald E. Osborn

A key element of success is to always be open to opportunities to learn and grow. You will never know it all, no matter how old you are or how successful you become. In fact, you should continually seek out opportunities to learn new things. A new prospect for success can be unearthed just about anywhere, so get out your shovel and start digging. There are so many exciting aspects of this world that you have not yet discovered. Do you wonder what you might be missing?

Your assignment today is to try to do something beyond what you have already mastered. Pick a subject area that interests you and dive in. No excuses. Take action and pursue something new. You will add to the volumes of information stored inside your brain, and you will also stay in shape mentally. You need to be sharp when you are in hot pursuit of success.

Margaret is ninety-three years old, and she has never stopped learning. She conquers a crossword puzzle every morning and constantly reads new books on a wide variety of subjects. She is even up for trying new exercises whenever she meets with her physical therapist. Margaret had a stroke last year, but she bounced back faster than most people her age. Part of the reason for her achievement is she constantly keeps her mind and her body active. She continues to absorb new information and new experiences. Margaret is a great example of success — especially after her stroke.

"An easy life doesn't teach us anything. In the end it's learning that matters — what we've learned and how we've grown."

Richard Bach

Your task today is to reflect on your past. When in your life have you learned the most? What exactly was going on that created a spike in your education? Some people assume they learned the most during their school years. Others disagree heartily with that idea and claim that their education really started when they got into the workforce and had to perform in a job. Their paycheck depended on learning a new skill, so they perked up and paid attention. Another group of people might point out that they learned the fastest when they were put in a crisis situation, either personal or professional. Maybe the welfare of their family or even their own life depended on learning something new. What has been your experience?

The quote above suggests that the difficult parts of your journey in life are your greatest teachers. Do you agree with that statement? Most of us would prefer an easy life to a hard one, but how much do we really learn during the effortless parts of our journey?

The next time you face difficulties, practice turning your dread and fear into a chance to engage and learn from your experience. This is a very difficult thing to do. It's hard to step out of panic mode and open up your mind to learn new ways to cope with your situation. Be brave and try it. The more you are able to approach tough times as an opportunity to grow, the faster you will speed toward success. These experiences have nothing to do with winning and losing. In the end, it's learning that matters.

Day 268

"Knowledge is love and light and vision."

Helen Keller

How would you describe the word knowledge? What synonyms come to mind when you ponder that word? Take some time to write in your journal today about knowledge. Then feel free to draw a picture or two that describes how you feel about knowledge, or use your creativity in another way to develop an accurate depiction of the word. Are your thoughts completely positive on this subject, or do you have a few resentments attached to it? Remember to always be honest when carrying out these assignments. You're only lying to yourself if you cover up your true feelings. These exercises are solely for your benefit.

Helen Keller offers a slightly surprising and very enlightening definition of knowledge in the quote above, considering the fact that she was deaf and blind. Imagine what it was like to feel as isolated as Helen Keller must have felt before she started working with her teacher, Annie Sullivan. How did she endure that solitary darkness with almost no way to communicate with the world around her? How could she ever have imagined she would have an opportunity to learn, much less become a successful author, lecturer, and political activist?

Annie Sullivan found a way to communicate with her. She broke through the wall that Helen Keller struggled against, and the knowledge poured in. It was love and light and, yes, vision to a woman who once was blind. Knowledge is transforming, and this historical relationship between a teacher and a student is a shining example of its powerful nature.

"Give me a fruitful error any time, full of seeds, bursting with its own corrections. You can keep your sterile truth for yourself."

Vilfredo Pareto

This quote is a terrific description of the benefits of mistakes. When you are learning something new, you really want to come across a big, juicy error. Why? Because it is bursting with seeds of opportunity. It is far more interesting to learn from your mistakes than it is to get everything right the first time.

Richard was a brilliant student. He had all the answers. His chemistry notebook was so neat it could have been a textbook. Nothing was scribbled out or written over. It was perfect. Richard was also bored out of his mind, because he was in possession of the sterile truth. He knew how everything was supposed to turn out, so he didn't need to follow the road to discovery. He took the shortcut and got no real satisfaction out of it.

David's chemistry notebook, on the other hand, was a disaster. There were scribbles all over the place, stains from experiments gone wrong, and questions written up and down the margins. David was having the time of his life! He was gobbling up the messy fruits of newly acquired knowledge, and he learned more through his mistakes than his triumphs.

Think about this: if you come to the correct answer right away, that's it. You're done. You deprive yourself of the learning process. It's like skipping to the back of a mystery novel to find out whodunit. Would you like to live your life like Richard, bored but correct? Or would you rather emulate David, a student who struggles but thrives in the search for knowledge?

Day 270

"I am learning all the time. The tombstone will be my
diploma."

Eartha Kitt

Don't ever stop learning. You don't want to hurry to get that lifetime
diploma, because when it's handed over to you, you're done with this
journey. Grab up every opportunity you have to get another degree.
Double and triple major. The wonderful thing about the lessons
you learn in life is that they're free. You're not going to have a big
lifetime student loan to pay off when you die. Take advantage of the
complimentary education that is offered to you every day in a variety
of ways.

Your assignment is to keep a notebook close by throughout the
day and jot down every new thing you learn. It doesn't matter how
insignificant it seems, write it down. At the end of the day, you should
have pages and pages of new information. If you don't, then it's time
to adjust your habits.

What can you do to ensure that you are continually learning? One
great exercise is to practice your sense of wonder. Stop assuming you
know the answers to everything that is important and start wondering
about the things you don't know. Did you ever wonder who makes
the first pot of coffee in the break room at work? Find out. Are you
curious about your carbon footprint? Do you even know what that is?
Learn more about it today. Would you like to know more about your
teenage son's favorite band? This one could be scary, but open up
your mind and be willing to receive a music lesson from your child.
Don't blow your opportunities to learn. Look for them. Practice a
sense of wonder.

"There is a hard law. When an injury is done to us, we never recover until we forgive."

Alan Paton

Forgiveness is yet another important ingredient for success. It sounds like a pretty easy task to take care of, but it is actually one of the hardest elements of success to put into practice. The next few days are going to be dedicated to the power of forgiveness and how it will help you achieve your dreams.

Your assignment for Day 271 is to make a list of the injuries that have been done to you. What were some of the biggest wrongs that you have experienced personally in your life? Write down the event; the person, place, or thing that caused the injury; and what happened as a result of it. Try to find injustices from your past that may have become roadblocks on your journey toward success. Those are the ones you want to deal with first.

Injuries can come from any part of your past. Maybe a kid in class made fun of your nose when you were in junior high school, and you have been embarrassed about your looks ever since. There are also physical injuries like abuse from a parent, spouse, or another person. An injury could also come from something that seems insignificant in the larger scheme of life, but it still bothers you personally. For instance, if one of your colleagues took credit for your idea at a meeting, it might provide irritation in the workplace and block you from continuing to give 100 percent to your job.

Write down these injuries, and when you are done, take some time to journal about how each one of them made you feel. This is the initial step toward forgiveness.

Day 272

"Forgiveness is the art of admitting that I am like other people."

Mother Teresa

Have you ever done anything wrong? Have you ever said something that made someone feel bad or made a choice that was not particularly honorable? Chances are, if you've participated in life for longer than about ten minutes, you've done something that requires forgiveness.

We're all human. Each of us makes mistakes — a whole lot of them, as a matter of fact. A very large aspect of participating in this world is screwing up from time to time. Absolutely no one is perfect.

That being said, why is it so difficult to forgive others for faults that we are very likely to have experienced in ourselves? Ego probably has something to do with it. Most people really don't like it when they feel they are not treated fairly. If they are injured physically or emotionally, they want retribution. There should be consequences for wrong actions. Societies all over the world are based on rules that spell out those consequences. Consequences are one thing, but forgiveness is also essential if you want to continue to move forward in life.

Look up one person from the list of injuries you made yesterday. Pull out one example of wrongdoing. Your task today is to write down everything you have in common with the person who wronged you. Forget about how different they are from you and concentrate on your similarities. In what ways are you alike?

"To err is human; to forgive, infrequent."

Franklin P. Adams

Stanley was an exceptional man. He wasn't particularly smart or funny or good looking, but he was the picture of success. Stanley was a widower. In fact, he had lost his entire family two years ago in a horrible car accident. His wife was driving their two young sons home from baseball practice, and they were hit head on by a drunk driver.

At first Stanley wanted the man who caused the accident to feel his pain and pay dearly for what he had taken away from him. His entire family was gone in an instant. Stanley encouraged the lawyers to file murder charges.

Stanley was driving to the trial months after the accident, and he was still filled with rage. He was talking on the cell phone with a friend and railing about how this man did not deserve to live. In an instant, Stanley gasped and slammed on the brakes. He hadn't been paying attention while he was driving, and he came inches away from mowing down a toddler who had wandered out into the street. When Stanley finally pulled himself together, he continued on to the courthouse. He realized as he traveled the last few blocks that he had almost committed the same crime. He was overwhelmed.

Stanley requested a moment to speak during the proceedings. He publicly forgave the man and asked that the murder charges be dropped. That man did not willingly kill his family. It was an accident. Stanley was finally able to forgive and move on and do something productive with his life.

If you want to truly be exceptional, learn to forgive. It is an uncommon trait.

Day 274

"Forgiving someone who breaks a trust does not mean that we give him his job back."

Lewis B. Smedes

It is very easy to confuse forgiveness with being a doormat. They are not the same thing. When you forgive someone, you are setting yourself — and the other person — free. However, it has nothing to do with condoning the actions of the perpetrator.

If one of your employees was caught embezzling money from your company, you would find it very helpful to forgive them. On the other hand, you would be a complete fool if you hired them right back and set yourself up to be robbed again. Forgiveness does not mean you have to lose your common sense. Trust must be earned.

A popular phase is "forgive and forget." It might be more beneficial to say "forgive and remember." You do not have to go through the insane task of repeating pervious mistakes in judgment. If someone injures you, bestow forgiveness freely, but think twice before you decide to get involved with them again.

Karen's daughter, Ellen, was an alcoholic in the early stages of recovery. Ellen had betrayed her mother's trust in a number of ways when she was active in her disease, including stealing from her on several occasions. Karen forgave Ellen for all of the things she did as a result of her alcoholism, but it took years before Ellen won back her mother's trust. Karen needed to observe Ellen in recovery and see that she was changing and growing into a more honest and trustworthy person. Forgiveness was immediate, but trust took time.

"Forgiveness is not an occasional act. It is a permanent attitude."

Martin Luther King, Jr.

It is very important to note that forgiveness is another one of those things that you must practice. You can't just do it once and check it off your list of steps to success. As Martin Luther King, Jr., says, it's a permanent attitude. It's not an occasional act.

Hopefully, you've gained some additional knowledge and insight into forgiveness over the last few days. You are armed with new information, so it's no longer good enough to hold on to righteous indignation. You've got to practice forgiveness all the time. Your own happiness and ultimate success depend on it.

Remember, forgiveness in no way condones the actions of the person who wronged you. You are not a sucker when you forgive someone. It doesn't magically erase your ability to have good judgment when it comes to decisions that affect your safety and well being. Forgive and remember what happened so you don't repeat mistakes from the past.

Finally, go back to the list of injuries you created on day 271. Have you forgiven the people involved in each one of those injuries? If not, it is the time to take action. Create a plan to forgive everyone on that list in some way. If it is not appropriate to see them in person, or if they are no longer alive or reachable, write a letter or write to them in your journal. You cannot be free of an injurious event in your past until you are able to forgive the perpetrator. Get it done as soon as you are able, so that it will no longer imprison you and hold you back from success.

Day 276

"Courage is not the absence of fear, but the capacity for action despite our fears."

John McCain

Over the next few days you will be studying courage. Now we're talking! Courage sounds like the real meat of success, doesn't it? It's a triumphant, strong, victorious, and proud word—all the things that one associates with achievement. Well, before you get all Cowardly Lion here, let's start with a definition of courage.

Courage is not the absence of fear. Fear is actually a good thing. It is an indication of sanity in many stressful situations. Courage is a quality that allows you to face your fears. When you have courage, you are able to put one foot in front of the other and take action in spite of your fears.

Who do you consider to be a courageous person? Find three or four examples, and write about them in your journal. Why do you think of those people as courageous? Search your feelings about why you chose those names. What do you admire about those people? How do they exemplify courage? What do you see in them that you would like to emulate?

Courage is like forgiveness. It is not something that you only do once, and it is not something that happens easily. It is a way of living and it requires practice. It is pretty frightening to act courageously the first time, but you will gain strength every time you practice courage, and soon it will be part of your character. Enjoy the next few days as you cultivate your courageous side.

"All serious daring starts from within."

Harriet Beecher Stowe

Harriet Beecher Stowe was an American author, and her first novel, *Uncle Tom's Cabin*, was quite a courageous work. It expressed very strong anti-slavery sentiment during a tumultuous time in U.S. history right before the Civil War. Harriet Beecher Stowe made a very important point about courage in the quote above. Courage is not something outside of you that you can somehow obtain. It starts from within.

The first step in cultivating your courage is to notice the impulse you have within you to be courageous. It's there, even if it's hidden under a big pile of fear. Spend the next few days noticing when your impulse to be courageous crops up. When you are at work and someone is badmouthing a colleague, you might have a twinge inside that is nudging you to stand up for that person. If it sounds like your neighbors are getting into a pretty heated domestic dispute one night, you might feel the impulse to do something to help. Would you have the courage to call the police? Let's say you are taking a college course in literature, and you're pretty proud of the essay you wrote. When the teacher asks if anyone would like to share, do you know what it feels like to have that urge to stand up?

All of those instances are examples of the innate impulse you have to be courageous. Practice recognizing them instead of burying them under your fears. Once you have identified an impulse to be courageous, see what happens if you follow through and act on it. Now that is serious daring!

"It takes a lot of courage to release the familiar and seemingly secure, to embrace the new. But there is no real security in what is no longer meaningful. There is more security in the adventurous and exciting, for in movement there is life, and in change there is power."

Alan Cohen

One of the things that strikes the most fear in people is change. It is very difficult to give up the familiar, even if it's not very good. At least you know what you're getting when you stick with what you've got. It is sort of a paradox, though, because change is actually more stable than staying the same. You can resist change with everything you've got, but you will never be able to maintain your lack of movement for very long.

How is it possible that change is stable? The stability of the world depends on the fact that it is constantly changing. Absolutely nothing on this earth remains the same for very long. So really the one thing you can count on as being permanent is change. There is no security in the status quo. If you believe you are playing it safe by refusing to let go of the familiar, you are wrong. You must update your thinking.

Embrace change. Have the courage to be adventurous, because you only have one ticket for this ride. Success is possible if you have the courage to move forward and embrace the new things that come your way in life. There is nothing secure about hiding in one place and never venturing out to see what the world has to offer.

Dare to change. Have the courage to explore. You will find security in how you evolve when you embrace change with an open mind. You will find power in the courage to release yourself from the familiar.

"Dare to be naïve."

Buckminster Fuller

Will hated feeling naïve. His fear of not being in-the-know could be traced back to a time when his family moved, and he was suddenly the new kid in school. He didn't know the routine of his new classroom, and the kids made fun of his ignorance on several occasions before he caught up. It left him with a feeling of inferiority that he secretly vowed he would try his best to avoid for the rest of his life.

Unfortunately, as Will was striving to become an expert in his field, he also ended up losing a very important ingredient to success—his ability to be teachable. Will wanted to know it all, to always have the answer. He continually demonstrated his knowledge and very seldom listened to new opinions. Therefore, Will left no room to grow. He was fearful of showing any ignorance, so he hid his questions and pretended he knew the answers, even when he didn't.

If Will had had the courage to be naïve, he would have traveled much faster along the road to success. When you are naïve, you are willing to admit you are an empty bucket that is ready to be filled with ideas. It takes courage to drop your ego and dare to be naïve.

Give it a try today. Dare to be naïve. It might feel a little insecure at first, but there will be power behind it, just like there is power behind change. Find out what it's like to be open to suggestions and to admit you don't know the answer. Have the courage to discover rather than instruct.

Day 280

"The best way out is always through."

Robert Frost

One final aspect of courage that will be studied in this section has to do with direction. It takes great courage to plow straight through a problem rather than find a way around it. Have you ever thought about that?

Many of us try to go around problems first. For example, you know your spouse is mad at you for some reason, but rather than asking what's wrong, you avoid them. It would be more courageous to find out from the source what you might have done to upset him or her, and it would probably save a lot of trouble in the future, but very few people take that route first.

Think about the direction you take when faced with an issue. Do you tend to attack it head on, or do you try a dance of avoidance first? Do you prefer detours when you are put in a sticky situation? Pull a couple of instances out of your recent memory and write about how you handled them. In what ways could you have been more courageous in dealing with those situations?

Don't be afraid to analyze your actions and practice a more courageous response the next time you face a similar situation. Successful people are constantly looking for ways they can improve their actions and live more authentically. Stare directly into the eyes of your problems and practice having the courage to deal with them rather than avoid them. The best way out is always through.

"Listening, not imitation, may be the sincerest form of flattery."

Dr. Joyce Brothers

Today your task is to explore how you respond to people around you. Think about how much you learn from the words and actions of others, good and bad. Are you paying attention to what is going on outside of yourself? Do you soak up outside influences, or do you prefer to cast your influence on others?

It's important to strike a good balance between what you take in and what you give off. Think of yourself as a light bulb. You give off light and heat, but you also need to bring in energy (or inspiration) in order to shine. You do not want to be imprudent about who you imitate. Not everyone is living the kind of life you want to emulate. You also do not need to impose your own criteria for successful living on others. They might have different priorities that don't necessarily match your own.

Dr. Joyce Brothers brings up an excellent point in the quote above. Listening may be the sincerest form of flattery. If you truly want to give someone respect, listen to them. You can make your own choices later, but it is almost never a bad idea to hear someone out. You may find you disagree with their views. You don't have to imitate them.

Listen to the people you come in contact with today. Respect their views. Learn from them. It does not mean you have to agree or follow their lead. Practice collecting information and reserve judgment for a later time. "That's interesting," is a great phrase to incorporate into your conversation. It does not mean you concur, but it does mean that you heard the other person's view. Open your ears and close your mouth today.

"Keep away from people who try to belittle your ambitions. Small people always do that, but the really great make you feel that you, too, can become great."

Mark Twain

Far too many individuals believe that they must stomp on the heads of their competition in order to achieve success. That is a completely false assumption. People who are truly successful and comfortable in their talents do not belittle others. They lift them up.

There is not a single first-place trophy that will be bestowed upon one individual at the end of this race. The potential number of people who will achieve success in the world is limitless. Every single one of us can finish first. It is critically important to realize that you do not have to push someone else down in order to pull yourself up the ladder.

You are not truly successful if your accomplishments are made to the detriment of someone else. Do you struggle with that concept? Does your competitive side long to beat out the competition? Address your beliefs starting today. Divide a page in your journal into two columns. In the left column, write down the instances when you belittled others. Did you point out a coworker's mistake without providing a useful alternative? Did you make fun of someone behind their back? Write down every time you remember raising yourself up by putting someone else down. In the right column, put down the times when you lifted someone up. When did you help a friend or encourage a family member? Did you teach anyone a new skill or congratulate them on a job well done? Now, your ongoing task is to increase the right column and decrease the left column.

"Flattery and insults raise the same question: what do you want?"

Mason Cooley

Cameron thought he had it all figured out. He had a very specific plan to climb the corporate ladder, and he took every opportunity to further his career. Cameron stuck his head in the office of his CEO at quarter to eight and congratulated him profusely on winning a new contract. That accomplished two things in Cameron's mind. It showed the CEO he had arrived at work fifteen minutes early, and it also laid on a thick coat of flattery that Cameron hoped would benefit him later. At a lunch meeting, Cameron did everything he could to shoot down a new proposal one of his peers presented. He scoffed and raised numerous questions so that the man was unable to complete a sentence and thoroughly explain his ideas. That accomplished another important task in Cameron's mind — picking off the competition. It was a good day . . . in Cameron's mind.

Was Cameron fooling anybody? Probably not. Flattery and insults are empty of substance. Successful people realize they are useless information and give them very little weight. What did Cameron really want? He wanted to get ahead. He probably didn't really admire his boss. He just wanted to *appear* to admire his work. Cameron also most likely didn't look very closely at his coworker's proposal. He just wanted to make sure his peer didn't get ahead of him in line for a promotion.

Remember that flattery and insults raise one question only, and that is: what do you want? Whether you are receiving them or sending them out, they are worthless. Practice mentally dismissing both whenever and wherever they appear.

"None are more taken in by flattery than the proud, who wish to be the first and are not."

Baruch Spinoza

An actor was interviewed for a national newspaper, and they asked her how she was dealing with the outpouring of praise she received from critics for her recent performance. Her response was enlightening. She said that if she allowed herself to believe the flattery, she would also have to buy in to the insults those same critics bestowed upon her under different circumstances.

Individuals who achieve great success are not affected by flattery — or insults. They develop a strong inner sense of their abilities, and that identity cannot be shaken. Flattery is something that influences those who do not have a strong core, those who wish they are something they are not. If you are confident you are following your destiny and doing your best, then it doesn't matter much what other people say about you.

Don't be concerned with flattery. It doesn't matter. It might be true, and it might just be someone sucking up to you because they want something else. Concentrate your efforts on honoring your gifts. You know what they are. You have done a number of exercises in this book alone to find out what you enjoy and where you excel in life. Are you still traveling toward goals that match your abilities and your passions? Take some time today to reach inward and center yourself. Realign yourself with your dreams if you have gotten off course. Are you on a path that brings out your best talents? Are you honoring your gifts and bringing them out in the open?

"I can spot empty flattery and know exactly where I stand. In the end it's really only my own approval or disapproval that means anything."

Agnetha Fältskog

Agnetha Fältskog is a successful singer who is well known as a member of the popular band ABBA. She is a terrific example of someone who knows exactly where she stands. This woman can spot empty flattery a mile away, and it has no effect on how she views herself or her success.

She points out a very important lesson. In the end, it is your own approval that means the most. Think about that for a moment. If someone lavishes praise on you, but you know deep down that you only gave a small percentage of your abilities, how do you feel about yourself? If you know that you could have done a lot better, then it's difficult to accept or believe that praise.

You are the only one who knows exactly what you are capable of achieving. If you hold back, you will know it. You can choose to pretend to believe flattery, but you always know the truth deep down. In order to live a successful, meaningful, and happy life, you must be authentic. That means you must use your talents and not hold back. How will you feel if you don't achieve overall success, and you know that you could have done better, but instead you chose to listen to empty flattery and quit when you thought you were ahead?

Take another day today to look inside and make sure you are being true to yourself. Are you using all of your talents? Do you approve of the efforts you are making today?

Day 286

"He who dies with the most toys is, nonetheless, still dead."

Unknown

Over the next few days you will be taking a look at what really matters — to you. What are the important things in your life? Are they toys? The quote above suggests that the stuff you collect doesn't really matter much in the end. If that's true, then what does matter?

Let's start this series with an awareness exercise. Make a list of the things you cannot do without. Next, make a list of the things that you enjoy, but you could live without. Finally, make a list of the stuff you probably don't need and wouldn't mind discarding.

After you complete this assignment, take a look at your three lists. What do you notice? Write in your journal about any conclusions you can reach by observing your lists with a critical eye.

When you think about what matters to you, it might also be important to consider whether or not *you* matter to others. Do you feel as though you make a difference? Are you significant to those around you? Write in your journal about how you influence your surroundings, human and otherwise, and what the world would be like if you suddenly went missing. Do you think anyone would notice? How would you be missed?

"Plenty of people miss their share of happiness, not because they never found it, but because they didn't stop to enjoy it."
William Feather

How high does happiness rank on your list of important things? Do you believe you deserve to be happy? Have you received your share of happiness, or are you still waiting for it to show up?

Many people wait their whole life for happiness, and frankly they feel a bit gypped when they see others getting more than their fair share. These people don't realize that happiness has shown up millions of times along their journey, but they never stopped to pick it up.

How do you make sure that you find happiness and scoop it up instead of passing it by? The first step is to be aware. Open your eyes and ears. Pay attention. Joy can be found just about anywhere. It pops up even in some of the most horrible situations. But you have to be looking for it.

Your assignment today is to look for happiness. Actually, don't just look for it as if you were looking for a pair of socks or a lost paper clip. Hunt for it like you are on a safari to find a hidden treasure. Seek out happiness. Find the things that bring you joy, and do them. You don't have to endure a long series of hardships in order to become a success. Part of reaching success has to do with hard work, but no one said it had to be devoid of joy. Happiness is necessary for success, so go out and cultivate it in your life.

"The greatest pleasure in life is doing what people say you cannot do."

Walter Bagehot

Do you really want to get a kick out of life? Then achieve the unattainable. You will receive a huge amount of satisfaction if you attempt the impossible. Work against the odds. You've got nothing to lose, and imagine what you have to gain if you beat them.

Think about the great inventors in history. Just about every one of them was told, "You can't do that!"

They responded with, "Why not?" and kept going anyway.

Adopt an inventor's attitude and find pleasure in doing what people say you cannot do. If you practice that one small change in attitude, you may be very surprised at what happens in your life. Can you imagine the unseen doors that might open?

Have you had any experiences in the past where people told you that you were not capable of doing something? They probably used words like "impossible," "not good enough," and "crazy" to put you in your place. How did you react? How did their words make you feel? Write in your journal about a few of those experiences if you can recall them.

Now is your chance to get even. No one can tell you what you cannot do. You know for a fact that you are the only one on earth who truly knows the power you hold within you. Ignore the naysayers and get to work. It's fun to prove them wrong! Pick up some joy when you mentally thumb your nose at the critics and go ahead and achieve your dreams in spite of their misgivings. Make them jealous. When you attempt things people say you cannot do, you are cultivating success.

"Dwell not on the past. Use it to illustrate a point, then leave it behind. Nothing really matters except what you do now in this instant of time. From this moment onwards you can be an entirely different person, filled with love and understanding, ready with an outstretched hand, uplifted and positive in every thought and deed."

Eileen Caddy

Mistakes people made in the past are heavy burdens that they often continue to carry with them for no apparent reason. They hold on to things that they regret and assume those things define them. The truth is that your past is not that powerful.

Karrie could have easily been characterized as a "mean girl" in high school. She only associated with the most popular students, and she often put down the teens that she considered to be nerds or geeks. She maliciously ruined the reputations of girls who didn't deserve it just because she considered them the competition, and she carried on as if she had no regrets.

The mistakes of her past caught up to Karrie. When she grew up a little, she realized that she didn't like the person she was in high school. Karrie wanted to change, but she felt as though her past defined her. She was a "mean girl," and that was it. Karrie continued to treat people poorly as an adult, because she couldn't let go of her high school image.

Your past is very useful as a teacher, but that's it. You are not your past. You have the opportunity to be anybody you want to be from this point forward. If you want to be kind, all you have to do is change your actions. Leave the past behind. Drop that heavy burden, and step into your true potential.

Day 290

> "There is no room in your mind for negative thoughts. The busier you keep yourself with the particulars of shot assessment and execution, the less chance your mind has to dwell on the emotional. This is sheer intensity."
>
> Jack Nicklaus

The routines that sports figures follow provide great examples of ways to achieve success. If you don't do the work and follow through, then you will lose. Even more importantly, if you don't believe you'll win the game, chances are you won't. If you believe against all odds that you can beat your opponent, you have a pretty good chance of making it happen. The worst player in the league has the potential to beat the number-one person if they believe they can do it. That's not a fairy tale. It has been done.

Many sports psychologists work with athletes in professional sports, the Olympics, and other high-profile venues, and they ask them to visualize sinking the perfect shot or getting the fastest time. They put the athlete's imagination to work and couple that with their training. If they can see it, then they have a chance of accomplishing it.

The exercise of visualization works across all areas where one is striving for success. You have to see your dreams in your mind's eye before you can make them a reality. If you don't believe you can be a success, there is no way it will happen. On the other hand, if you imagine success and visualize how it would look on you, then you start to believe it is not an unattainable goal. When you believe, you have a chance to achieve.

Do you believe you are capable of achieving your dreams? Close your eyes and visualize how it will happen. See your success — then achieve it.

"You cannot change your destination overnight, but you can change your direction overnight."

Jim Rohn

Craig felt completely hopeless. He was buried under a pile of credit-card debt, was two months behind on his mortgage, and to top it off, he had recently been laid off from his job. Success did not look probable. Instead, Craig was on a train headed straight for bankruptcy.

Ever since he lost his job, Craig was frozen in fear. He was afraid to answer his phone, because he was sure it was creditors calling. He didn't want to hang out with his friends. They would see he was a complete failure. In addition, Craig had no idea where to start to look for a new job. He had been with the same company for twenty years and had never even considered looking for a new position elsewhere. The future looked grim.

Sometimes the outlook is pretty scary. It seems as though you are headed for disaster, and there is no way out. Remember that no matter what you are facing, you always have options. You might be teetering on the edge of a cliff, but you can change your direction at any time.

Take a look at your current situation. If you were on a train, where would you be headed? Is it really where you want to go? If not, what can you do to get off at the next station and change direction? In Craig's case, he could alter his route immediately by choosing some positive actions. He could make an appointment with an employment agency or call his creditors and explain his situation. Craig was not out of options. He could choose to continue to live in fear, or he could change direction overnight.

"Opportunity is missed by most people because it is dressed in overalls and looks like work."

Thomas A. Edison

Would you recognize opportunity if it knocked? What do you think it looks like? Unfortunately, opportunity does not look like a shiny new car or a million-dollar house. It looks like work. In other words, an opportunity might come in the form of a friend who needs you to help them with a catering job, an appliance that needs fixing in your own home, or even a local radio contest.

You never know when opportunity is going to show up, but if you are willing to put in a little extra effort—especially when you don't have to—then you might be inviting opportunity in. You can't predict where these seemingly minor tasks will lead you. You might meet a future employer on the night you help your friend with a catering job. You could very well discover a new invention when you're trying to fix a broken appliance. A radio contest might give your new brainstorm just the exposure it needs.

Your assignment today is to actively search for new opportunities. Opportunity almost never looks like a winning lottery ticket or an unexpected inheritance. It is more likely to come to you in the form of something you don't have the time or energy to take on. Nevertheless, seize that opportunity. Do the right thing when someone requires your help or a better solution needs to be worked out. Take the time, and you will reap the benefits.

"Work is either fun or drudgery. It depends on your attitude.
I like fun."

Colleen C. Barrett

You've read several times in this book that achieving success will require some work on your part. Do you sigh and roll your eyes every time the idea of work comes up? Work sounds like, well, work. It doesn't sound like fun. Success sounds like fun! Work sounds boring.

That does not have to be the case. Today you have an opportunity to change your concept of work. It does not have to be drudgery. Work is exhilarating if you're doing something that inspires you and makes you think and grow.

Your assignment is to adopt a new definition of work. Start with your old beliefs. Write down words that describe work that you dislike. You might begin with "boring" and "hard." Next, create a new description of work and start with words like "fun" and "exhilarating." If you dislike work now, change your definition of it so that it is more appealing. Then look for work that fits your new concept.

Now, if you are currently earning a living in a job you intensely dislike, you may associate work with negative concepts. But wait a minute! You chose that job you hate. You can change direction and work at finding a more interesting and fulfilling position. In that case, the word "work" might be a new and exciting opportunity.

You can systematically exchange negative work that you are currently engaged in for more promising work that might help you reach success. Both of them require effort, but one is a whole lot more fun than the other.

"I know the price of success: dedication, hard work, and an unremitting devotion to the things you want to see happen."
Frank Lloyd Wright

This price of success that Frank Lloyd Wright talks about in the quote above involves a wonderful and almost magical kind of work. It's the work that will lead you to straight to success. Can you describe how this type of labor is different from the kind of work that is considered a chore?

One very important difference is conviction. People who attain awe-inspiring goals are almost single-minded in their purpose. They really believe in what they are doing. They feel like they are fulfilling a greater purpose through their exertion. They are excited about it and want to do whatever it takes to see it accomplished.

It is like the difference between climbing a mountain and working on a chain gang. Both tasks require a great deal of effort, but one is awe-inspiring and the other is hell. Not many of us would sign up for a chain gang if it wasn't forced upon us. Similarly, it is likely that you will only be willing to pay the price of success if you are able to find something that inspires you. If you find your passion, then anything can be endured to see it to fruition. You won't care if people tell you it's impossible. You will find superhuman effort within yourself to see it through. That kind of drive and devotion creates the magic you need to become a success. Nothing less will do the trick. Are you willing to go that far?

"Work while you have the light. You are responsible for the talent that has been entrusted to you."

Henri Frederic Amiel

Here is another little spin on work. Work is the utilization of your talent. Talent doesn't just appear on its own. You have to engage it in an activity to bring it out in a useful form. You are responsible for the gifts you have been given. They were entrusted to you. Are you going to waste them, or are you going to use them?

So get to work now while you have the light. You have a responsibility to turn your talents into something the rest of humanity can enjoy. Could you imagine how much we would have missed if Mozart had decided to play billiards all the time instead of writing down the beautiful music he had inside of him? Evidently, he sometimes did both at the same time, but that's beside the point. He had an extraordinary talent, and he was responsible for bringing it into the light. Mozart worked and played with equal ferocity. He was a prolific composer, and he also performed all the time. That kind of schedule probably wasn't a walk in the park, but Mozart must have understood that the gifts that were entrusted to him needed to be shared with the world.

It is your job to use the talents you have. If you are already doing so, it feels pretty good, doesn't it? You know in your soul when you are engaged in something you were meant to do. That's when work is pure joy. If you continue to be unsure of where your true talents lie, get to work on finding out. Journal about your questions and seek the answers. Success is born out of putting your talents to serious work.

Day 296

"Joy is the best make up."

Anne LaMott

Cheryl was bursting with happiness. She finally discovered her true talents after months of searching, and she felt a renewed sense of purpose that invigorated her from the inside out. Cheryl had a lot of work ahead of her, but she was bursting with joy at the thought of taking a new direction. She showed up at work bright and early, and everyone she came across noticed the change. Joy looked great on her! People asked her if she got a haircut, a makeover, a face lift, liposuction—each comment was funnier than the one before. The simple fact was that Cheryl was bursting with happiness. She found joy, and it made her look radiant. No amount of plastic surgery could have done a better job than the makeover she gave herself from the inside out.

Are you finding the joy in your life? Don't despair if you're not quite there yet. Sometimes it takes a little practice. Start with small things. Do old black-and-white movies make you happy? Then rent one tonight. Do you enjoy babysitting your niece or nephew? Call up your sister and make plans to do that sometime very soon. Do you like to cook? Get in the kitchen and get busy. Don't underestimate the power of joy. You don't have to wait for it to come. You can make it happen as often as you want.

If you had a chance to experience even a little bit of joy every day, wouldn't you take it? What's stopping you right now? You can make the conditions right. You deserve to have overwhelming joy in your life. It's the best make up.

"The secret of joy in work is contained in one word—
excellence. To know how to do something well is to enjoy it."
Pearl S. Buck

During the last several days, you've been reading a lot about joy and
work. The best way to combine the two is to strive for excellence.
When your work reaches the definition of excellence, it is of such high
quality that it is exceptional. It is not the norm. You stick out in a
crowd.

That is exactly what you want when you strive to achieve your
dreams. Your ultimate goal is not to make a lot of money. That is a
byproduct. The definitive prize is to achieve excellence. You want
to shine brightly in this world, and you will when you learn how to
do something very well. Let's go over the basic steps on your path
toward excellence. They are the following:

1. Find your passion.

2. Work very hard at learning how to do it extremely well.

3. Experience joy in the excellence you have achieved.

Money and fame will come later. If you find joy in working very hard
on your passions in life, then you will be making a contribution that
is worth recognition and reward. Write down these three basic steps
and stick them on the mirror in your bathroom. Ask yourself if you
are adhering to them every day.

Day 298

"The great teachings unanimously emphasize that all the peace, wisdom, and joy in the universe are already within us; we don't have to gain, develop, or attain them. We're like a child standing in a beautiful park with his eyes shut tight. We don't need to imagine trees, flowers, deer, birds, and sky; we merely need to open our eyes and realize what is already here, who we really are—as soon as we quit pretending we're small or unholy."

Unknown

Every single tool you need for success is already within you. You have everything you need. The greatest deterrent to success is the limitation you place on yourself. You are not small. You are not unholy. You are a unique gift, and no one possesses your particular talents. It is imperative that you stop selling yourself short and start accepting your brilliance.

Find a quiet place today and take your journal with you. Write about your gifts. Close your eyes and visualize the power you hold within you. The tools for success are not hidden somewhere out in the universe. You don't need to go on a long expedition to find them. They are inside of you at this very moment waiting to be put to work. It is so incredibly important to realize and accept that simple fact. You don't have to wonder if you've got the goods to be a success. You do. So you can stop asking that question. You have the answer.

Your task now is to take action. Don't put off your achievements because you are unsure of yourself. Honor the peace, wisdom, and joy that are part of you already. Find out today what you can achieve by using the gifts you already possess.

"Sometimes your joy is the source of your smile, but sometimes your smile can be the source of your joy."

Thich Nhat Hanh

Are you starting to get sick of all this lofty talk about the power you possess within you? Are you just not feeling it? Then today's exercise was created especially for you.

There will be days when you simply don't feel the joy. You know you should be grateful for your talents and working hard to achieve success, but you are not experiencing the happiness inside that you think you should be feeling.

The good news is that happens to everyone. It's hard to maintain a high level of happiness all the time. Emotions dip, and you will hit times when you feel a little blah about the whole endeavor. Those low energy times can be expected, but you can control how long you wallow in them. If you are traveling along the path to success, and you fall in a mud puddle, you decide how long you are going to roll around in it before you get back up and move on.

You do not have to sit and wait for joy to show up. That could take quite a long time. Take action and coax happiness back into your life. The quote above provides one great way to do that. Sometimes joy is the source of your smile. If it's not, then try starting with the smile. That might become the source of your joy.

When you are feeling low, practice being happy. Smile in spite of yourself. Do something nice for someone and enjoy their reaction. Complete a task you've been putting off for months. Find at least one positive thing to do. Joy will come if you coax it.

Day 300

"If you were all alone in the universe with no one to talk to, no one with which to share the beauty of the stars, to laugh with, to touch, what would be your purpose in life? It is other life, it is love, which gives your life meaning. This is harmony. We must discover the joy of each other, the joy of challenge, the joy of growth."

Mitsugi Saotome

Congratulations! You made it to Day 300. Spend some time today considering your journey thus far. Are you making changes in your life? Your metamorphosis started out small, but by now you might be seeing a significant change in yourself.

Write about how you have evolved over the last three hundred days. Do you like the person you are becoming? What else needs to be done to complete the metamorphosis? Do you feel like you're getting ready to spread your wings and take flight, or is fear still holding you on the ground?

You have come a very long way, and there are only sixty-five days left to complete this year-long journey. This milestone is a good time to remember that you are not on this road alone. Your interaction with others is what gives your life meaning. Did you block yourself off from those around you while you were hard at work achieving your dreams?

Think about ways in which you can draw people into your life and discover the joy of each other. This isn't a solo mission. Life is so much richer when you share it with others. Have you been talking about the changes you have experienced with anyone else? Have the people who are close to you noticed a change and asked you what you're up to? Maybe now is the time for you to begin to relate this extraordinary journey to others. Share your recent challenges and growth. You may find friends who have had similar experiences.

"I just wish my mouth had a backspace key."

Anonymous

Who among us hasn't said something we regret at some point in time? It's a horrible feeling, isn't it? It would be nice to install a backspace key somewhere in the mouth area, but until a brilliant mind comes up with that feature, you need to consider other effective remedies. Clean up your poorly chosen phrases, especially those that cause harm to others.

When you spout off to a coworker, a friend, a spouse, or a family member, what do you typically do next? Do you ignore your outburst? Do you pretend it didn't happen? Do you spend the rest of the day trying to talk yourself into the rationalization that you were in the right? Or do you apologize immediately — or eventually?

People who are successful and content with their lives are often those who are quick to remedy their mistakes. It is not a sign of weakness to go back and apologize for something you said. It is a sign of self-awareness and a sign of respect to those around you.

Your assignment today is to be quick to make amends. Own up to your mistakes. If you said something mean to a coworker, go immediately back to their desk and apologize for it. It doesn't really matter if you spoke the truth and your sin was a cruel choice of words. If you hurt someone, make it right, and don't delay. This is not a one-day assignment. Work this pattern into your everyday life by practicing your ability to have some humility and admit to your wrongs. You will make bad word choices from time to time. A successful person finds a way to use the backspace key.

Day 302

"Gather up all your excuses, carry them outside, and bury them deep in the ground. When you're bored of success dig 'em back up."

Seth Simonds

Excuses suck the life out of success. They are absolutely useless on your journey to follow your dreams. In fact, they are major roadblocks. Excuses send you on a detour away from your true destiny, and the crazy thing is you can't blame anyone but yourself for them. You can't shake your fist at some unseen construction worker. You put the big detour sign right in the middle of the road all by yourself when you pulled out an excuse instead of taking action.

The quote above provides a beautiful image. Take all of your excuses and bury them outside. Get rid of them. There is absolutely no reason you will ever need them again. If you decide at some point that you're bored on the road to success, you are more than welcome to dig up an excuse or two, and you'll be back on that detour route. However, if you really mean it when you say you want to achieve your dreams, you must be willing to give up excuses for the long haul.

How often do you replace action with excuses? Pull out your journal and write about that for a half hour or so. Can you think of instances within the last week when you pulled out an excuse instead of taking care of business? Did you decide it was too cold outside to go for that walk? Did you blame traffic for arriving late to work? How many excuses did you utilize in the last seven days? Try to come up with a comprehensive list. Then make a plan to reduce the number of excuses you utilize in the week to come.

"If you're not failing every now and again, it's a sign you're not doing anything very innovative."

Woody Allen

Failure has been a topic to ponder in previous months, and now you have a chance to look at it again as it relates to your success. Today you will take a little time to solidify some of your new views on how success and failure depend on each other.

Failure is not optional if you want to achieve success. It is an important ingredient of achievement. As Woody Allen states in the quote above, if you don't fail, then maybe you're not doing anything very interesting or innovative. If you want to break new ground, you must be willing to fail. Go toward failure fearlessly. It's actually desirable to fail every once in awhile. Unlike excuses, failure is not a detour. It is like getting a special jet pack to propel you toward your dreams at a faster rate.

Why is failure an important aspect of success? Write your answer to that question today in your journal. You may come up with a number of different responses. If you're not convinced failure is an integral part of achieving success, then write about your doubts.

It is a tricky thing to learn. The opposite words play with your mind. You think you want one but not the other. But failure will point you in the right direction to achieve success. When you find out what doesn't work, you've narrowed down the scope of possible solutions. You also find energy in the pursuit of your dreams, and failure is a kind of fuel that drives you toward your ultimate goal. A thousand failures will lead you to ultimate success. Can you say the same about excuses?

Day 304

"Problems are not stop signs, they are guidelines."

Robert Schuller

There are three types of people in this world: problem seekers, problem solvers, and problem see-ya-laters. Which one are you?

A problem seeker is someone who likes drama. They thrive in chaos and seem to attract plenty of it. You know who you are. You think life is boring if it's in balance. You point out the difficulties in your life in order to define who you are and why you have not yet achieved your dreams.

A problem solver is a person who enjoys balance and finds excitement in making the puzzle pieces fit together. They are happiest when providing the answers, not creating more questions. It drives a problem solver crazy to leave things open-ended. The problem solver sounds like the star pupil, but sometimes they are afraid to venture into new territory. They try to be content with the puzzle they've completed.

The problem see-ya-later personality is probably one we've all visited at some point in time. This person simply hides from problems. If you ignore it, maybe someone else will take care of it . . . or it will go away. Is that a problem over there? See ya later!

Think about these three types of people and then examine how you deal with problems in your life. Are problems guidelines for future action? Or do you look at a problem and see a stop sign? Do you attack problems, attract problems, or run for cover whenever you see one coming at you?

"Fault finding is like window washing. All the dirt seems to be on the other side."

Unknown

Fault finding is another sure way to ruin success. If you find fault in others, you give away your power. If all the grime is on the other side of the window, you have to wait for someone over on that side to clean it up before you get a clear view. Do you really have the time or the desire to sit there looking at dirt until someone else takes action?

Let's be honest for a moment. There is something about human nature that makes us feel momentarily very good when we shift the blame to someone else. Your tax guy screwed up the accounting numbers, and that's why you're being audited. It's not your fault! Whew. Nevertheless, you're still going to owe the government a huge fee when it all gets straightened out.

If a big rock sits in the middle of your road to success, it really doesn't matter who put it there. You're not going to get to your ultimate goal until you move it. Stop worrying about where to put the blame, and start working on a solution. That is how you achieve success.

Have you ever taken responsibility for something that wasn't your fault? If you haven't, give it a try. It's a strangely powerful feeling. Taking the high road and working on a solution feels ten times better than shifting the blame to someone else. Your assignment is to reduce the number of times you find fault in others and increase the occasions when you take responsibility and take action.

Day 306

"The most important trip you may take in life is meeting people halfway."

Henry Boye

Katy felt like she had run into a brick wall on her road to success. She was in a midlevel corporate job, and she didn't feel like she had a lot of respect from her underlings or her superiors. She was stuck and having difficulty building her success.

What Katy did to become unstuck was revolutionary. Instead of concentrating on her personal achievement and finding ways to stick out as an individual, she started to take a critical look at how she worked with others. Katy realized that she was very seldom willing to meet people halfway. She did not like compromise. If she had a great idea for a new project, she tended to have a take-it-or-leave-it attitude about the whole thing. She discounted any new concepts that her coworkers tried to add to the plan, because they didn't mesh completely with her vision.

Once Katy was aware of this character trait, she started to practice compromise. She intently listened to new ideas and worked to incorporate the suggestions of others into a common solution. Suddenly, she wasn't stuck anymore. Katy started to shoot up the corporate ladder, and she also gained the respect of others in her company. They began to view Katy as a collaborator instead of a dictator.

Is there something you can take away from Katy's experience? Are you good at meeting people halfway, or do you have more of a take-it-or-leave-it attitude? What can you practice today that will bring compromise into your life as a tool for success?

"Compromise is but the sacrifice of one right or good in the hope of retaining another—too often ending in the loss of both."

Tryon Edwards

Yesterday you read a bit about the positive side of compromise. However, there is also a negative side to consider. It would be far too easy to say that compromise as a general rule is a great idea. It isn't all the time.

A compromise is usually a settlement of differences where each party makes some concessions to meet in the middle and find a common solution. It is also thought to be the halfway point between two extremes. It is the balancing point. On the other hand, compromise is a negative when it has to do with giving in to the pressures of others. For instance, it's usually not a great idea to compromise your principles.

Do you compromise even when it comes to the things that you feel very passionately about? Have you ever compromised your ethical or spiritual beliefs?

Come up with some personal examples of compromise—good and bad—and write about them in your journal today. Think about the areas where you are willing to compromise and the areas where your ideas and beliefs are very strong and you would not be willing to compromise. It is very important for you to know where you stand on these issues. If you have a fervent belief, then it's okay if you're not willing to compromise. Maybe the strength of your convictions will draw people to your views. That is a leadership quality, as well.

"Compromise is the essence of diplomacy; and diplomacy
is the cornerstone of love."

Unknown

Today you will have another chance to look at the positive aspects
of compromise. Compromise is a very useful tool for diplomacy. But
wait a minute, why do you need to be diplomatic if you're rising to
the top of the heap? As you know after spending nearly a year on the
subject, you cannot reach success or maintain it on your own.

Success is not about conquering a foe and ruling alone. You do not live
on this earth by yourself, and therefore an integral part of success is
learning to respect others and live and work with them in a mutually
beneficial way. Compromise is a very important part of living in
harmony with the people around you.

What do you think about the statement above? It takes it one step
further and says diplomacy is the cornerstone of love. When you are
willing to give up something and meet someone halfway, it shows
that person that you value them. Their views have meaning to you,
and you are willing to give up some piece of your own self to take
them into account. That is love in action.

Compromise isn't always about giving up something that is important
to you; it can also be about giving to someone outside of yourself.
Brainstorm ways that you can use compromise to honor the important
people in your life. Follow through on at least one of those ideas this
week.

"Never cut short your waiting with compromise. Simply put, the waiting's not over until the waiting's done."

Duke Rohe

Here is an example of a kind of compromise that is deadly to your success — the shortcut compromise. If you give up on your original goal and settle for something that isn't as wonderful but can be obtained faster, then you will linger waiting for ultimate success forever. Shortcuts don't work when your goal is to achieve your dreams.

For example, let's say you really want to become a doctor, but then you find out how much time it would take to obtain your degree. You're impatient to taste success. You don't want to wait that long to get your reward. So instead you look into becoming a medical assistant.

Now, there is absolutely nothing wrong with being a medical assistant. It is a very worthy profession and requires quite a bit of talent. However, if you chose it simply because you would get that degree quicker than you would get an MD, then you are compromising your success. You are picking an easier, faster solution and not owning up to your true potential.

Your assignment today is to be willing to wait. Success is almost never immediate. You have to be willing to put in the work, and then you have to be willing to wait for it. Don't be lured by temptations that look like they will get you to the finish line faster. They will not fulfill your dreams.

"Some people never learn the art of compromise. Everything is either black or white. They do not recognize, or will not concede, that the equally important color gray is a mixture of black and white."

Waite Phillips

Today you have one more chance to spend some time considering the art of compromise. It is just that—an art.

Imagine if you were an artist, and you were only allowed to use pure black and pure white in your color scheme. It wouldn't give you a lot of choices for shading and contour, would it? How will you make your work come to life and give it dimension?

Compromise incorporates the equally important color gray into your life, and suddenly you see depth. You experience what was once a two-dimensional object in 3D. The black and white are still present, but when they combine, they offer additional opportunities for a creative mind.

If you are willing to give up a few of your stubborn notions through the art of compromise, then you make room for new thoughts and different perspectives to emerge and become part of your palette. A fresh outlook may completely change the scope of your reality and take you places you couldn't imagine when you were stuck in your black-and-white world.

Your assignment today is to remove a few of your preconceived notions and make room for new ideas. Be willing to compromise when the opportunity presents itself. Try something new. Dabble in colors you haven't used before, and find out what you've been missing.

"Time is fun when you are having flies."

Kermit the Frog

What do you do for fun? Kermit likes flies, but he's a frog. What makes you happy? Have you taken time out recently to do some of the things that make you smile? Taking time off for fun is not a luxury. It's mandatory if you want to achieve your dreams. Your dream for success is probably filled with happiness. So it doesn't make sense that the road to success should be filled with drudgery. You have to experience a little levity along the route if happiness is your goal.

There is no truth to the myth that you have to work like crazy and have no fun in order to reach the upper levels of success. You need to balance hard work with joyful play. So what's it going to be today? A hike in the woods? Ice cream? Playing basketball? A road trip? A game with your five-year-old nephew? Schedule your fun time with equal reverence as the time you set aside for work. It is no less important. Do something that makes you really happy today.

Make a list in your journal of all the things you can think of that would be fun to do at this very moment. Don't limit yourself to affordability, time, or location. Let your mind enjoy the exercise. Come back to this list often and add to it whenever you are feeling weighed down by your work responsibilities. Make sure you do some of the things on that list. The assignment isn't over until you've given a few of those ideas a whirl. Take time to have your flies. Life is too short to save up all of the fun for the final chapters.

Day 312

"If it's not fun, you're not doing it right."

Bob Basso

You have studied the importance of fun in your life throughout this book. There is a reason for that. Nobody wants to spend their days toiling away. That is no way to achieve your dreams. We all need a little softness and light to balance out the hard stuff.

Spend some time today going back through your dreams for success. You have written about them a number of times in your journal. What do those dreams look like to you? Are they full of misery and pain? That is highly doubtful. Dreams are happy, fun, joyful, and hopeful. If for some reason your dreams are not full of fun, then you're not doing this right. Throw away your journal, and start over at Day 1.

What do you really want?

Most of us just want to be happy when we get to the core of our dreams. You can obtain some happiness today—right now if you want. Just do something fun. This does not have to mean quitting your job and spending your life savings on a trip to Disney World.

Stop your chores for five minutes and play with the family pet. Read a funny story on the Internet. Listen to your favorite music. Look at a piece of artwork that fills your heart. None of those things cost money, and they all invite a little fun into your life. That fun is like getting an infusion of energy, and you will be better equipped to go back to the tasks you want to complete today. Life should be fun every day. If it's not, you have no one to blame but yourself. You control the joy you let into your life. If it's not fun, you're not doing it right.

"People rarely succeed unless they have fun at what they are doing."

Dale Carnegie

Lee absolutely hated his life. He hated his job, he hated his car, he hated his house, and he wasn't that fond of his dog, either. He was a brilliant engineer specializing in robotics, and he had used his talents to rocket to a pretty lofty height in his profession. Now he found himself as an upper level manager. He was no longer building robots. Instead, his job was to tell other people what they were doing wrong when they built robots—at least that's how he saw his job.

He was outwardly successful, but Lee was not having any fun. He liked building robots, and his job no longer required that skill. He liked people, but he spent most of his day on the computer in his spacious office and his evenings in a big, empty house out in the suburbs. He liked dogs. His best buddy growing up was a mutt his parents rescued from the local shelter. But a former girlfriend got him a purebred something-or-other, and it was high maintenance and no fun at all.

Lee was not a success. He made a lot of money, and he owned a few things that gave him the appearance of being a successful person. However, Lee didn't have fun in any aspect of his life. He had not yet achieved his dreams.

"A well-composed book is a magic carpet on which we are wafted to a world we cannot enter in any other way."

Caroline Gordon

You've had a chance to consider some of the ways in which you can incorporate fun into your life, and you have your own list of activities from which to choose. The quote above suggests a cheap form of entertainment that may not have made it to your list yet. It is a magical opportunity for fun that is often underrated: reading.

You may not have the cash or the vacation days available to take a trip to Spain or France, but you can pick up a copy of *The Sun Also Rises* by Ernest Hemingway and fly away to the bullfights and festivals without leaving your living room.

Reading is fun, it's a form of entertainment, and it is also a very easy way to get your creative juices flowing. When you read, you transport yourself into a world that the author suggests and you inhabit through your own imagination and life experiences. The words have the power to transform you. Reading is a great way to spark new and innovative ideas, because it takes you out of your immediate surroundings. The altered perspective works like a kaleidoscope to change a picture you thought you knew into something fresh when seen through the creative eyes of the author.

What do you like to read? Do you prefer mysteries, romance novels, or history books? Maybe you enjoy short stories or magazine articles instead of full-length novels. There is an endless variety of reading material out there. Your assignment today is to take some time to read.

"If you obey all the rules, you miss all the fun."

Katharine Hepburn

Today let's begin with a quick check-up. Have you followed through with your compromise plan from Day 308? Did you find a way to use compromise to honor someone who is important to you? If you have not completed that assignment yet, today is the day to do it. Get to work! If you have, congratulations! How did it feel?

What do you think about today's quote? Is breaking the rules on your list of things to do for fun? If it isn't, maybe you should add it. This is not a suggestion to become a criminal. It simply points out that sometimes it's really fun to break the rules.

When Kevin was six years old, his parents had a rule in the house that eight o'clock was bedtime. However, whenever his Uncle Steve came over to babysit him, they broke the rules and stayed up late watching movies and eating popcorn. The two of them had a great time "being bad," and as far as Kevin knew, his parents never found out. Kevin is an adult now, and the times he broke the rules and stayed up late with his uncle are precious, happy memories.

Your assignment today is *not* to obey all the rules. You can certainly think of a few more subversive examples of rule breaking than Kevin's beautiful childhood story. Remember, you're not looking for an arrest record — but have fun. You won't get a gold star at the end of your journey if you followed every single rule. There is no award for that. Let loose and disobey a rule now and again. If you don't, you'll miss some of the fun.

"Life is change. Growth is optional. Choose wisely."

Karen Kaiser Clark

Change is not an option. The world will continue to change and evolve whether you want it to or not. Growth, however, is an entirely different matter. That one is up to you.

Jackie's life was in a constant state of flux. She was a salesperson, and her territory changed all the time. New and exciting opportunities landed in her lap almost daily. On the other hand, her sales numbers remained flat. She had accumulated years of experience as a salesperson, but she did not learn and grow from the knowledge she had collected. Jackie continued to repeat the same mistakes and miss the same types of opportunities. She refused to grow, and therefore she chopped off her success at the knees.

Life is change, and that's one of the beautiful aspects of it. Every day you will have new opportunities for success in an ever-evolving world. If you feel stuck now, wait a little while, and things will alter to provide you with an opening to a new path you never considered before.

Growth is optional, so pay attention if you want to achieve your dreams. Are you growing? Do you continually take in new information, process it, and use it to build your success? Gulp down those nutrients all around you, and change your life for the better.

Your assignment today is to think about whether or not you are using every opportunity you have to grow. Are you constantly learning? Do you pay attention to others? Do you observe as much as you perform? Growth is optional. Choose wisely.

"You've got to do your own growing, no matter how tall your grandfather was."

Irish Saying

Before looking at today's quote, it's time to check in on a previous assignment. How are you doing with your Reality Check Day assignment from Day 257? Your assignment was to initiate Reality Check Day once a week for two months and find out if it helped inspire you to push harder and strive to give just a little bit more than average effort. Did this assignment affect your output? Did you find yourself pushing harder than usual toward success? Write about the results in your journal.

Now, let's turn to today's quote. It actually coincides with Reality Check Day. The reality is you have to do your own growing. No one can take on that assignment for you. It doesn't matter if you were born into wealth and privilege. You can't rely on what has been given to you or the work completed by someone else who came before you. Anyone can give you money or things, but you have to develop knowledge and respect and compassion and all of the things that come together to make a successful person on your own. Success is not something you can outsource. It grows from the inside out.

Are you growing? Or are you leaning on the reputation of your father, mother, grandparent, boss, coworker, or friend? Take responsibility for your success today. It's time for you to grow.

Day 318

"Growth begins when we accept our own weakness."

Jean Vanier

When a plant becomes weak, it needs something to regain its strength—usually water or sunlight. Can you imagine what would happen if a plant didn't accept water or if it hid from the sun? It would wither and die. A plant needs those things in order to grow. When it takes them in—when it accepts them—it thrives.

What do you need in order to grow and achieve success? Have you developed a list? Your weaknesses should be on that list. Weaknesses are not shortcomings. They are opportunities for growth. Develop a list today of the things you need to grow and achieve your dreams.

Is education an area where you are weak? Great! Put it on the list and start to consider your options for education, so that you can grow and build your strength in that area.

What about your health? Is it a challenge for you to eat right and exercise? Write that down. Then look for a solution that will help you to turn around your bad habits and incorporate diet and exercise into your life.

Are connections a weakness? Do you feel like you just don't know the right people in your desired field? Put it on the list. Then brainstorm about clubs or associations you can join that will help you meet the appropriate mentors to guide you on your path.

Pinpoint your weaknesses, and then use them as opportunities to grow.

"There are no such things as limits to growth, because there are no limits to the human capacity for intelligence, imagination, and wonder."

Ronald Reagan

Guess what? Good news! There are absolutely no limits to your growth potential. You can be a giant in the area of success, and your growth only stops when you say so. Growth is not rationed out to each individual like a morsel of food in a soup kitchen. You can be a complete glutton when it comes to growth opportunities. Eat them up. Consume everything you can get your hands on.

You will never reach a point where you are done learning, where you have sopped up all of the intelligence in the universe, and there is nothing left that you don't know. Thank goodness! That means life will never be boring, unless you shut yourself off to growth opportunities. Your capacity for intelligence, imagination, and wonder is infinite.

Your assignment today is to respect the infinite human capacity for growth. Take some time out to learn something new. Study an interesting tidbit of history on the Internet. Learn a new phrase in a foreign language. Work a crossword puzzle. Look up at the stars and wonder about the universe. Use your imagination to create a new bedtime story for your children. Expand your growth potential in some way, and revel in the knowledge that you can do this a million different ways for the rest of your life, and you will never reach capacity.

Day 320

"Conformity is the jailer of freedom and the enemy of growth."

John F. Kennedy

Ty moved from a small town in Wyoming to a suburb of Boston with his family. He was a junior in high school, and he stuck out in his new school. They treated him like he was from another planet. The students all dressed pretty much alike. They looked to Ty as if they were about to spend the day at the yacht club. Ty showed up in cowboy boots and a western-style shirt. He did not conform in any way to their unspoken dress code, and at first he drew quite a few stares and some immature comments.

Luckily, Ty was pretty comfortable with himself, especially for a teenager. He was content with his clothes, and he had no intention of changing his style just because he was in a new location. Within a month or two, cowboy boots started to show up as a new fashion trend in his school.

How often do you conform to your surroundings? Do you tend to follow the lead of others and imitate what they do, or are you the one who sets the trend?

Conformity can really slow down your growth. You stop thinking for yourself when you conform. Instead, you follow the decisions someone else made for you rather than coming to your own conclusions and making your own choices. Write in your journal today about the ways in which you conform to societal pressures. What changes can you make in your daily life to lessen your conformity and increase your opportunity for growth?

"Solitude is as needful to the imagination as society is wholesome for the character."

James Russell Lowell

There are times when it's good to be around other people, and there are times when you need to be alone. Both will help you to grow in different ways. Do you have a good balance between the time you spend participating in society and the time you spend in solitude? Some people are the life of the party, but they're afraid to be alone. Others are very uncomfortable in social situations, but they cherish their alone time. Where do you fall on that continuum?

Draw a line on a piece of paper and write "social butterfly" on one end of the line and "hermit" on the other end. Then draw a big X on where you think you fall along that line. Do you enjoy solitude more than companionship, or is it the other way around? It is important to make an honest diagnosis of where you sit right now before you start to even think about making any possible adjustments.

Next, start a new page in your journal and write down all of the advantages of taking an active part in society. Act as if you have just become the PR representative for society, and you have to come up with a new ad campaign. What are the best things about having the ability to interact with others? Then turn the page and do the same thing for solitude. You are now on the solitude campaign. What's so great about being alone? Talk up all of the advantages of taking some time for yourself.

Solitude and society are partners in your journey toward success. Take some time today to explore the advantages of each of them.

Day 322

"If you don't like being in your own company, what makes you think others will?"

Anonymous

A very important part of being comfortable in your own skin is to be able to spend time alone without going crazy. Does it make you uncomfortable to spend time alone? Maybe you would love five minutes to yourself, but you don't know when that will happen because your life is packed full of people and obligations.

The importance of solitude cannot be stressed enough. You have to nourish your soul by giving yourself some breathing room every once in awhile. The best way to do that is to spend a few moments alone.

It doesn't matter whether you are comfortable with solitude or not, you must make it a part of your weekly — if not daily — routine. If you enjoy your solitude already, then this will be a fun exercise. If you are afraid to be alone, it will get easier with practice. You will have a much more difficult time achieving your dreams if you don't take the time to reach inward and spend some minutes in your own company.

Your assignment is to find at least ten minutes every day to be alone. If you live in a busy household, that might mean setting your alarm ten minutes early or staying up a little while after everyone has gone to sleep. Why is this so important?

If you are asking that question, then you probably haven't stopped and taken the time to get to know *you*. Don't you think it might be a good idea to interview the main character? As the quote above suggestions, if you don't like being in your own company, what makes you think someone else will?

"A solitude is the audience chamber of God."

Walter Savage Landor

Today you have another opportunity to consider the advantages of spending some time in solitude. When you are alone, you aren't truly alone. You are spending time with God.

You don't have to be a believer to feel the power of this statement. God can be anything you want it to be. God may be the power of the universe or the power of the potential that lies within you. God might be all of the things you have yet to learn. You get to pick your image or understanding of God when you spend time alone. No one will tell you you're doing it wrong.

When you sit in solitude, you get to tap into your intuition and let your dreams flow without being inhibited by the influence of others. You get to taste your true potential when you spend time alone. If you are skeptical, practice being by yourself and see what happens. Many people find that some of their greatest innovations float to the surface when they take the time to seek out a quiet place to be by themselves for awhile. Solitude also allows you to slow down for just a moment. It's incredibly refreshing to stop doing for awhile and just be.

Your assignment is to spend at least twenty minutes alone today and ponder your own understanding of God. Enjoy your solitude.

"We live in a very tense society. We are pulled apart . . . and we all need to learn how to pull ourselves together . . . I think that at least part of the answer lies in solitude."

Helen Hayes

Sophia lived the life of a typical working mother in the twenty-first century. Her day was a swirl of cell phones, computers, commuting, kids, and family. Her hectic schedule was not unique. Sophia's fears and hopes were much the same as anyone else's. But Sophia seemed a little more "together" than her counterparts at corporate meetings and soccer games. What was her secret? It was a love affair . . . with solitude. She made a date with solitude every single day.

Helen Hayes makes a very good point in the quote above. We live in a tense society. Thanks in part to technology, we are capable of rocketing through life at lightning speed. Our speedy society also has the power to pull us in a million different directions at once. A whole host of distractions compete for our attention at any given minute.

The good news is that there is a solution, and that solution is solitude. Sophia spent at least thirty minutes every morning by herself. Sometimes she listened to music, other times she read a book, and every once in awhile she just listened to her own breathing. She used that quiet time to pull herself together, to take the scattered pieces of her life and collect them again so that she felt whole. When she took some time to be alone each morning, she was given a gift of serenity and a new inner power to face the day.

Have you incorporated some alone time into your schedule yet? If you haven't, make it a priority today. You may be very surprised to find out how it affects the rest of your day.

"Solitude never hurt anyone. Emily Dickinson lived alone, and she wrote some of the most beautiful poetry the world has ever known . . . then went crazy as a loon."

Matt Groening, *The Simpsons*,
spoken by the character Lisa Simpson

For the last several days you've heard about the advantages of solitude. Today you will have a chance to entertain your thoughts on the negative side effects of spending too much time alone. Even a good idea can go bad if you take it too far.

The quote above is funny, but it also has a bit of truth hidden within the humor. Spending some time alone is healthy. Spending too much time alone can make you crazy as a loon.

Your assignment is to take a few weeks and find the right balance for you. Jot down some notes in your journal every day about the percentage of time you spend with others and the percentage of time you spend alone. Then rate the success of your day. Did you feel annoyed at the end of the day, because it seemed like everyone was bothering you all the time? Did you long for a little quiet time? Or did you find yourself talking to the cat one afternoon, because you had not seen another human in several days?

Pay attention to the days that feel balanced and happy, and look at what you did to make that day successful. If you simply jot down a few notes each day, you will probably see a pattern emerge. You know intuitively what you need to stay healthy and sane. Pay attention to your internal warning signs, and then take charge of your schedule and create the environment that works best for you.

Day 326

"Don't you wish there was a knob on the TV to turn up the intelligence? There's one marked 'Brightness,' but it doesn't work."

Gallagher

Today you have an opportunity to look at those nasty little habits that tend to suck your time, energy, and intelligence. Any initial thoughts on what those might be? Make a list of the activities you take part in that probably send you on a detour away from your success.

This is not a case for cutting all of the fun out of your life. In order to achieve success you do not have to be constantly working. Time for rest and relaxation is just as important as the time you spend actively building your achievements. However, there is a thin line between relaxation and procrastination. It's important to choose your downtime activities wisely so that they don't suck the life out of your dreams.

One big time-sucker is television. It's great for a diversion, but it can put you in a trance if you're not careful. Another black hole is the Internet. Again, it's a useful tool in some respects but a complete waste of time if you cross the line to listlessly surfing the net. Technology is a powerful part of our society. On the other hand, it is easy to become a zombie when you're clicking through 200 channel options on TV or sifting through over two million responses to a Google search on "things to do when you're bored."

Your assignment today is to find fun things to do that don't sap your talent and energy. What might spark your creativity instead of sucking it out of you?

"Stop the mindless wishing that things would be different. Rather than wasting time and emotional and spiritual energy in explaining why we don't have what we want, we can start to pursue other ways to get it."

Greg Anderson

George couldn't concentrate. He sat at his desk staring at a pile of work that got bigger and bigger as the days and weeks went on, but he couldn't bring himself to dive in and take care of business. He wasn't sure when it started—and he was in a panic about when it would end—but there was a tape in his mind replaying the missed opportunities of his life over and over again. George felt useless and hopeless. Why even bother? If only things had been different.

Have you ever felt like George? It can be extremely difficult to shake yourself free of that kind of despair. Do you want a minute? Okay, time's up. Now get back to work!

Sitting around and wishing that things would be different serves absolutely no useful purpose. It's a waste of your time. Stop it. It really doesn't matter how you "feel" at this particular moment. If you want things to change, you have to actually do something. Try a new workout at the gym, work late and get ahead a little, or do something nice for someone else without expecting anything in return to snap out of your rut.

If what you are doing right now is not working, and you aren't finding the success you dreamed about, then do something else! If you're anything like George, it certainly can't get worse. Pursue a new strategy. You are only stuck if you want to be. You have two choices: continue to play the "poor me" tape, or change. What will it be?

"Time is the coin of your life. It is the only coin you have, and only you can determine how it will be spent. Be careful lest you let other people spend it for you."

Carl Sandburg

Have you ever watched children pick out a special item at the store? Jonelle recently took her daughter to redeem a gift card at a local toy store, and a ten-minute errand turned into a very detailed assessment of possibilities that took no less than forty-five minutes. Jonelle was a bit impatient as she watched her daughter survey every toy and take her time to come to the best possible decision, but she actually could have learned something from the little girl. Her daughter had a valuable gift, and she wanted to spend it wisely.

Do you spend your time with the same kind of care? Most people do not. Very often, time is given little value. It is wasted on meaningless activities and given away to people who are undeserving. The tragedy about that is you can't get time back. You lose a little every second.

Your assignment today is to answer a few questions:

1. Are you in control of your time?

2. Do you spend your time wisely?

3. Who or what gets the majority of your time?

After you have had a chance to answer those questions, think of time as a precious and fleeting commodity. Is there anything you want to change about how you spend it?

"Regret for wasted time is more wasted time."

Mason Cooley

Hopefully, yesterday's reflection did not send you into a tailspin of despair over the time you've wasted. It was meant to heighten your awareness, not bring you grinding to a halt. Here is the catch: you waste even more time if you sit around feeling bad about the time you wasted.

What is the solution? Action. (You have probably learned by now that action is almost always the solution.) Stop regretting and start moving. What can you do today to increase the value of your time? Start by making a list of the top ten most wonderful ways to spend it. What are the most valuable things you have done with your minutes? Unfortunately, there is no roll-over plan in real life, so you should really pick the best of the best. Is it playing with your children? Volunteering? Creating something new? Hiking in the woods? Reading a great book? You decide.

Spend some time today writing down valuable ways to spend your time. Then put your journal away, and do the things on your list. Journaling will help give you direction, but no amount of writing or wishing will get the job done. Take action.

Stop wasting time. Use it today as if it were more precious than gold or jewels or even ultimate success. Time is not unlimited, and it slips out of your grasp faster than you think.

Day 330

"A single day is enough to make us a little larger."

Paul Klee

For the past several days, you have considered the tragedy of wasted time. Today, you will have an opportunity to look at a slightly more positive spin on the concept. Time gives you limitless possibilities. Time is opportunity.

You have an opportunity every single day to follow your dreams. If today ends up being a bad day, tomorrow you have a brand new opportunity to shape your destiny. You can start over at any point in life and change your circumstances for the better. You don't have to wait until you circle back to the starting line. You can call a do-over right now, if you want. Did you have a bad morning? Change it. Take control of this moment and change the way your day is shaping up. You, and no one else, are charting the course of your life.

Today is enough to start the process. As the quote above states, a single day is enough. What do you want to do to make yourself just a little bit larger? Do you want to learn a new skill? Do you want to practice kindness?

You can also change someone else's life in a single day. You can make them smile if they are feeling down or helping them with a task that is difficult. What else can you do in a day? Put yourself in the superhero mode that you practiced way back on Day 21. What incredible things can you accomplish in just one day? Stretch yourself. Remove your limits. Find out what you're really capable of achieving.

"Personally I'm always ready to learn, although I do not always like being taught."

Sir Winston Churchill

Are you teachable? That might not be as easy to answer as you think. Sometimes pride gets in the way. It's a wonderful feeling of empowerment when you get to teach someone else. Sharing your knowledge feels good. However, when you are on the receiving end, do you gracefully accept help and become a good student? Or do you turn away a potential teacher because you don't want to admit they know more than you do?

Winston Churchill makes an interesting point in the quote above. You can be ready to learn at any time but not always enjoy being taught. Why is that? Some people feel like it puts them in an inferior position, or they just don't like people telling them what to do. They would rather struggle to learn a skill through their own personal study than talk to an expert and learn faster in a one-on-one situation.

How do you learn? Do you prefer the do-it-yourself method, or are you willing to accept help from someone who has more knowledge on a particular subject than you do? Write in your journal today about the most effective ways that you learn. Think about whether or not you slow down your success when you don't accept help from someone who would like to teach you.

Pride is a roadblock on your road to achievement. Practice accepting help, and remove that obstacle from your journey.

"Swallow your pride occasionally, it's non-fattening!"

Unknown

Today you will have an opportunity to continue to work on pride as an obstacle to success. One of the hardest things to do is swallow your pride. On the other hand, if you can manage to do it, you will see terrific results — and it's non-fattening!

Make a list of the times that you have had to swallow your pride. Write extensively about one of your experiences. Next, make a list of future opportunities you might have to swallow your pride and then detail the positive things that might come out of taking that action.

At ninety years old, Leroy knew that he was no longer a good driver. He still had a valid license, but his eyesight had gone bad, and he wasn't as quick to react to hazardous driving conditions as he used to be. It was a very difficult task, but Leroy finally swallowed his pride and admitted to his daughter that he didn't think he should drive anymore. It felt like defeat at first, but Leroy's daughter was impressed with his ability to acknowledge the fact that things had changed. She was proud of him for being strong enough to do the right thing. As it turned out, Leroy's daughter took the time to drive him where he needed to go, and their relationship deepened when they had more time to spend together in the car.

Swallowing your pride is not a failure. It can be an example of strength of character. Learn to swallow your pride occasionally — it's non-fattening!

"Generosity is giving more than you can, and pride is taking less than you need."

Kahlil Gibran

Sometimes a little bit of pride isn't such a bad thing. Vicki was out of a job and looking for work. She finally swallowed her pride and went to a local shelter where they were handing out gently used clothes in addition to a hot meal. Other women were snatching up as many items as they could carry, but Vicki only took one thing: a navy suit that would give her a professional appearance as she interviewed for new jobs. Vicki needed clothes badly, but she took less than what she needed in order to leave some clothes for other women. Her pride in this case turned into an act of generosity.

Two years later, Vicki went back to that shelter. The blue suit had helped her to land a respectable job at a local firm. She had worked hard, learned everything she could about the business, and had eventually built her way up to a lower management position. Vicki was successful, but she still didn't have a lot of clothes. She kept barely what she needed to get by and then bought new clothes to give to the shelter that had helped her when she was in need. Vicki also volunteered at the shelter, cooking meals three times a week. She had become a success, and her generosity increased right along with her achievements.

Your assignment today is to give more than you can and take less than you need. Think of others before yourself. You will soon see that a big dose of generosity and a small dose of pride are very useful tools to help you achieve your dreams.

"Pride makes us artificial and humility makes us real."

Thomas Merton

Take a look at the quote above and write in your journal for at least thirty minutes about your thoughts on it. Create your own definition of pride and your own definition of humility, and journal about the advantages and disadvantages of each. Try to keep your pen moving at all times to allow your stream-of-consciousness thinking to ramble on without censorship. When you are finished, read through what you wrote. What were some of the major themes?

Let's take a look at pride first. How does pride make you artificial? Do you believe when you are full of pride that you have an accurate view of yourself? It may be possible that you give yourself a little too much credit when you are in a prideful state of mind. Some people would define pride as healthy self-respect, while others consider it to be an overly high opinion of oneself. How do you define pride?

Now, let's take a look at humility. Many definitions of the word are not flattering. Humility is sometimes equated with meekness, lowliness, and having a submissive nature. That doesn't sound like someone who is reaching for success. Another definition of humility is lacking false pride or having modesty. Those might be useful traits. In the quote above, Thomas Merton says humility makes us real. Humility could simply be an acceptance of your shortcomings. No one is perfect. There may be advantages to being humble. Use your definitions of these words today to help shape your self-awareness and move you along the road to success.

"Proud people breed sad sorrows for themselves."

Emily Brontë

Jerry was a proud man. He had accomplished much, and everyone who came across him knew before he opened his mouth that he thought very highly of himself. From his perfectly coiffed hair to his impeccably shined shoes, Jerry was the picture of success — outwardly. He looked down his nose at anyone in close proximity and made it quite clear that he was on a higher plane. Jerry could barely stand to hold a conversation with his inferiors. They had nothing useful to give him. He knew it all.

Unfortunately, Jerry found out that it was lonely at the top. If he was better than everyone else, who would he find interesting? Who could teach him something new?   He never even considered sharing his brilliance with others. Jerry's pride set him so far apart from the pack that he didn't identify with anyone. He constantly looked for ways in which he was different, so he lost sight of the similarities he had with his fellow humans. Yes, it was very lonely and dull at the top, but Jerry created his sorrowful world. He had no one to blame but himself.

Draw a picture of yourself when you are full of pride. What do you look like? What emotions surface when you are proud? Have you ever taken pride too far and ventured into the kind of world Jerry created? What was it like? Now, draw a picture of yourself when you think you have just the right dose of pride. What colors emanate from you then? How do you relate to those around you? Consider how pride might alienate you from your peers, and work instead to strengthen connections with others today.

Day 336

"I finally figured out the only reason to be alive is to enjoy it."
Rita Mae Brown

What do you want out of life? Why are you here? If you could get only one thing out of your time here on earth, what would it be? Many people simply want to be happy. Others prefer to collect as much stuff as possible. What are your goals? Are you enjoying life?

It is really important to consider your overall happiness while you are sifting through your daily activities, so you don't get stuck in the minutia and forget to have a little fun. If it all ended today, would you wish you had enjoyed your life a little more?

You have completed assignments throughout this book to discover what activities will bring enjoyment into your life. You've done your homework. Have you used what you learned? Are you living a joyous life? Have you done anything fun today? If not, get out there and go for it!

Enjoying life has nothing to do with blowing off your responsibilities. There are a million fun things you can do that don't take you away from the work you also plan to complete. If it's a nice day, take your lunch outside. If your kids, in a moment of random silliness, ask for pancakes for dinner, make them! Enjoy the unexpected things that come up during the day. You may not have a second opportunity to experience them. If you enjoy life today, you are a success. Go with the glitches in life, and you may find yourself on an interesting and rewarding new path. If you don't find happiness for yourself, try to give a dose to someone else. That will also put you in the success category.

"Not what we have but what we enjoy constitutes our abundance."

Epicurus

Everyone has the right to live an abundant life. The primary purpose of this book is to guide you toward living abundantly and achieving your dreams. How are you progressing? Are your dreams coming into view? Has your idea of abundance changed at all since you started reading this book?

The quote above suggests that abundance has nothing to do with possessions. You may be thinking, "Ahhh! Here's the catch. The book says I will achieve my dreams, but now they're going to try to tell me that all my dreams should be of the emotional variety, and I don't need material abundance."

Don't worry. There is no catch. You have every right to live an abundant life—emotionally, financially, and any other way that makes your dreams come true. The point of the quote above is to expand your thinking concerning the word "abundance." It does not have to be limited to possessions. You deserve more than that.

What do you enjoy? Do not look back to any previous pages of your journal to answer that question. Turn to a new page and make a fresh list of the things that make you happy. How do those items coincide with achieving your dreams?

No one is stopping you from living abundantly right now. Do the things you enjoy, and abundance will follow. Help others, and you will be rewarded. Follow your dreams and drop your fears, and you will know happiness.

"Enjoy the little things, for one day you may look back and realize they were the big things."

Robert Brault

Eric had a million and one things to do. He was behind at work, and his to-do list at home was also several pages long. So what was he doing? Babysitting.

He sat across from his three-year-old nephew at the kitchen table.

"So what do you want for breakfast, big boy?" Eric asked the child.

"Everything."

Eric laughed. He forgot about all of the things he "should" be doing and enjoyed the unplanned play day with his sister's kids. He would look back on this day years later at his nephew's graduation and realize that he had strung together a lot of little, special times with his niece and nephew. Before he knew it, all those seemingly small things turned into one very big thing—an abundance of love and a family bond that was stronger than ever.

Pay attention to the little things in your life today. Don't put off a chance to help, a chance to love, a chance to laugh. Open the windows and enjoy a beautiful spring day. Stop in a gallery just to look at the artwork. Ask a co-worker who's going through a tough time if there's anything you can do. Buy those Girl Scout cookies when your nine-year-old neighbor shows up at the door. Little things become big things. You don't get abundance all at once. It comes in unexpected increments from all angles when you least expect it.

"You only live once. If you don't enjoy it, it's your fault, nobody else's."

Duncan Bannatyne

Brace yourself—here comes one of the most important themes of this book: you are responsible for your life. If you want to blame someone or something else for your state of affairs, then toss this book in the trash and get on with your miserable life. If you aren't having fun yet, it's your own fault.

That may sound a little harsh, but we don't have a lot of days left in this year to get that point across. It's time to look at the bottom line. If you have not yet chosen to enjoy life, your time is up. Do it today. Stop concentrating on the negative things and start enjoying where you are right now. Stop wishing for whatever you don't have, and start being grateful for what belongs to you at this moment. You cannot achieve success if you don't believe you deserve happiness, and you can't be happy if you continue to focus on the negative aspects of your life.

Every single time a negative, self-deprecating thought comes to the forefront of your mind today, knock it out of the ballpark. Stop and replace it with a positive thought. You have to practice happiness if it doesn't come naturally. If negative thoughts are overwhelming you, then get out of yourself completely by doing something for someone else.

Do you really want to achieve your dreams? Then you must get down to the business of enjoying life every single day from here on out. Live a life full of joy, and your dreams will have fertile ground to grow.

"If you can't learn to do it well, learn to enjoy doing it badly."

Ashleigh Brilliant

You have spent a lot of time throughout this year discovering your talents and pursuing them in various ways in order to achieve success. What if there is something you enjoy doing, but you display no talent for it whatsoever? Do you have to leave it behind, because you'll probably never be the best? Not necessarily.

Roger was a horrible singer. He could barely carry a tune. But he loved to sing, and yodeling in the shower just wasn't enough. Was he destined to sit on the sidelines and never experience the joy of making music with others? Absolutely not. Roger joined a very large community choir. He surrounded himself with singers, and there was safety in numbers. He sat right between two strong basses, and they helped anchor him to the correct pitch (or drowned him out when he was completely off key). Roger was finally able to achieve his dream of singing. He participated in numerous successful choral events with the group, and he contributed a kind of enthusiasm for music that boosted morale even in the most tedious rehearsals. He didn't have natural talent to bring to the table, but Roger did have unbridled joy and a passion for music that was contagious. He became an important member of the group.

If you can't learn to do something well, don't worry about it. You can learn to enjoy doing it badly! Or you can become a supporter of those who do have talent in that area. Get a little creative and find alternate ways to fulfill your dreams if the first route doesn't work.

"We make zero percent of the shots we don't take."

Michael Jordan

Wouldn't it be nice if achievement just landed in your lap or showed up in your mailbox one day? Unfortunately, that's not how it works. You have to practice success. You must work on the skills you need to achieve a victory, and really, that's part of the fun. As Michael Jordan states in the quote above, you make zero percent of the shots you don't take. If you want to capture your dreams, you have to get out there and make the shots. No one will sink those baskets for you. You have to reach for your own goals.

The question for you today is: are you taking the shots? Are you actively pursuing success or just dreaming about how nice it would be to have it? Let today be another "Reality Check Day," just like the habit you started on Day 257. Take some inventory and honestly assess whether or not you are truly reaching for your dreams. Is there anything you've been putting off that would bring you closer to your goals? Now is the time to do it.

Get out there and take the shots. Practice success. You won't improve if you don't put your ideas into practice. Instead of dreading the work it will take to achieve your dreams, try enjoying the experience. Practice can be fun. Think about how great you feel after a good workout at the gym. It might be hard to get there, but the experience is invigorating. You will need to practice new skills in order to achieve success, but that's exciting. It can be fun to learn something new. Train your mind to enjoy the process as much as the result. Then you can have fun during every play, not just at the end of the game.

Day 342

"The people I distrust most are those who want to improve our lives but have only one course of action."

Frank Herbert

You've seen the ads: Get rich quick using the Internet! Find financial freedom through this pyramid scheme! Lose weight by eating only peanut butter for a month! What do you think when you read those headlines? Are you instantly skeptical? Good!

You will not achieve success through a single course of action. It's a fact. Get over it. Everyone wants that quick fix, and that's one of the reasons there aren't as many successful people in the world as there could be. You are actually going to have to put a bit more effort into real success. Shortcuts just don't work in the grand scheme of things.

Your assignment today is to make a commitment to get in this journey for the long haul. You have your whole life ahead of you. Stop looking for band-aid solutions and start building a solid foundation for success.

Open up your journal to a new page and write a pledge to yourself today. Take an oath that you will follow every step on the path to your dreams. Promise yourself that you will not try the shortcuts, but you will stay on the road you need to take to reach legitimate success. That means you must be willing to devote time to your project. Make a pledge in this document to practice your skills, learn from others, and help those you meet along the way. Make a promise to yourself that you are worth the effort. You deserve abundance. Show that you are willing to take the less-popular but more-rewarding road to get there.

"Trust only movement. Life happens at the level of events, not of words. Trust movement."

Alfred Adler

Yesterday you considered things you don't trust. Today you can latch on to something you can trust: movement. Taking action is the surest way to success.

Think of the people you know who really live life to the fullest. Describe their characteristics. Why do you consider them people who get the most out of life? What is it about them that feels vibrant and exciting? Which of their characteristics do you want to emulate in your life?

Life is a series of events. Words and thoughts are reflections on those events, but life happens in the actions that you and others take every day. You cannot live out a fruitful life in your mind or on paper. Life requires action.

The twins were almost two years old, and they were a whirlwind of activity. Grandma sat on the floor watching Kate play the drums and Sam "read" a book. Then Sam took over the drums, and Kate decided to make breakfast in their playhouse. Within minutes, Sam took over the breakfast duties, and Kate fired up the miniature vacuum to clean house. Suddenly, Sam became a DJ blaring music on a CD player while Kate danced. Grandma smiled at the pandemonium created by those two blonde cuties. It was a banner day filled with an endless series of events strung together to form a bond between brother and sister and between grandparent and grandchild. Are you enjoying the events in your life? Trust movement.

Day 344

"You cannot change anything in your life with intention alone, which can become a watered-down, occasional hope that you'll get to tomorrow. Intention without action is useless."

Caroline Myss

Randy saw his co-worker coming down the hall, and he ducked into the restroom. Her mother had recently died, and he had intended to send a sympathy card but never got around to it. Best just to avoid her until she recovered from her loss, he thought. During lunch, Randy checked his bank balance online. Rats! He was overdrawn again. He had intended to transfer funds from his savings the day before, but he forgot about it. Randy arrived home at six o'clock at night and found a note on the kitchen table from his wife. She wanted a divorce. He stared at her handwriting on the page, and a deep feeling of emptiness started to creep into his heart. He had intended to tell her how much he loved her . . . but he just never got around to it.

Intention without action is useless. You can be filled with good intentions, but nobody knows it until you do something. Randy had no proof to show his wife that he really did love her, because his actions didn't reflect his feelings.

Your assignment today is to openly display your intentions. That does not mean simply talking about the things you want to do. It means getting out there and doing them. Don't get caught in the trap of good intentions. They are useless and will do nothing to help you achieve your dreams. Intentions are not real until you take action.

"Nobody made a greater mistake than he who did nothing
because he could only do a little."

Edmund Burke

A little bit makes a difference. If you ever feel overwhelmed by the
tasks in front of you, know that taking any action, no matter how
small, will make a difference. Pick up a piece of trash if you see it on
the sidewalk. Put your loose change in the can for muscular dystrophy
at the grocery store check-out line. Plant some flowers in your front
yard. Help your kids with their homework. When lots of people do
little things, great things will be achieved. It is much worse to stand
by and do nothing. Every little thing you do has a ripple effect on the
rest of the world. You are more powerful than you think.

Give what you can give today; do what you are capable of doing
today; help the people you can help today. Don't give up because you
can't save the world. No one can accomplish great things alone. It
takes time and action—continual action—to exact real change.

It is a mistake to do nothing, but it is never a mistake to do even a
little bit. Do what you can today, and when you go to sleep tonight,
congratulate yourself on taking action. When you wake up tomorrow
morning, do it again. You can reach your dreams through a series of
small steps, but you can't get there by doing nothing.

Day 346

"Humility does not mean thinking less of yourself than of other people, nor does it mean having a low opinion of your own gifts. It means freedom from thinking about yourself at all."

William Temple

You will have an opportunity for the next few days to consider humility as it relates to your success. Humility sounds like a bad word to many people. It's a little too close to humiliation. In actuality, humility is not the same thing as humiliation. Humiliation happens when you are in a state of public disgrace or shame. Humility is a personality trait of being humble or modest.

We talked about humility in relation to pride back on Day 334 and discussed its positive and negative connotations. Now you will have a chance to look at how humility can be a useful tool for success.

Humility doesn't put you at a lower station than those around you. It also doesn't mean that you do not consider yourself worthy of success. William Temple described it beautifully in the quote above. Humility is freedom from thinking about yourself at all.

As you move toward success, you will travel the road faster if you turn your attention outward to those around you rather than becoming self-absorbed. You have worked through lots of exercises in this book to allow your talents to emerge and to reveal your personal gifts. You know you have the ability to achieve your dreams. Now is the time to look around and find ways to make a difference in this world. It may sound kind of funny, but you are not the centerpiece of this endeavor. Stop thinking about yourself and start thinking about what you can do for those around you. Then success will be yours.

"We are all worms, but I do believe I am a glowworm."

Winston Churchill

Jim looked up at his drill sergeant with a gleam in his eye. He had been beaten up both physically and mentally in Officer Candidate School—told he was worthless and didn't measure up over and over again. He was lower than dirt. Jim smiled from the dusty ground as he completed his last twenty pushups. The sparkle in his eyes revealed the sheer will rising in his stomach. He wouldn't be broken. Maybe he was nothing but dirt, but he would turn that dust into a tornado of success that would tear through the camp before his time was up.

Sometimes it's beneficial to be knocked off your pedestal, to find out your shortcomings and look them straight in the eye. Humility will work for you as long as you never, ever give up. The quote from Winston Churchill above takes a mischievous view of how to deal with your humanness. Maybe you look at the talents you have to offer, and you think you're not that special. That is when you need to let your drive to succeed take over. Take what you've been given and make it special. Give everything you've got, and that will be enough. You will have what you need to achieve your dreams if you're willing to give one more big push.

Write in your journal today about how you can go further than you have gone up to this point. What can you do to push harder toward success? How can you go one step further than everyone else? You don't have to be smarter, funnier, or better looking. All you have to be is willing to go the distance.

Day 348

"It is far more impressive when others discover your good qualities without your help."

Author Unknown

Rhonda was a walking, talking résumé. If you had an extra minute, she would surely take the time to bend your ear about her latest triumphs. It was nauseating. People started to avoid her in the halls. What Rhonda didn't understand was her friends and co-workers really didn't care how great she thought she was. Her daily recaps of her successes either bored them or made them feel inadequate themselves. They wanted action. They would much rather witness her change the world than hear her talk about it.

Do you share a little of Rhonda's desire to let people know about your good qualities? It's a fairly common human trait. We all want recognition for our good deeds. There is a much better way to do it. Shut your mouth and move your feet. Others will undoubtedly discover your successes if you just put one foot in front of the other and accomplish them. Your actions will have an effect on others, and you want it to be a positive one. So get things done, and stop talking about yourself.

Remove yourself from the focus of conversation today. Ask people about what is going on in their lives. Listen to the answers. You may find new opportunities to be helpful and also contribute your unique talents to situations. Your actions will allow others to discover how great you are, not your words. Words are often a waste of time when you are working to achieve your dreams. People don't need your help to discover your good qualities. They will be obvious when you use them.

"Nobody stands taller than those willing to stand corrected."
William Safire

Phil knew where he was going—at least he thought he did. He had taken these back roads millions of times as a young man. Phil's wife wasn't so sure his memory was solid. She pulled out their navigation system and punched in the proper coordinates.

"I think you should have turned back there, honey," Phil's wife offered as she stared at the glowing screen.

"Nonsense! I know exactly where I am," Phil replied with a smug grin.

An hour later, they stopped at a gas station to confirm his wife's suspicions. They should have turned back there.

Do you listen to words of caution as you travel the road to success? When you find out you've gone the wrong way, how long does it take you to admit it and turn around? How bad does it have to get before you will ask for help?

There is no shame—no humiliation—in being willing to stand corrected. You do not have all the answers, and that's just fine. There is a living, breathing encyclopedia of knowledge all around you. Do you willingly absorb new information from people who might know a little more than you? Or does it really bother you to admit you don't have all the answers?

You will achieve your dreams if you continue to follow the right path. The trick is to remember you don't always hold the navigation system. You can't do this alone. Admit when you've taken a wrong turn. Seek help. Then you will find the right path again.

Day 350

"Modesty: the art of encouraging people to find out for themselves how wonderful you are."

Anonymous

You don't have to give up any of your awesomeness to be modest. You are very special! Admit it. It's true. Just don't tell everyone else. It is much better if they find out for themselves how wonderful you are.

Your assignment today is to stop trying to convince yourself and others that you're special. Give up wondering whether or not you're going to achieve your dreams. You have no way of predicting what your future will hold, and whether or not you think you deserve success is pretty irrelevant, too.

The basic truth is you are already wonderful. The day you were born, the world changed. Now, how are you going to go about showing people how wonderful you are? We've already established that lip service won't do it. The answer is simple. Do wonderful things.

In addition to your long-term goals, find some things to do this week that will immediately help someone else. Demonstrate your unique gifts by putting them to work. Are you a great organizer? Help you brother or sister organize their basement over the weekend if they need (and want) the help. Do you have a friend who is down in the dumps? Surprise them by showing up at their work and taking them to lunch. (Spend the lunchtime listening rather than talking.) Are you a good teacher? Offer to tutor a student in need. Encourage people to find out just how awesome you are through your actions.

"When you are grateful fear disappears and abundance appears."

Anthony Robbins

Jodi could never get enough. She was always reaching her hand out for more: more money, more food, more friends, more clothes, more interesting opportunities at work, more praise for her accomplishments — she was never satisfied. Jodi spent most of her life wanting and wishing for more, and therefore she was unhappy a lot of the time.

What would happen if Jodi made one small change? Every time she felt that twinge of wanting more, what if she instead stopped and gave a short, silent thank-you for what she had at that exact moment? Could that change her attitude?

A simple attitude of gratitude will lead you to a life of abundance. Do you believe that is true? If you don't, here is your challenge: try it. Every time you find yourself wanting more, stop for a moment and be thankful for what you have. You don't have to wait until you have the biggest house on the block, three cars, and a huge bank account to feel like you live an abundant life. All you need to do is practice gratitude every day, and a feeling of abundance will follow.

When you are able to be grateful for what you do have, then you squash out the fear of not having enough. You free yourself to live happily, and ultimately that will open doors for you. Fear has a way of immobilizing you on the road to success. On the other hand, gratitude allows you to celebrate the gifts you have been given and build on them. You can move forward with a positive attitude and live abundantly today.

Day 352

"The world is full of abundance and opportunity, but far too many people come to the fountain of life with a sieve instead of a tank car . . . a teaspoon instead of a steam shovel. They expect little and as a result they get little."

Ben Sweetland

What do you expect to get out of life today? Do you expect abundance in real time, or are you waiting for it to show up some day down the road? Write in your journal about your daily expectations, and answer those two questions as honestly as you can. Are you walking up to the fountain of life with a teaspoon, or are you backing a steam shovel up to it? When you see opportunity in plain clothes on an average day, do you ignore it? Do you only siphon off a small portion for now and assume you will take more later? Why do you make that choice?

Abundance is all around you on an ordinary day. You may be sitting on the curved edge of a fountain waiting for a big rainstorm of opportunity, but right behind you is a continual flow of abundance that you can be drawing from constantly. Did you notice it? Why aren't you drinking from the fountain of life at this very moment?

Expectations can be self-fulfilling prophesies. If you expect only a little bit out of life, then that is exactly what you will get. Practice changing your view today. Look around you and notice a world that is full of abundance and opportunities. You basically have two choices. You can concentrate on the things that limit you, or you can concentrate on the opportunities that are plentiful and within reach. Which one of those choices will lead you to achieving your dreams?

"Expect your every need to be met. Expect the answer to every problem, expect abundance on every level."

Eileen Caddy

Today you will have another opportunity to change your expectations. Your first task is to write in your journal about what you expect to happen today. Make a list of your expectations for the next twenty-four hours.

Now, take a look at that list. Are you aiming low, or do you have pretty lofty expectations? What did you write down? Your expectations for this day might be a laundry list of mundane tasks that you hope to accomplish: pick the kids up from school, go to the gym, finish the laundry, get the tires rotated, attend a mandatory meeting at work . . . boring! What would happen to your outlook if you added something fun to your list? Today I will: start a new book; plan an impromptu date night with my spouse; take the day off and go hiking just to spend some time meditating and surrounded by nature; take the kids to a movie after school. Puts a little spring in your step, doesn't it?

If you don't plan for abundance, it's not going to happen. Expect it. Put it on your to-do list. If you expect to be baffled by life today, then you will be. If you expect to be frustrated at work, it'll happen. If you expect to be annoyed by the guy next door who goes to get his newspaper in his underwear, chances are you will be.

Take charge right now. Alter your expectations. Expect to come across new opportunities to be happy. Plan for an abundant life — today!

"Life is a lottery that we've already won. But most people have not cashed in their tickets."

Louise L. Hay

First there was the flashing red light, then the endless sound of falling coins. Bells and whistles started going off everywhere, and people gathered around. Curt stared at the machine. He had been going to Las Vegas once a year for the last twenty years, and in the past he always walked away a loser. He never lost more than a hundred dollars. It was just fun to play. He didn't expect much more than that. Sometimes he was up fifty dollars or so, and that was when he should have quit, because he always ended up losing it again. It was just the way it went. Nevertheless, he enjoyed pulling the lever on the slot machine and tasting that far-off, elusive chance for big money.

Now, here he was—a winner! One magic pull on the right machine and he was a millionaire! It happened. He won the lottery. People were patting him on the back, and a smiling casino employee wrote him a ticket to redeem at the cashier's booth. He won. Curt stood up shakily, put the ticket in his pocket, and shuffled out of the casino without redeeming it.

What?!

No one in their right mind would do that!

Actually, many of us do just that every day. Life is a lottery you have already won. You are incredibly lucky to be here and take part in this crazy play. Have you cashed in your ticket yet?

"Life in abundance comes only through great love."

Elbert Hubbard

For the last several days you've read about abundance and how you can have it right now, but most of us don't take advantage of the opportunities that will lead us to an abundant life. You could be living abundantly today, so what are you waiting for?

I don't know. You may be thinking. "Fine. I'll stop waiting and go for it. Sign me up. How do I start?"

You need one very important ingredient in order to live life in abundance, and that is love. Abundance is easy to obtain, but it's not exactly free. You have to willingly give of yourself in order to see abundance flow back to you. There's always a catch, isn't there?

This catch is a wonderful surprise, though. You will get back so much more than you give. If you practice great love for everyone around you, you will see incredible abundance flowing your way—and not just in the form of hugs and nice words. Don't worry. You don't have to go out and hug that annoying neighbor who always gets his newspaper in his underwear. That would be creepy. You could practice tolerance and let the guy do his own thing without plastering unflattering pictures of him on the Internet, though.

You must look for ways in which you can enrich the lives of others. What can you do to make someone's day better? Practice bringing your talents to the table and sharing them. Take action all the time, and make sure that it is not only for your own benefit. This is not a one-day experiment. Practice great love for those around you, and you will be rewarded with an abundant life.

Day 356

"To be nobody but yourself in a world which is doing its best, night and day, to make you everybody else means to fight the hardest battle which any human being can fight; and never stop fighting."

E. E. Cummings

Your secret weapon for success is *you*. No one else has your unique combination of abilities. That means you have talents to share that not one other person on this earth can put out there. You own a monopoly, and it's inside yourself. You've spent some quality time throughout this year discovering your talents, and you will continue to do so throughout your life. Now, here is your battle: you must continue to fight to be nobody but yourself.

The quote above from E. E. Cummings points out how easy it is for you to sabotage your dreams by trying to be something you are not. It seems as though this world is doing its best, night and day, to make you into everybody else. Remember that your ultimate strength is your uniqueness. Don't let anyone try to mold you into something that doesn't feel like you.

Your assignment today is to write down all of your unique traits. Write about your quirky habits, your endearing behaviors, and your special talents. If you were going to write an ad about yourself, what would it say?

This exercise can be slightly uncomfortable for many people. It's hard to talk about how great you are. It feels self-centered. Nevertheless, do this exercise. You're not going to share it with anyone else. It's a reminder that you are an amazing work of art, and you should be constantly working to utilize your secret weapon—you!

"God has given you one face and you make yourself another."

William Shakespeare

Sheila loved women's magazines. In a way, they gave her an identity. She would buy a handful of them every Friday night and pour over the fashions and the makeup throughout the weekend. Sheila flipped through the glossy pages and plucked her eyebrows to resemble one model, dyed her hair to look like another, and created her wardrobe after all of the latest fashions. If someone asked Sheila what her favorite color was, she would probably consult *Vogue* before she answered.

What was she doing? Sheila was looking outward to find her inner beauty. It wasn't necessary. We are all influenced by our surroundings, and that can be a positive thing. However, it is extremely important to discover your unique characteristics from the inside out rather than from the outside in.

What are you doing to stay true to yourself today? Are you constantly trying on the masks of outside influences instead of appreciating the face God has given you, as Shakespeare put it? Remember, you are the secret weapon for success. You can't let your unique talents emerge if you are constantly covering them up with the status quo.

When you are bombarded with outside influences today — and you will be — think before you act. Are you picking up that new bestselling book just because it's popular, or are you really interested in the story? Did you choose the shoes you're wearing today because you like them or because you saw a famous actor wearing them in a magazine? Let your face emerge as a powerful influence today.

Day 358

> "We are so accustomed to disguising ourselves to others that in the end we become disguised to ourselves."
>
> François Duc de la Rochefoucauld

Carl was going to do what it took to fit in at his new law firm. One of the partners asked him if he played golf, and he blurted out, "Of course!" Hundreds of dollars in lessons later, he was a passable player. Carl hated the game, but he thought he needed to be out there with the other guys. That wasn't the only new thing that he adopted. Carl's wardrobe changed from modest navy suits to Armani designs and flashy cufflinks, he got a Blackberry and a membership to the country club, and finally, he traded in his Honda for a BMW.

Carl caught a glimpse of himself in the hall mirror when he came home one night. Who is that guy, he thought, as he stared at his reflection. Who is that pompous jerk with the slicked-back hair, the man who is living far above his means? Carl stepped closer to the mirror to try to find a hint of his true colors somewhere in the persona he had spent months creating.

What do you do to disguise yourself? Are you good at becoming a chameleon and fitting into almost any situation? Do you tend to adopt the behaviors and attitudes of those around you in order to fit in? Be careful. That's an easy way to lose yourself. Practice worrying less about how others perceive you and more about honoring your own identity. The right friends, the right job, and even the right significant other will come to you if you don't disguise yourself. If you reveal who you truly are, you will attract the people who will most complement your life.

"Never be bullied into silence. Never allow yourself to be made a victim. Accept no one's definition of your life; define yourself."

Harvey Fierstein

Your voice is important.

You are a significant influence on this world.

You are not a victim.

You get to define yourself.

Write each of the four sentences above on a separate piece of paper in your journal, and then fill the rest of the page with your thoughts. Are you defining yourself, or are you letting others do it for you?

If you want to achieve your dreams, you must remember these four messages. They are essential to finding the strength you need to succeed. Take control of your life and your future. Define yourself. It is so exciting to realize that you don't have to hold back or cover up your true self. Unleash your potential. Don't let anyone stop you from following your path to success. Find people with common goals and work with them. Help others along the way, but never let someone else tell you who you are or what you are capable of accomplishing. You are the only one who can do that.

Accept nothing less than what you know to be true about yourself and your potential. Don't worry if others laugh at your dreams. They don't get to vote on your future. You're in charge of that. Define yourself today . . . and think big!

Day 360

"Let the world know you as you are, not as you think you should be, because sooner or later, if you are posing, you will forget the pose, and then where are you?"

Fanny Brice

Do you feel like an actor pretending to be you in real life? Are you play-acting at one thing, when you know you are something else? It's stressful to try to imitate all of the right moves and make people believe you are someone you're not.

Maybe you are pretending to be really knowledgeable about a certain technology at work, but the truth is you have no idea what you're doing. Unfortunately, it's only a matter of time before the curtain comes down and that scene is over. What is going to happen when they find out the truth?

Think through your life today. Are there areas where you are posing? Are you pretending to be something you think you should be? As Fanny Brice mentions in the quote above, sooner or later you're going to forget the pose. Do you really want to go through the embarrassment of admitting you were pretending to be something you're not? Not only is that dishonest, but it also carries the connotation that you're ashamed of who you really are. Are you?

You have absolutely nothing to be ashamed about. The world wants to see you just as you are. No one is interested in the poser. We want the real deal. So throw away all of your costumes and take off that horrid makeup. Reveal your true self and seize control of your future. Let the world know you as you are, not as you think you should be.

"A journey is best measured in friends rather than miles."

Tim Cahill

You are now nearing the end of your year-long journey to achieve your dreams. How do you feel? Have you experienced any significant changes in your life over the past year?

During these final few days you will have a chance to explore your journey thus far, starting with ways in which journeys can be measured. Read the quote above and write in your journal about your personal reaction to that sentence.

There are so many methods you can use to measure a journey. One significant way is through the friends you have made along the way. A journey is always a success if you have had a chance to meet new friends and develop lasting relationships with people who inspire you and help you to thrive. Measure your journey in friends over this past year. Have you made any new friendships? Have you deepened the friendships you already have?

It is never too late to start measuring your journey in friends. Solid relationships with others are so important in helping you to live an abundant and happy life. The road to success is not a solitary one. Relationships also give you a chance to reach out and lend a hand to someone in need — a critical ingredient for success.

If you haven't spent a lot of time cultivating friendships this year, don't beat yourself up about it. Change your pattern of behavior right now. Build your friendships one step at a time. Learn more about others. Find out how wonderful your friends are, and your life will become richer in the process.

Day 362

"Too often we are so preoccupied with the destination, we forget the journey."

Anonymous

Julia was from Finland, but she had many relatives who lived in the United States. Her mother promised her when she was a little girl that she could go and visit them when she turned sixteen. Julia could hardly wait. As her sixteenth birthday approached, there was only one thing on her mind—Disney World! Julia was a Disney freak, and it was a lifelong dream of hers to visit the Magic Kingdom.

The exciting day finally arrived, and Julia boarded a plane for New York City. Her relatives picked her up and drove her to their home in Connecticut. Then, after she had a chance to rest up and meet many members of her extended family for the first time, they embarked on a road trip to Florida. Julia was so filled with anticipation to see Disney World that she remembered almost nothing about the journey. Numerous interesting sights flowed by her window on the long trip, but she was preoccupied with dreams of Cinderella and Mickey Mouse. It was unfortunate that she missed rich aspects of the journey because she was preoccupied with the destination.

Have you been a little like Julia this year? You most likely picked up this book because you want to achieve your dreams. Have you missed some of the journey because you were preoccupied with the destination? Have you not stopped to enjoy your minor successes because you were focused on achieving the ultimate success of realizing your dreams? Don't forget the journey as you travel on. The destination is only a brief moment. The journey is a lifetime of interesting experiences.

"Success is a journey, not a destination. The doing is often more important than the outcome."

Arthur Ashe

Yesterday you were reminded to not miss the beauty of your journey while you strive for ultimate success in life. Today you will take that one step further: success is the journey, not the destination.

You are actively achieving—not waiting for—your dreams right now. You are a success at this very moment, because you are doing things that move you forward in life. You are grabbing fruit from the tree of your dreams and tasting it. You're not just looking at the tree.

Whenever you cultivate a friendship, learn a new skill, offer a smile to a stranger, practice taking a leadership role in a situation, or actively follow any of the steps and examples we have discussed in this book, you are a success. Success is the journey. It is motion, not completion. It is full of life and change and excitement.

Your dreams have probably changed a little over this year, and that serves to clarify the point that success is a journey. It is a fluid thing. Your life is evolving all the time, and if you go with the flow and are willing to learn and grow constantly, you will achieve your dreams every single day of your life. Stand in your success today. The destination is not important. The doing is the key.

Day 364

"The secret to a rich life is to have more beginnings than endings."

David Weinbaum

You were probably hoping to find the secret to success somewhere in this book. Well, here it is (drum roll please): start more than you can finish.

As David Weinbaum suggests, the secret to a rich life is to have more beginnings than endings. It's interesting that the secret is not necessarily to complete more tasks than everyone else. It's to leave plenty of loose ends in life, so that you are always open to new inspiration and fresh opportunities. Life is not neat. You do not work on a single item, complete it, put it away, and then bring out the next thing. If you operated that way, you would miss all of the cool things that show up unexpectedly.

If you were studying a new technique at work and someone offered you a chance to go on a hot air balloon ride over the weekend, would you ignore them because you had not finished your project? Of course not! Unless you are afraid of heights, you would take advantage of the experience over the weekend and then go back to work on Monday refreshed and exhilarated.

Celebrate the beginnings in your life. Endings are not that exciting. Beginnings have an element of the unknown that is thrilling. You will have new opportunities every day if you look for them. Rejoice in the new beginnings you find today.

"I wish you a very good journey to an unknown you've never seen."

Pieter V. Admiraal

Here you are at Day 365. Congratulations! What an incredible journey this year has been. Do something special to commemorate this day. You have spent a year discovering and nurturing your unique talents. You have developed ways to celebrate your successes every single day and enjoy the journey as it unfolds. Give yourself a party today!

You are achieving your dreams right now, but the end is nowhere in sight. I wish you an exciting journey, a pleasant journey, a fruitful and joyous journey. Bring happiness to others, and it will return to you abundantly. Push a little harder, and you will be surprised by the rewards. Experience and celebrate the little victories along with the major milestones. Don't wait to be happy.

My parting hope for you is that you travel forward into the unknown with open eyes and an open heart. Gather up your dreams and use them every single day. You have already achieved so much. Just imagine what lies beyond the next curve in the road.

Summary

If you took the time to do the lessons I offered here, you probably learned quite a bit about yourself. It is likely you discovered areas of your life that were problematic, some of which surprised you.

You know that change requires effort. It does not always have to demand a lot of work, but you will never move forward by standing still. As you have learned with the 365 lessons here, you can make a positive change in your life, one day at a time.

The life you lead is the result of the choices you make. You can choose to be gloomy, negative, frustrated, or envious. You can decide to believe that you've been punished with a string of bad luck and cave into what you see as destiny. Or you can stand up and recognize that you are the one who steers your own life journey. In which direction do you want to head?

It all began with the very first lesson: Open your mind to the possibility that you can have more. Give yourself permission to dream.

I designed the lessons and assignments presented in this book to help you untangle your thoughts and ideas so that you could proceed with a clear path. I know it is impossible to achieve your full potential if you cannot even see what the "best possible you" looks like.

On Day 17, I asked you to examine your targets in your personal and professional life. Did you find a sweet spot that would bring you to a better place, either physically or emotionally?

In my experience as a life coach, I work with people who know they want to elevate their lives to something more purposeful, to obtain results that seem out of their reach. Together, we work to scrape away the layer of confusion that blocks their view. We create a game plan and then establish accountability to ensure they stick to that game plan.

Remind yourself of this message from Day 42: If you do nothing, that's exactly what you'll get.

In your 365-day journey toward living your dream life, did you hold yourself accountable for completing the assignments? Some of them were as simple as writing a quote on a piece of paper and keeping it with you (Day 60). It doesn't get much easier than that! Did you do it? On Day 72, you had the assignment of describing your perfect life. Did you write it down or just give it casual thought?

The amount of positive change you experience through this 365-day trip toward your dream life is directly proportional to the amount of effort you are willing to put into achieving that change. When an assignment asked you to write something down or make a list, it's because the act of picking up a pen or pencil and committing words to paper is more concrete than just pondering them in your mind. It can define the difference between wishful thinking and thoughtful action.

Be honest with yourself. Did you complete the assignments with your full attention, thought, and effort? If not, you are only cheating yourself of the results you could have attained. We all have days that get away from us, where distractions and chaos force us to veer off our regular path. When that happens, get back on track as soon as possible. Start from where you left off. Don't skip a day. Don't rush through two or three lessons on one day in an effort to "catch up".

Living your dream life is not a race. You won't "win" by moving faster through the paces, and there are no shortcuts—because there is no destination. As I shared with you on Day 364, the secret to a fulfilled life is to engage in more beginnings than endings. Explore. Discover. Experience. Do not close doors behind you, continue moving forward and opening new ones.

In writing *Achieve Anything In Just One Year*, my goal was to give you the tools to discover the dreams that matter to you and then turn them from vague ideas to actions. I wanted people to realize that they are in control of their joys as well as their misery. They must revel in life's victories, not dwelling on the misses, but rather using them as opportunities to achieve more victories.

I have experienced my own challenges and used this same 365-day process to overcome them. I often return to the book and revisit certain assignments to refresh my dream life mindset. By completing this book, you have made important progress toward the life you want, but I suggest you keep it close by for the occasional refresher course. At the end of the day, pick it up and pick a page—randomly or purposely. Just like you might return to the photos of a vacation to revisit those memories, come back to this book and remind yourself of the journey.

I hope *Achieve Anything In Just One Year* helped you discover and live the dream life you deserve! Please share your experiences with me at JasonHarvey.com and let me know if any particular assignments, advice, or insight has helped you on your journey.